THE NATURAL WONDER
OF SOUTHERN AFRICA

AUTHOR'S DEDICATION
For my parents, to whom everything is due

PHOTOGRAPHER'S DEDICATION
To Ingrid and Frisky, for all the precious hours
we lost while I was away

THE NATURAL WONDER OF SOUTHERN AFRICA

TEXT BY
ALF WANNENBURGH

PHOTOGRAPHS BY
J.R. DICKSON

C. Struik Publishers, Cape Town

AUTHOR'S
ACKNOWLEDGEMENTS

In preparing the text of *The Natural Wonder of Southern Africa* I gained information from a large number of scientific publications, without which the present work would not have been possible. A select bibliography appears on page 158. I would like to thank the publisher's editors, Ailsa Smith and Leni Martin, for their guidance and assistance in bringing the work to completion, and the consultants Cecil Keen and Colin Greathead for their meticulous reading of the manuscript and their many useful suggestions. I am also grateful to Dr John Rourke of the Compton Herbarium for his valuable comments on the Fynbos chapter.

ALF WANNENBURGH, CAPE TOWN 1984

PHOTOGRAPHER'S
ACKNOWLEDGEMENTS

I would like to thank Pieter Struik for his bold decision, and the editorial and production staff of Struik Publishers for their encouragement and help. In particular my thanks go to Walther Votteler for his superb use of the photographs in the book's design.
The help received from the Zimbabwe Tourist Board, the Nature Conservation and Tourism Division of the SWA/Namibia Administration, and the Natal Parks Board was invaluable and much appreciated.

J.R. DICKSON, CAPE TOWN 1984

CONSULTANTS
Dr Cecil Keen, PhD, Senior Lecturer, Department of Geography, University of Cape Town
Colin Greathead, MSc, Consultant Geologist

C. Struik (Pty) Ltd
Struik House, Oswald Pirow Street, Foreshore, Cape Town 8001
Reg. No. 80/02842/07

First published 1984
Second edition 1987
Casewrapped edition 1987

Copyright (text) © Alf Wannenburgh
Copyright (photographs) © J.R. Dickson, except for the following which were reproduced with the kind permission of D. Archibald (140); R. Böck (19); De Beers Consolidated Mines Ltd (70); M. Reardon (157, 163, 166); C. Ward (38, 39, 40, 41, 43, 137, 138, 139, 142, 143, 144, 145).

Maps by Anne Westoby, Cape Town
Consultants for the geological map: Dr Clive Stowe and Dr Christopher Hartnady of the Precambrian Research Unit, University of Cape Town

Design by Walther Votteler, Cape Town
Dustjacket design by Janice Ashby Studios, Cape Town
Set by McManus Bros (Pty) Ltd, Cape Town
Lithographic reproduction, printing and binding by Tien Wah Press
(Pte) Ltd, Singapore

ISBN 0 86977 420 4
ISBN 0 86977 421 2 (casewrapped)

1. *One of the highest waterfalls in Africa, the Malutsinyane Falls mark an early stage in the Orange River's long journey to the Atlantic Ocean.*
2. *The Fish River has carved a tortuous canyon through the barren rocky landscape of a desert plateau.*
3. *Rocks swirled by churning floodwaters of the Blyde and Treur rivers have gouged a spectacular assembly of potholes at Bourke's Luck.*

CONTENTS

MOMENTS IN ETERNITY
THE SHAPE OF AGES PAST

Africa south of the Zambezi encompasses an amazing diversity of natural wonders within a relatively small area. A third of the subcontinent is thirstland. Parts are true desert. But also there are lush tropical and temperate forests, high mountain grasslands and soaring snow-capped peaks. Lagoons and estuarine lakes fret the coastline. Deep inland, once-great lakes have become vast salt flats blistering in the sun, and rivers that flowed into them are now silent, sand-choked valleys. Elsewhere, mighty rivers carve gaping canyons through mountain ranges, thunder over stupendous waterfalls and dissipate in swamp wonderlands. These are places of pilgrimage, continually drawing people to marvel at the glories of nature, reflect on the events of inconceivably distant ages and meditate upon their own place in nature and time.

The splendid landscapes of southern Africa are passing scenes in a pageant of creation spanning so great a period that, had the full performance been compressed into a year, barely the final three hours would have been played to a human audience. Were all the words in this book spread evenly over the period, no more than 20 would describe the entire natural and social evolution of man. The earth's crust is some 4 600 million years old; fewer than two million encompass the whole story of mankind.

From the time the crust formed on the accretion of gas, dust and space debris that became the planet, its surface has perpetually been transfigured and transformed. Forces curmurring within the earth have disgorged new rock over old, raised mighty mountain ranges and plunged them beneath the sea. Sun and wind, water and ice have broken them down, carried them off and reconstituted them elsewhere. Huge masses have sundered, drifted apart and become separate continents. Various climates at different times have sculpted them into new shapes, ultimately composing today's landscapes, coloured by the floral arrangements favoured by the climates of our time.

On occasion, the awesome events that gave substance and relief to Africa and the other continents must have produced some spectacular bursts of volcanic pyrotechnics, but the most profound changes were wrought gradually, protracted over aeons, and were probably no more dramatic at the time than are the changes taking place today.

The genesis of the subcontinent's natural wonders is indistinguishable from the origin of the earth itself. In the beginning, heat generated within the growing planet separated the original material into an iron-nickel core and an enveloping silica mantle. As this mass cooled, molten silicas at the surface crystallized into basalt lava, while gasses and water released by eruption became the planet's first atmosphere and seas. Air and water weathered the basalt, producing sediments which were later compacted and cemented into conglomerates, sandstones and shales. Beneath these ancient sedimentary rocks, subsequent upwellings of molten silicates hardened into granite when they cooled underground, or, if they broke through the crust, emerged as lava and cooled more quickly on the surface.

Most of the ancient sedimentary rocks were later eroded away, but remnants in southern Africa, which were transmuted into tough schists by the heat of the upwellings, are among the oldest rocks on earth. Dating back some 3 300 million years, they form the so-called 'gold belts' in Zimbabwe and occasional ridges across granite country, such as the Murchison Range in the eastern Transvaal and the mountainland around Barberton.

The old granite is the major component of the Basement Complex, the foundation on which the sediments and lavas of subsequent geological systems were laid. It forms two vast, continuous 'shields', or 'cratons', one extending beneath most of the Transvaal and deep into neighbouring provinces, the other underlying most of Zimbabwe, typified scenically by the granite hills of the Matopos.

Deposited some 1 800 million years ago on the eastern flank of the old granite in Zimbabwe, the quartzites of the Umkondo and Frontier systems today form the Melsetter Plateau and Chimanimani Mountains. Considerably older are most of the geological systems formed on the Transvaal craton.

Older by about 700 million years, the Dominion Reef System consists chiefly of lava, with minor layers of quartzite and the gold-bearing conglomerate now mined near Klerksdorp. A far more abundant source of the precious metal, however, is the succeeding Witwatersrand System, comprising shales, quartzites and conglomerates that collected in a large basin in the old granite, extending from east of Johannesburg, across the southern Transvaal and into the northern Orange Free State. The ensuing period of intense volcanic activity buried large areas of these earlier rocks in the west and south-west beneath lava sheets of the Ventersdorp System.

Subsequently, the sediments of the Transvaal System accumulated in another enormous depression, extending more than 1 000 kilometres across the central Transvaal, westward into Botswana and south-west as far as Prieska. Quartzites at the base of this system form the powerful krantzes of the Transvaal Drakensberg, such as those dominating the Blyde River Canyon. The deposition of these quartzites was followed by the chemical precipitation of a vast body of dolomite, which occurs in a narrow band directly west of the Great Escarpment in the eastern Transvaal and underlies the rolling plains west of the Witwatersrand, reaching south-west to near Klerksdorp, and north-west beyond Lichtenburg to Lobatsi, in Botswana. In the northern Cape it forms the great triangle of the Ghaap Plateau, with its southern tip at the confluence of the Vaal and Orange rivers. Quartzites higher up in the system form the ridges of the Timeball Hill, Daspoort and Magaliesberg ranges of the Bankeveld, between Johannesburg and Pretoria. West and south-west of the Ghaap Plateau, the upper quartzites, banded ironstones and lavas of the system form the Kuruman Hills and the Asbestos Mountains.

The completion of the Transvaal System, some 1 900 million years ago, was followed by the creation of one of the geological wonders of the world, the Bushveld Igneous Complex. First, a gigantic inverted double cone of gabbroic rock intruded the older rocks. From above, the tops of the cones can be imagined as two enormous, intersecting

4. *Complex, twisted patterns in the rocky precipices of the Swartberg Pass testify to the intensity of the folding that formed the mountain ranges of the southern Cape.*

conglomerates of the Waterberg System form the rugged topography of the Waterberg, Blouberg and Soutpansberg ranges in the northern Transvaal. Related rock formations of the Matsap System are responsible for the Langeberg and Korannaberg in the northern Cape.

If any more recent geological systems accumulated upon the ancient landmass of the Transvaal craton during the following 1 600 million years, no trace of them remains. From the completion of the Waterberg System until the commencement of the Karoo System, some 300 million years ago, this whole region was dissected by erosion, shorn of its eminences and shaven down to a generally level plain. The material carried off by ice, wind and water became the substance of new systems elsewhere.

The geological history of the land surrounding the cratons is quite different. In the western part of South Africa the Basement Complex consists of granite-gneiss that came into existence about 1 000 million years ago. It extends from southern Namaqualand to north of the Orange River, and eastward from the Richtersveld to Prieska. As similar rocks of comparable age also occur in the Basement Complex of Natal, it is believed that they continue beneath the younger rocks of the interior, linking the two areas on opposite sides of the subcontinent. In the west, however, the Basement Complex does include older rocks; ancient sediments and volcanics, folded by disturbance and altered by volcanism to quartzite, slate, marble and schist more than 1 800 million years ago. Although most prevalent between Prieska and Upington, remnants occur frequently along the Orange River all the way to the Richtersveld.

An enormous trough, open to the sea in the west, was the receptacle of sediments that became the sandstones, quartzites, shales and limestones of the Nama System. Magnificently displayed in cross-section by the cleft of the Fish River Canyon, these rocks underlie much of Namibia's interior plateau. They extend northward from the Orange River to the Naukluft Mountains, and eastward from the Namib Desert to Upington, with lesser showings further south near Springbok and Vanrhynsdorp. Submarine subsidence over much of what is now central and northern Namibia led to the accumulation of Damara System sediments, subsequently folded and extensively altered by granite intrusion to quartzite, marble and mica schist.

In the south-western Cape, another huge trough filled with thick sediments

circles, together covering 66 350 square kilometres. In the second stage, a sheet of red granite spread over the centre of the complex. Although all this took place far below the surface, large areas of the complex were afterwards exposed by erosion, while today other areas are covered by more recent formations. In

Zimbabwe, rocks similar to those of the first stage occur in the Great Dyke, which is five to ten kilometres wide and runs roughly north to south across the country for 480 kilometres.

Deposited 50 to 150 million years later on Bushveld and earlier rocks, the brightly coloured shales, sandstones and that became the limestones, grits and characteristic blue shales of the Malmesbury System. These underlie Cape Town itself and the low, rolling hills of the Swartland, from the Cape Peninsula to west of Citrusdal. To the north and east, smaller exposures occur as far afield as Vanrhynsdorp and the Little Karoo. Folded some 600 million years ago, these Malmesbury rocks were invaded at about the same time by Cape Granite, which today forms the rugged headlands at Saldanha Bay, an almost continuous range of hills from St Helena Bay to Paarl Mountain, and the smooth slopes below the sandstone ramparts of Table Mountain.

Planed to an even surface over a period of some 100 million years, the Malmesbury rocks and Cape Granite were the foundations upon which the Cape System was built. Once again a vast depression, extending across the whole of the south-western and southern Cape, became the depository of sediments eroded from areas lying to the north. Accumulating under fluctuating conditions from about 500 million to about 400 million years ago, they formed successive layers of shale and sandstone, to a total thickness of several thousand metres. From them, subsequent erosion and disturbance of the earth's crust shaped Table Mountain, the ranges running northward from Cape Hangklip to the Cedarberg, and the parallel folded ranges of the southern Cape, including the Outeniqua and Swartberg which enclose the Little Karoo.

Towards the end of this period, a great basin-shaped depression, extending well beyond the present eastern coastline of the subcontinent, developed between the newly formed Cape System and the much older geological systems in the north. It became the cradle of southern Africa's last great geological system, the Karoo System.

Some 300 million years ago, immense ice-sheets converged on the basin from surrounding high ground in Namibia, Griqualand West and the Transvaal to the north, and adjoining landmasses to the east, south and west that have since been replaced by the Indian and Atlantic oceans. The whole of southern Africa was then a frozen waste, above which only the tips of the highest mountains projected. When eventually the ice melted, the pebbles, clays and coarse rock fragments that had been transported many hundreds of kilometres in the icy grip of glaciers were dumped on the surface, where they were cemented into a type of conglomerate known as tillite. The so-called Dwyka Tillite forms the first layer of the Karoo System.

As the deepest part of the original basin was near its southern extremity, the strongest movement of ice was towards the south, and consequently it was here that the greatest thickness of tillite and subsequent sediments of the Karoo System accumulated.

The earliest sediments deposited on the tillite originated in highlands lying outside the present coastline. Along the southern margin of the basin they formed shales and sandstones to a total thickness of 3 000 metres. Further north the deposits were much thinner. North and east of present-day Bloemfontein, sediments carried by running water from the east and north-east settled in river systems that had their deltas in the basin. Here they formed shales, sandstones and conglomerates, alternated with seams of coal produced by the large masses of vegetation rotting in the swamps of that time. Fine sediments filtering through from all sides formed an unvaried sequence of shales in the central region. All these deposits are grouped together in a subdivision of the Karoo System called the Ecca Series.

In these drab Ecca sediments the typical fossils are of plants – seed-ferns, which are intermediate between ferns and cycads, and tree-sized varieties of today's club-mosses – belonging to a distinct type of vegetation that evolved in the southern hemisphere after the Dwyka glaciation. In the brightly coloured strata of the succeeding Beaufort Series, however, it is possible to trace the evolutionary progress of creatures, from early amphibians and reptiles, to reptiles displaying mammal-like characteristics. The red, purple, blue and green sequence of shales and mudstones containing their fossil remains are interbedded with sandstones that have weathered to a yellowish shade. Forming the surface of a far larger area of South Africa than any other rock series, these sediments cover virtually the whole geographical region known as the Karoo, completely encircle the Natal

5. *Its aperture clearly visible from the sea, the offshore formation known as Hole in the Wall is a familiar landmark of the Wild Coast.*

6. *Early morning mists shroud the hillside behind the sparkling still waters of Knysna 'lagoon'.*

Drakensberg and Lesotho highlands, and extend northward to Kroonstad and eastward to the Transkei coast.

While the Beaufort sediments were accumulating, the older rocks in the southern Cape began crumpling under pressure from a landmass lying south of the present shoreline, forming ranges of folded mountains roughly parallel to the coast, from near Worcester to Port Elizabeth. The folding continued throughout the period that sediments of the ensuing Stormberg Series were amassing in the inland basin, and a second zone of folding produced the ranges that parallel the western Cape coast.

The Stormberg Series forms the mountainous region of Lesotho and the fringing area in South Africa. Its lowest levels terrace the landscape with coarse grey sandstone and bluish shale, comprising material eroded from the southern Cape mountains. Plant fossils present in these rocks disappeared in the massive red and purple mudstones laid upon them in the shallow waters of alluvial flats as the climate became progressively more arid. Dinosaurs are the

typical fossils of these Red Beds, and of the fine-grained Cave Sandstone formed from sand dunes that covered the Beds when desert conditions eventually prevailed. Named for the shallow caves characteristically hollowed in their exposed faces, these former desert sands are displayed to their greatest perfection by the sheer pink and cream cliffs of Golden Gate.

Initiated by ice, the Karoo System was completed by fire. Some 180 million years ago it was given a massive basalt capping by lava erupting from the earth at many points. Piling flow upon flow in rapid succession, to a total thickness of more than 1 400 metres, the lava spread out over most of southern Africa. But subsequent erosion has removed the capping from all except small portions of the vast area it once covered. The Erongo Mountains, in Namibia, and the Batoka Plateau, in which the Zambezi River cut the Victoria Falls, are scattered fragments. Even the mighty buttresses and towering peaks of the Natal Drakensberg and the Maluti Mountains are no more than isolated, though spectacular, remnants.

Throughout the extensive area covered

by Karoo sediments, underground disturbances continued for some time after these massive eruptions. Enormous quantities of molten material thrust up through weaknesses in the shales and sandstones, until checked by the newly formed basalt mantle. Eventually cooling underground, this material formed dolerite 'dykes' in vertical weaknesses, and 'sills' where it spread out into horizontal weaknesses between sedimentary layers. Anything from less than a metre to more than 300 metres thick, these dolerite sills are responsible for the commonest features of the Karoo basin, forming the flat tops of kopjes and raised table-lands, where the softer rocks above and about them have been eroded away.

At this time, Africa did not exist as a separate continent. With Antarctica, South America, Australia, Madagascar and Peninsular India, it was part of a super-continent, Gondwanaland. Thus the rocks of the Karoo System have equivalents in what were then adjoining parts of these continents. It is possible that the disturbances that caused the folding of the Cape mountains, the copious eruptions of the Stormberg lava and the widespread formation of dolerite dykes and sills, were early symptoms of loosening ties between the continents, which would lead to the dissolution of Gondwanaland 45 million years later.

When Africa emerged as a separate entity about 135 million years ago, running water immediately began channelling down to the new coastline, carving out deep valleys, broadening them and creating a widening belt of lower land along the coast. The basalt of the Drakensberg, which initially extended all the way to the east coast, retreated inland as fast-flowing streams and rivers ate back into it and gradually eroded it away. Having removed the basalt capping, they progressively exposed dolerite-riddled Cave Sandstone and older mudstones, shales and sandstones of the Karoo System, which now form the surface of Transkei, the Natal Midlands and the foothills of the Drakensberg. On the Wild Coast and in the Valley of a Thousand Hills they uncovered great blocks of sandstone similar to the sandstone of the Cape Peninsula, as well as tracts of Basement granite.

As the continents drifted further apart, massive adjustments took place in the earth's crust, causing the 'uplift' of the whole African continent some 65 million years ago. But the land was not all raised to the same extent. The result was a vast interior basin, rimmed by a broad, mountainous ridge. Known as the Great Escarpment, this ridge is built by several geological systems. In Zimbabwe, the Eastern Highlands are of Stormberg-age basalt, Basement granite and Frontier quartzite. South of the Limpopo, the principal component of the Great Escarpment is Transvaal quartzite. Further south, it is formed by the mighty basalt wall of the Drakensberg. From east to west across the southern end of the subcontinent it separates the Upper and Great Karoo regions with a dolerite-capped ridge of Karoo System sediments. Up the west coast it is chiefly composed of rocks of the Cape, Nama and Damara systems.

Subsequent major uplifts, 20 million and five million years ago, invigorated the erosive power of streams and rivers by causing them to flow faster as they descended to lowered sea-levels. The material they excavated and bore to the coast accumulated offshore as marine sediments. The most extensive of these deposits, nearly 1 200 metres thick in the vicinity of Lake St Lucia, rose from the sea during the last major uplift, about two million years ago, adding the broad

coastal plain of Mozambique and northern Zululand to the subcontinent.

Since the most recent uplift, the growth and shrinking of polar ice-caps have caused the sea-level to fluctuate several times. During the ice ages, more of the planet's water was held in the ice-caps, and the sea-level dropped. As the ice-caps melted, releasing water into the oceans, the sea-level rose. Some 10 000 years ago, after the last European Ice Age ended, the rising sea 'drowned' the lower valleys of rivers, creating the lagoons and lakes associated with estuaries at many points on the coast.

Rivers draining westward through the Orange River system excavated Karoo sediments in the interior and transported them to the Atlantic Ocean at Oranjemund. From there, the north-flowing current carried them up the coast to create the great dune fields of the Namib Desert. When arid climates prevailed, desert winds spread red Kalahari sand over a third of the subcontinent, from south of the Orange River to the Zaire watershed, and from western Zimbabwe to Etosha Pan.

Through the ages, the climates that have shaped the natural wonders of southern Africa have ranged between the extremes, producing glaciers, swamps and deserts in the same places at different times. As in ages past, climate continues to change the landscape, although its effects may not be apparent over such a short period as a human lifespan. Yet considering that every year some 400 million tonnes of soil are stripped from the land and deposited in the sea by rainwaters draining into South African rivers, it is not difficult to imagine the effects of such erosion over hundreds of millions of years.

Southern Africa lies in a subtropical zone of high atmospheric pressure, skirted to the south by a belt of westerly winds that blow perpetually around the south pole. In winter, the belt extends further north and these winds bring heavy rain to the coastal regions of the southern and south-western Cape. Inland at this time, however, intensified high pressures promote dry, stable conditions. During the summer months, a tongue of equatorial low pressure reaches in over the interior from the north-east, bringing rain to northern and eastern areas. The high, east-facing mountains of the Great Escarpment, which interrupt the flow of moist air before it reaches the interior, receive the highest rainfall. These winds usually shed their moisture before they reach the western side of the subcontinent, where persistent high pressures and the effects of the icy

Benguela Current sweeping up the coast from the Antarctic account for the arid and semi-arid conditions in the Kalahari, the Karoo, Namaqualand, Bushmanland and the Namib.

Despite the apparent simplicity of the general pattern, there is a fairly wide range of climatic conditions. Seasonal movements in the atmosphere determine the general pattern, and distance from the equator controls the amount of sunlight that may be received. But local factors, such as height above and distance from the sea, as well as the nature of intervening topography, all have a strong bearing on rainfall and temperature and help create a large variety of localized climates.

The diversity of climates and the variety of soil types derived from and deposited on the old rock formations have created an intricate mosaic of vegetation over the land. There are in southern Africa several major groupings of plant species, one of which is the temperate forest, and another is the fynbos vegetation of the winter-rainfall area. Karoo, tropical forest, savanna and grassveld are other vegetation types, and these occur in the area that receives its rain in summer. Fynbos is probably the oldest, and in former times it appears to have spread far beyond its region of origin in the south-western Cape.

As the continuous mountain ranges in the east and south provide a variety of climatic conditions and usually receive more rain than the plains, they have been the principal route along which the fynbos and tropical types of vegetation have advanced and retreated in response to climatic changes. The pattern is continually changing, and today it is the Karoo vegetation that is the aggressor, conquering territory formerly held by the other floras.

Early humans, living on the wild fruits of nature and the flesh of the animals they hunted with primitive weapons, made no more impact upon their environment than any of the other animals that shared it with them. But over the past thousand or so years, and especially in the present century, the greatly intensified pressure of humans on the land, and the ways in which they exploit it, have made them one of the most potent forces at work on the landscape. In their economic endeavours, they have accelerated the processes of erosion and deposition and radically altered the vegetation over much of the subcontinent. Little of what we see today is as it was a century ago. Even less will appear as it is today a hundred years from now.

EXPLANATION OF GEOLOGICAL MAP

ERA (Million Years)	SEDIMENTARY SEQUENCES	IGNEOUS/METAMORPHIC COMPLEXES
CENOZOIC	KALAHARI, NAMIB and COASTAL PLAIN sands	
70 m.y.	COASTAL MARINE sandstones, shales and limestones	
MESOZOIC		
	KAROO	
230 m.y.	DRAKENSBERG basalts	(N) MESSEN, ERONGO, BRANDBERG, NUANETSI
PALAEOZOIC	ECCA, BEAUFORT 'STORMBERG' sandstones and shales	
	DWYKA Tillite (glacial)	
570 m.y.	CAPE sandstones and shales	
PRECAMBRIAN LATE PROTEROZOIC	MALMESBURY, NAMA, DAMARA and KATANGAN quartzites, shales and limestones	CAPE, DAMARA and KATANGAN granite
1080 m.y.		DAMARA and ZAMBEZI gneissic complexes
MIDDLE PROTEROZOIC	UMKONDO, FRONTIER, WATERBERG, SOUTPANSBERG, 'MATSAP', KAAIEN quartzites, shales and lavas ORANGE RIVER lavas	NAMAQUA-NATAL, IRUMIDE and MOZAMBIQUE granite-gneiss complex
2 070 m.y.		(P) PILANESBERG and PHALABORWA alkali complexes
EARLY PROTEROZOIC	TRANSVAAL, GRIQUALAND WEST and LOMAGUNDI quartzites, dolomitic limestones, ironstones and shales	
	VENTERSDORP lavas, quartzites and conglomerates	Layered complexes of various ages (GREAT DYKE, BUSHVELD, KUNENE and others)
2 600 m.y.	WITWATERSRAND and DOMINION conglomerates, quartzites, shales and lavas	URUNGWE and GABORONE granites
ARCHAEAN	PONGOLA conglomerates, quartzites, shales and lavas BARBERTON, MURCHISON, BULAWAYAN and SEBAKWIAN GREENSTONE BELTS lavas and sedimentary rocks	'OLD' granite
3 700 m.y.		LIMPOPO gneiss complex
4 600 m.y.	No known rocks	

Fold trends

Fault

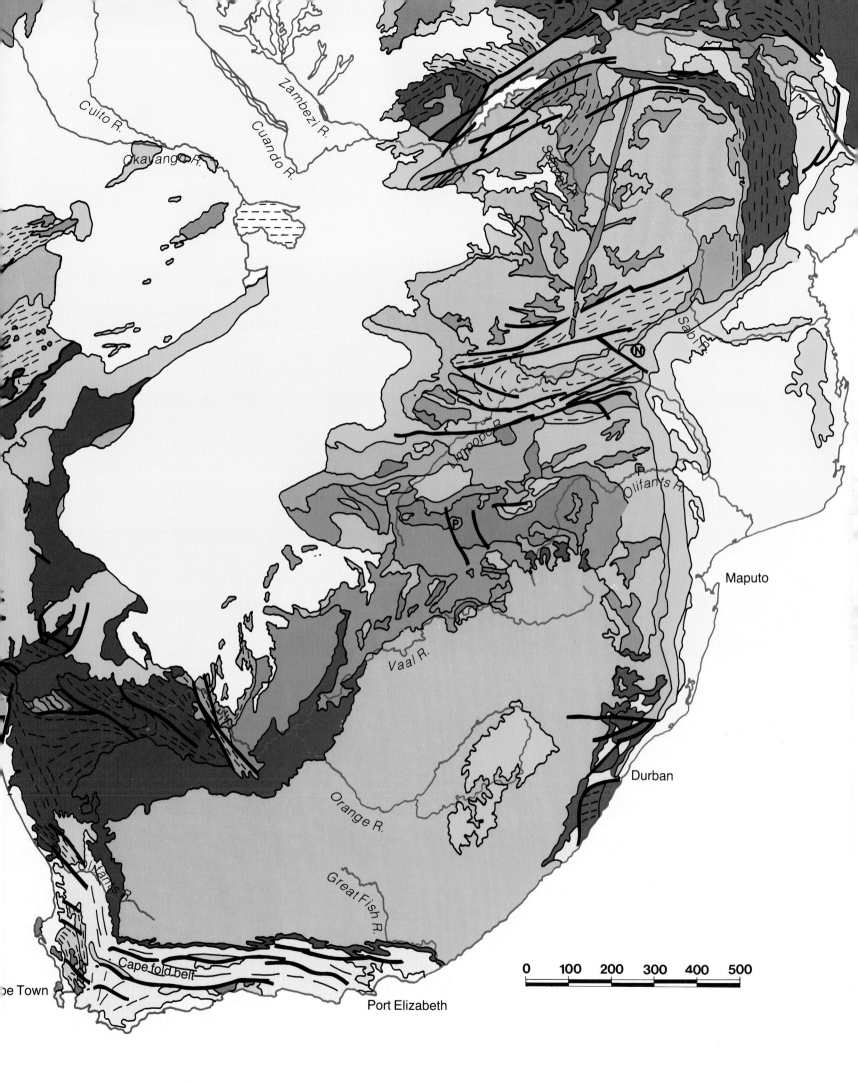

THE MATOPO HILLS
WHERE A NATION'S SPIRITS DWELL

The Matopos have worked their singular magic upon all whose historical paths have crossed the south-western corner of present-day Zimbabwe. The enchantment of this fantastic assembly of granite domes and weirdly balancing boulders is tacitly acknowledged in the finest works and recognized in the most sacred observances of those who have fallen under its spell. The Bushmen, who once hunted undisturbed among these hills, celebrated their wonderment with the pigments they used to embellish the walls of their shelters in the rock. Here, later, the Shona established oracles which spoke with the voice of their national deity, the Ndebele entombed their first king, and European colonists erected shrines to their transient conquest of the land and its earlier inhabitants. It may have been that to some the wild landscape spoke of the primal chaos upon which religion, art and science attempt to impose order, and so seemed to require symbols of their own dominion. Perhaps it was the great age of the rock itself that spoke to them, inspiring in them instinctive reverence for these granite hills.

Between Bulawayo and the Matopos one passes through a belt of red soil decomposed from some of the oldest rocks on earth: ancient sediments and lava flows that at one time covered most of Zimbabwe, including the whole region of the present hills, continuing southward to where the Limpopo River flows today. About 2 500 million years ago immense masses of molten rock pressed up beneath these older rocks. The great heat converted them into rocks colloquially known as green schists, while the molten material cooled gradually and crystallized out as the enormous granite and gneiss batholiths that underlie Zimbabwe's central plateau. Very much later, in Karoo times, sedimentary and volcanic layers mantled the old surface. Subsequent readjustment in the earth's crust produced the Zambezi and Limpopo troughs, and a swelling of the surface

7. In late winter, even before its new leaves have sprouted, a lucky bean tree growing beneath the remnants of a castle kopje raises dense heads of scarlet flowers on the ends of naked stalks.

between them, forming a broad watershed from south-west to north-east across the whole country. The slope on the southern flank being the steeper, rivers and streams draining into the Limpopo eroded the surface more thoroughly, removing the younger rocks completely and leaving only remnants higher up of the ancient green schists, which today are called the 'gold belts'. Lower down, the streams and rivers, drawing added strength from tributaries, have erased all traces of the older rocks, and the great smooth domes and angular stone columns of the Matopos have been shaped from the solid granite that the schists formerly rested on. South of the hills even the granite eminences have been reduced to a broad plain, shelving down into the Limpopo Valley.

Gigantic rounded boulders, which seem set to roll off the summits of massive whaleback hills, and fantastic kopjes that resemble planless stone castles built with haphazardly jointed granite cubes, create an impression of rocky disorder typical of the Matopos viewed from the ground. But seen from the air, the apparent chaos of shapes resolves into a general pattern in which valleys cut by watercourses systematically box the countryside.

The blueprint for this pattern is inherent in the body of the rock itself. When originally the granite cooled and hardened underground, the stresses set up by contraction produced vertical planes of weakness in the rock, one set running roughly from north to south, and another intersecting it from west to east. The major rivers that flow through the Matopos have scoured their beds in the north-south weaknesses. Their tributaries, however, enter them along those that trend from west to east, while the smaller streams that feed the tributaries again follow the north-south weaknesses. Enmeshed in this net of watercourses, the Matopos are being gradually eaten away. In time, this inexorable process will level the hills, as it already has the land between them and the Limpopo.

Within the areas boxed by the rivers and streams lie the great whalebacks and castle kopjes that are the most striking features of this region. While vertical weaknesses, on a much smaller scale than those ordering the landscape, also help shape its specific features, the massive whalebacks owe their domed outlines to arched horizontal weaknesses which probably developed in the granite as the pressure of older rocks weighing down on it was relieved by erosion. Hot days and cold nights cause the surface rock to expand and contract. This initiates a type of weathering reminiscent of an onion

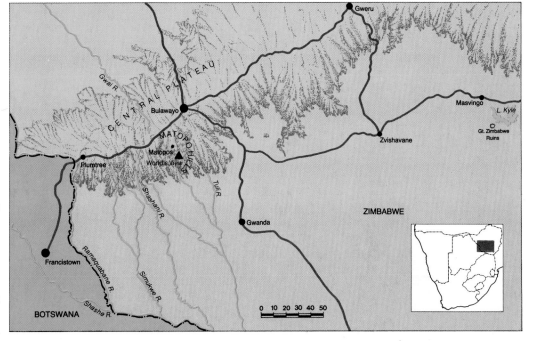

shedding successive layers, as the outer skin is loosened from the inner mass at the arched weakness nearest the surface. The expansion and contraction, and water percolating into fissures, also split up the loosened layer of rock along lesser vertical weaknesses into large, detached blocks. Some of these may linger on the crest, weathering into rounded boulders, but eventually they all slide or tumble down to end in a jumble at the base of the whaleback. There they slowly decompose into the sand that fills the valley bottoms, while the whole process is repeated on the smooth new surface above.

Where the arched weaknesses are not well developed, the vertical fractures take the lead and break the granite mass into roughly rectangular blocks, stacked one upon the other as if by some giant hand, to construct the castle kopjes. But while it is tempting to see the kopjes as the handiwork of some supernatural master builder, they are in fact what is left of the original mass after the surrounding rock has fallen away. The blocks nearest the bottom generally retain their squared edges and corners, but higher up they have been exposed to the weather longer, and so become increasingly rounded towards the top. Early in its development a castle kopje is usually squat, seeming short in relation to its girth, but eventually it may narrow to a slender column of precariously balanced boulders. Finally the balance is upset and it topples, or crumbles away slowly, growing shorter, until it is no longer a feature in the landscape.

Whalebacks, castle kopjes and balancing boulders may be found wherever areas of old granite are exposed,

but nowhere else in such profusion as here. One of the reasons for this is the contribution made by rainfall to the weathering process. Although the Matopos lie in a comparatively dry region, they receive more rain than the plateau immediately to the north because they form a kind of escarpment above the Limpopo Valley, and so benefit first from the moist air carried up the valley from the Indian Ocean by south-easterly winds. Most of the 600 millimetres of rain received here each year falls in spring and summer, but even in winter there is occasional drizzle and the hills are periodically wreathed in mist.

Owing to the higher local rainfall in the Matopos, the many species of plants typical of the central plateau are here supplemented, and in some cases replaced, by those more common to wetter regions. These include tree ferns, lucky bean trees and Cape chestnuts, in Zimbabwe usually associated with the evergreen forests of the Eastern Highlands. Brightly coloured lichens cling tenaciously to the smooth granite surfaces. Where soil collects in small cracks opened in the rock by weathering, mosses and delicate ferns establish themselves; and where the cracks are wider and the soil is deeper, aloes of many kinds raise flaming heads of yellow, orange and red. Tall trees grow where the hills are more broken and there is enough soil to allow their roots to spread. Among these are the paperbark albizia, the paperbark commiphora and the candelabra tree. But the most prevalent and prominent tree is the misleadingly named mountain acacia. Really a species of *Brachystegia* and like its better-known

8

and more widely distributed relative, the msasa, its new foliage is ablaze in spring with the reds and oranges usually associated with autumn. Ferns, shrubs and herbs thrive in their moist shade, and grass fills the intervening open spaces, while red-hot pokers, mauve ground orchids, lilies and purple gladioli brighten the banks of vleis and streams.

The list of animals seems endless, for the wetter climate and rugged topography of the hills favour more species than are maintained by the surrounding thornveld and mopane country. They find shelter and abundant food among the rocks, in the rich vegetation of the valleys and well-wooded kloofs, and around the watering places. In days gone by there must have been many more, especially of the larger species, for the advent of man has depleted them in number and kind.

Baboon troops wander about, overturning stones in search of insects and grubs. Multi-coloured lizards blend into the bright fabric of lichens on rock surfaces. Solitary duiker, steenbok and klipspringer forage for tasty shoots among the broken rocks, where basking puffadders appear to doze. Black-faced vervet monkeys pluck berries among the branches, while a variety of reptiles conceal themselves in dense valley vegetation. Sable antelope graze in the open areas, their fearsome horns ready to defend their young against leopard hunting from lairs in the kloofs. Hares, dassies, a host of rodents, insect eaters and lesser predators of many kinds have their places in the food chain. The air is alive with the hoarse cries of loeries and exultation of larks and babblers and chats,

to name but a few of the scores of resident and migrant bird species. Among the raptors riding the thermals above the hills, the black eagles, their eyries perched on the highest cliff faces, are supreme.

With the profusion of plants and animals for food that must have been available there in early times, the Matopos were a paradise indeed for primitive hunters and gatherers. It is tempting to speculate that this was the 'Eden' of the Bushmen; the place where, according to the mythology of these people still living in the Kalahari thirstland, all animals were human and all spoke the same language. Certainly the Matopos offered them the leisure and inspiration to paint naturalistic masterpieces; timeless studies of animals and scenes that could have been drawn from nature today, although the residence of Bushmen and their ancestors in the Matopos goes back at least 50 000 years.

For the black peoples, who came long afterwards, the hills acquired a mystical significance that survives to the present in the observance that certain of the hills may not be pointed at. The Kalanga, who were the first of the Shona tribes to populate the central plateau, occupied the Matopos during the first millennium AD. The Rozwi, who settled further east, around Great Zimbabwe, although their power afterwards extended over most of the plateau, sent priests to live in the Matopos in the fifteenth century. The caves that they and their successors occupied became holy places of pilgrimage for all Shona, and the principal cave, at a hill named Njelele, is

still visited today by people who come from near and far to consult the oracle.

When the warlike Ndebele, originally from Zululand, settled just north of the Matopos in 1836, they subjugated and assimilated the Kalanga, adopting their spiritual cult, consulting and giving tribute to the oracle in the Matopos. The Ndebele king Mzilikazi, when told that the hills were called Madombo meaning 'the rocks', is reputed to have renamed them Matobo, 'the bald heads'. After his death in 1868 his remains were interred in a cave on a hill that ever since has been known as Ntumbane, 'the burial place'.

It was in the rugged Matopos that the Ndebele made their last stand against British colonizers in 1896. Here, six years later, the spirit behind the conquest, Cecil John Rhodes, was laid to rest. The site he had selected for burying national heroes was on a hill he named View of the World, long venerated by earlier inhabitants as Malindidzimu, 'the dwelling place of the spirits'.

A revolution later, the new rulers of Zimbabwe have removed his statues from public places, but in the Matopos he has been left to dwell undisturbed among the spirits that at different times have ruled the land.

8. *Probably because of its colour, Ififi, meaning 'blue jay', is the name given to this typically shaped granite whaleback in the Matopos.* **9.** *A former whaleback, reduced by weathering of fractures in the granite to a heap of huge boulders.* **10.** *Seemingly poised to roll off, great boulders group on Malindidzimu, 'the dwelling place of the spirits', renamed View of the World by Cecil John Rhodes, who chose this hill as his burial place.*

9

10

THE CHIMANIMANI MOUNTAINS

GATEWAY TO MONOMOTAPA

Centuries before Europeans began settling in southern Africa, Arab merchants on the Mozambique coast were trading their wares for gold extracted from the ancient green schists in the Shona Kingdom of Monomotapa, centred commercially and administratively around what are now the stone ruins of Great Zimbabwe. Travelling from the coastal lowlands to the Zimbabwe plateau, one of the routes taken by traders lay through a gap in the precipitous escarpment bordering these two countries today. The gap was known locally as Chemamemame, meaning 'pincers', while the mountain mass it cut through bore the name Mawenje, which means 'steep'. But the first white settlers in this area misunderstood the locals and took the name of the gap for that of the mountains, and so the latter have been called Chimanimani ever since.

The huge white massif from which the mountains have been carved belongs to the aptly named Frontier System. Together with the blue quartzites of the Umkondo System which form the Melsetter Plateau to the west of the mountains, they were deposited on the sloping eastern flank of the Basement granite between 1 600 and 1 900 million years ago. At this time the whole of present-day Mozambique was covered by the sea. These quartzites are perhaps better envisaged as parts of a single system, in which the white quartzite was formed further out to sea, in deeper water than the blue.

Subsequently, in late Precambrian times, tremendous mountain-building pressures from the east thrust the white quartzite up on to the shoulder of the blue quartzite plateau, folding, shearing and shattering the Chimanimani massif in the process.

Seen from the Melsetter Plateau, the upper faces of the mountains seem to have a waxy lustre which may, depending on the light, be tinted blue or grey, pink or a creamy shade. But the summit and valleys of the thrust faults recall the age of upheaval. Here are jagged outcrops and the debris of splintered boulders, grotesquely weathered, like gargoyles, and daubed with red, orange, brown and green lichens.

From the Mozambique plain the summit of Binga, the highest peak, rises 2 440 metres above sea-level. The Chimanimani are, therefore, a barrier to the moisture-laden winds blowing across the lowlands from the Indian Ocean. Sudden storms strike without warning, the peaks are often draped in showers of light rain, and mists drift through the valleys, creating a wonderland of clear streams, sparkling waterfalls and deep, peat-stained pools.

Cooler temperatures and higher rainfall than on either plateau or plain have arrayed the summits and slopes, gorges and foothills in floral splendour. As the mountains are on the chief route along which plants have migrated in Africa, there are communities that have lingered here from the time when the Cape fynbos advanced into North Africa and then retreated, and of tropical species that once extended far to the south, but which elsewhere are found only much further north today.

Five aloe species grow on the highest peaks, where the Cape type of vegetation is represented by golden everlastings, three species of erica and two of protea, all of which found a congenial environment at these high altitudes. On the grass-covered high plateau areas, small-leaved brachystegia form open woodland, while bracken and philippia, a shrub related to the ericas, mantle the upper slopes. Evergreen forests choke the ravines, in which typically Cape forest species, such as real yellowwood and mountain cedar, dominate. On the forest margins and on rocky hillsides flourish the Chimanimani tree hibiscus, red mahogany and mvule trees, up to 60 metres tall. These create unbroken canopies that shut out the sunlight among the eastern foothills, while along the lower watercourses there are mahobohobo trees, screw-pines and raffia palms, whose 18 metre-long leaves are among the largest in the plant kingdom. Ferns and mosses carpet the ground and cluster at the feet of the forest trees whose branches are hung with epiphytic orchids and trailing festoons of old man's beard.

Just as the Chimanimani form an age-old bridge that the northern and southern varieties of plantlife have passed over, they serve too as a meeting place for birds of many kinds from the extremities of the continent. Malachite and doublecollared sunbirds from the south coexist with their bronze, yellowbellied and olive relatives from the north. There is a local species of bokmakierie, once thought to occur only in South Africa and Namibia. The magnificent crowned eagle, which inhabits forests below the Great

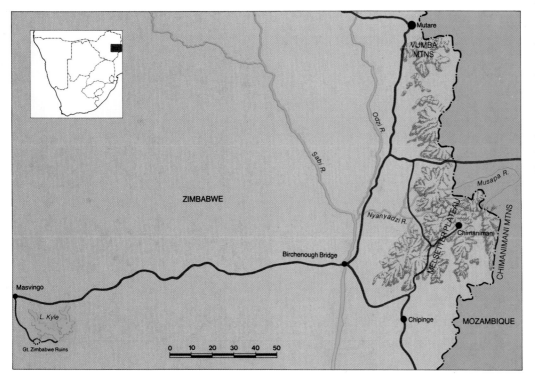

Escarpment from Knysna to Ethiopia, perches atop the tallest trees, scanning clearings for prey to leave the safety of cover. Purplecrested loeries and crested and trumpeter hornbills, all more prevalent further north, provide flashes of vivid colour in the forest green, and fill the air with their noisy chatter.

Scimitar-horned sable antelope graze according to the seasons along circular routes on the high mountain grasslands, where small herds of eland are common. Ever alert to possible dangers, rubbery-hooved little klipspringers perch precariously on quartzite boulders, and leopards hide in thickly wooded gorges. Buffalo, reclusive blue duiker, shy but pugnacious bushbuck and dark green samango monkey thrive in the dense foothill forests, while elephant survivors from the ivory-hunters' purge find sanctuary in all accessible parts of the mountains.

Although the Chimanimani abound with wildlife, they did not hold the same attraction for man, probably because the soils here were less suitable for growing staple grains. An extinct relative of man, *Australopithecus*, and our early ancestor, *Homo habilis*, passed this way some two million years ago on their southward

11

migrations down the well-watered highlands from their East African genesis. Stone artefacts, rock art and potsherds discovered in caves indicate that different peoples have lived in these mountains through the ages, but never in large numbers.

When the political climate was favourable towards the old Arab traders, there were easier routes than the Chemamemame gap by which they could reach the interior plateau, through the river valleys of the Zambezi in the north, and the Sabi to the south. Thus the hidden beauties of the mountains were not violated. They are still only accessible on foot, along old trails trodden by elephants. And so, the Chimanimani Mountains have remained one of the few unspoilt places in southern Africa, one of unique beauty, where frothing streams of amber water plunge into rugged quartzite gorges.

11. *In an eland sanctuary a few kilometres north of Chimanimani (formerly Melsetter), the white lace of Bridal Veil Falls cascades down a cliff into a pool which is said to be haunted.* **12.** *One of the routes by which Arab traders from the coast reached the interior plateau of the gold-rich Kingdom of Monomotapa lay through this cleft in the mountains, the Chemamemame gap.*

12

13

14

13. North-west of the Chimanimani Mountains, towards Cashel, the border between Zimbabwe and Mozambique roller-coasts over ridge after ridge of paling blue mountains.   **14.** The huge quartzite massif of the Chimanimani Mountains is continually changing colour, from blue to grey to pink or cream, depending on the light.   **15.** More commonly a tree of the Lowveld in the Zambezi, Sabi and Limpopo valleys, the baobab was first identified and described by the French explorer Michel Adanson. It is endowed with many supernatural associations in African folklore, including the tale that the hyena, instructed by God to plant its first seed, planted it upside down. The tree is noted for its squat, thick trunk and root-like branches. Individual trees with trunks nine metres in diameter are estimated to be over 3 000 years old.   **16.** Forest trees hung with trailing festoons of old man's beard.   **17.** The Chimanimani range has its share of colourful flora, like this seeroogblom or poison bulb, so-called because local tribesmen used poison from the plant on their arrow tips.

THE WITWATERSRAND
GOLD FROM FOSSIL RIVERS

The quest for gold in Africa is probably as old as the mines that supplied King Solomon. Gold extracted by ancestral Shona from the ancient green schists on Zimbabwe's central plateau enticed Arab and Portuguese adventurers to seek their fortunes in the old Kingdom of Monomotapa. In the seventeenth century, dreams of procuring the wealth of Monomotapa spurred the Dutch at the Cape to send several expeditions into the unknown interior to find the legendary kingdom. With their ignorance of African geography, none of the expeditions came near to finding it. But by amazing coincidence, the Dutch speculated that its capital lay in the vicinity of present-day Pretoria – hundreds of kilometres south of Monomotapa, but virtually within sight of the ridge where the world's richest gold deposits would be found some two centuries later: the Witwatersrand.

On the surface, the Witwatersrand seems less a natural wonder than an economic miracle. But it is the gold in the natural rock that caused the 'miracle', and the pursuit of economic interest has been responsible for revealing a natural wonder concealed beneath the surface.

The rainwaters of the Transvaal Highveld are divided between the Limpopo and Vaal rivers by quartzite ridges that form an escarpment through Johannesburg and run from west to east for a distance of 56 kilometres. Named the Witwatersrand, 'ridge of white waters', for its clear streams, by Boer trekkers who settled north of the Vaal in the late 1830s, the escarpment is today obscured by buildings.

Although the quartzite ridges form the highest ground, they are actually peripheral outcrops of the lowest level in the sedimentary rock sequence

comprising the Witwatersrand System. They rise above the later deposits here in much the same way that a basin rises above its contents at its rim.

The Witwatersrand basin is moulded in what was once a huge depression in the old granite shield, similar in age and character to the old granite shield exposed in the Matopos. Its contents are sediments derived from weathered fragments of even older rocks, equivalent to the 'gold-belt' schists in Zimbabwe, which many millions of years ago formed the surrounding high ground.

Since the multi-layered succession of Witwatersrand quartzites, shales and conglomerates were deposited, they have been covered over by younger rock formations. As a result, they are visible at the surface only at a few places near the rim of the basin, and in the centre. Here, much later, a dome of solid Basement granite, 40 kilometres in diameter and known as the Vredefort Ring, pressed up through the floor of the basin, folding back the younger rocks around it, and carrying the underlying Witwatersrand sediments to the surface on its shoulders.

The full extent of the original basin in which the earlier quartzites and shales were deposited is uncertain, because the margins of these formations have been eroded away. By the time the later quartzites and conglomerates were deposited, however, the basin of actual deposition had shrunk towards the centre.

As these conglomerates are the prime source of gold in this region, systematic drilling by the mining companies has established the shape and size of the reduced, but nevertheless extensive basin. It includes the whole area between Krugersdorp and Springs in the north and north-east, and Klerksdorp and Welkom in the west and south-west. Drill probes and mining operations thousands of metres below the surface have in fact

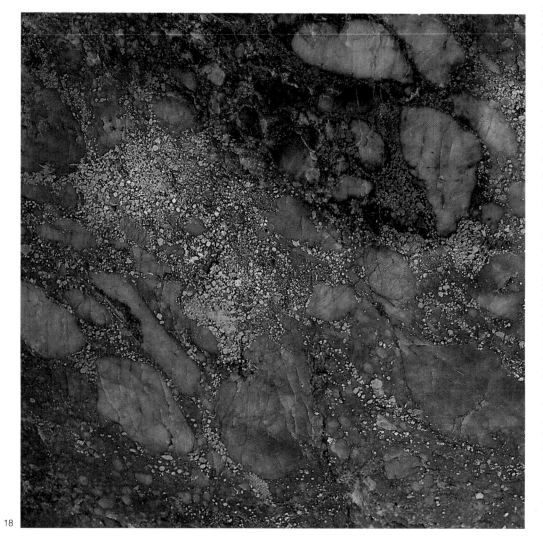

18. *Called 'banket' by early miners because of its resemblance to a Dutch cake, this gold-bearing conglomerate was deposited by rivers that flowed in the Transvaal some 2 800 million years ago. The gold particles are usually microscopic and what appears to be gold is often iron pyrite, also called 'fool's gold'.* **19.** *Clearly defined within the surrounding white quartz, there is no mistaking this vein of gold.*

produced a fairly detailed picture of this ancient basin, in which are discernible the deposits and channels of powerful rivers that once flowed here, into an inland sea, some 2 800 million years ago.

Because the Witwatersrand sediments were laid down over a period of hundreds of millions of years to reach a combined thickness of nearly 8 000 metres on the Central Rand, the drill-cores provide not one but many pictures at various levels, each depicting a different stage of deposition. Strung together, these pictures become individual frames in a film sequence of the evolution of the whole Witwatersrand System.

The huge, slowly subsiding depression in the old granite, into which streams and rivers poured water and detritus from surrounding high ground, stretched from the northern Free State, across the southern Transvaal to Natal. During the time that the lower 5 000 metres of sediments were laid down, the depth of the water in this vast natural sump was not constant, as the rate at which the sediments built up did not keep pace with the rate at which the depression was subsiding. Consequently there were long periods during which fine sediments settled in deep water to form thick layers of shale. Layers of quartzite, formed from coarser sediments that accumulated when the water was shallower, separated these shale layers. Later, however, a balance was struck between the rate of subsidence and the rate of deposition. As a result, the upper layers of the Witwatersrand System, deposited in shallow water, consist of the coarser-grained quartzites and conglomerates.

Recent studies of these sediments show that they were deposited principally by rivers entering the basin at four points around its margin, then fanning out over deltas of their own making to distribute ever more widely the material they carried. The most significant contributions were made by rivers entering the north-western part of the basin, near Krugersdorp, on the West Rand, and through the Boksburg Gap, between the Central Rand and the East Rand. Somewhat lesser contributions were made by rivers entering west of Klerksdorp and south of Welkom.

As the flow slowed and the carrying power of the rivers diminished upon entering the basin, the heaviest fragments were naturally dumped first. The sediments are consequently thickest and composed of the coarsest material where they are closest to the points of entry, and become thinner and finer further into the basin. The minute particles of gold,

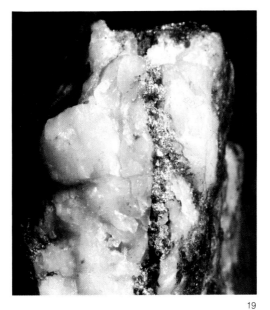

19

because of the metal's high specific gravity, were deposited with the larger rock fragments. The richest concentrations of gold thus occur in the conglomerates that have the greatest proportion of large pebbles, because they were formed in the main channels along which the rivers transported the sediments.

The most productive goldfields in the world are based on the gold deposited in these channels and cemented into the conglomerates. However, it was in the quartzites that gold was first discovered on the Witwatersrand in 1853, and the man responsible for the discovery, a British mineralogist named John Henry Davis, was summarily deported by the Transvaal government. Their fears that his find would lure a flood of foreign fortune

seekers were not unfounded, for the discovery of gold in the conglomerates 30-odd years later revived British interest in the Transvaal and led eventually to the Anglo-Boer War.

Diggers had been panning gold in the eastern Transvaal for several years when, in 1885, an accomplished amateur geologist, Fred Struben, realized that the real wealth of the Witwatersrand lay in the conglomerates, which locally were called 'banket' because they resembled a popular Dutch almond confection of that name. But while Struben was busy proving his claim to his own exacting satisfaction, George Walker, an English mill-hand who had formerly worked for him, and an Australian gold-digger named George Harrison, stumbled on an outcrop of the main Witwatersrand reef on the farm Langlaagte. Two months later, in September 1886, the area was proclaimed a goldfield, and the rush was on.

It would not advance our purpose here to go more deeply into the growth of gold mining as the main pillar of the South African economy. It is, however, worth observing that, whereas the impact of man on scenery is usually most evident in his contribution to erosion, the great minedumps that are to be seen everywhere on the Witwatersrand today show him as an agent of deposition. As the great forces of nature have converted mountains into valleys and valleys into mountains, so through the agency of man, rock from thousands of metres underground has been crushed and refashioned into large, flat-topped hills that in places fill the skyline.

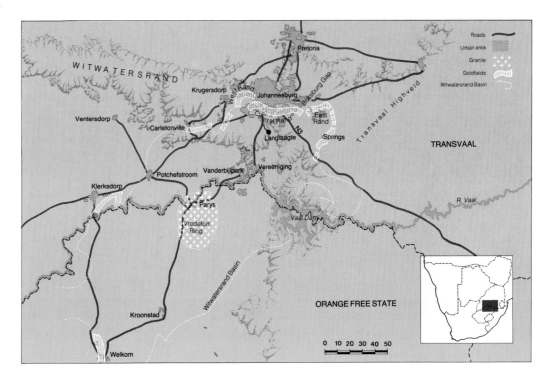

THE BLYDE RIVER CANYON

RIVERS OF SORROW AND JOY

Plunging more than a thousand metres to the Lowveld from the highlands of the Transvaal Drakensberg, the Blyde River cuts away the massive escarpment to carve out the only true canyon in South Africa. Where it emerges from the mountains between Marepe and Swadene peaks, towering quartzite krantzes frame an unbroken vista of bushy lowland, reaching beyond the horizon towards Phalaborwa in the north-east, and eastwards to the sea.

Viewed from a height of some 700 metres, the river threads through the canyon like a slender silver ribbon. Between lofty pink krantzes and thickly grown slopes, it descends rapidly from the high-mountain grassland at its source, through bands of fynbos and temperate rain forest to the dense pile of tropical bush on the plain.

Like the Chimanimani Mountains, the Transvaal Drakensberg is a bridge over which northern and southern varieties of

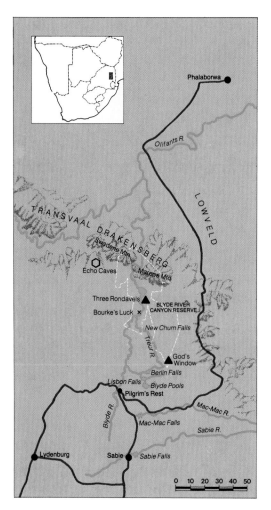

plantlife have migrated through the ages. It too is a link in the chain of ranges that forms the Great Escarpment down the eastern side of Africa.

Here in summer the tall, east-facing ramparts intercept moist winds from the Indian Ocean, forcing the warm air to rise, so that, suddenly chilled, its moisture condenses out before the air passes on to the interior as a dry wind. Thus the Blyde River, until it leaves the mountains, lies in the so-called 'mist belt'.

The quartzites that determine the clean-cut features of the Transvaal Drakensberg escarpment are the fundamental rock formations of the Transvaal System. They were deposited in Precambrian times in a vast inundated depression in the old granite shield. Today they define the extreme eastern margin of the System with powerful krantzes rising abruptly from the granite plain along a 240-kilometre front, from Carolina to Letaba Point. The most striking crags are on Marepe Mountain, where the quartzites are 762 metres thick. On either side of Marepe they become progressively thinner, while north of Letaba Point the quartzites have disappeared altogether, and the escarpment is formed by the old granite itself.

Formerly the quartzites were covered by the dolomites and other later series of the Transvaal System. The dolomites are still prominent, with a thickness of more than 900 metres near Pilgrim's Rest, where the Blyde River has its source. But above the canyon, and elsewhere along the escarpment, these coverings have been stripped by weathering. Streams cutting downward exposed the resistant quartzites. What started as little more than quartzite steps in the landscape broadened into soaring precipices as the unprotected granite surface to the east was denuded faster. And where erosion bared underlying granite, it went on to shape the granite into steep slopes and break up the escarpment in places into a series of long spurs.

20. *Dominated by powerful quartzite krantzes, the Blyde River winds through its canyon in the Transvaal Drakensberg. Behind the cone-capped summits of the Three Rondavels, massive Marepe (right) and Swadene guard the river's exit from the mountains.*

Not surprisingly, the massive resistant quartzites, their high relief and the heavy rainfall have produced many waterfalls in the Transvaal Drakensberg, of which the Sabie, Berlin, Lisbon and 60 metre-high Mac-Mac falls are the best known. But none matches the grandeur of the great canyon sliced through the quartzites by the waters of the Blyde River.

Draining an area of some 3 000 square kilometres that receives upward of 2 000 millimetres of rain a year, the headwaters of the Blyde River flow north from the Pilgrim's Rest hills on a shale bed through a broad dolomite valley. Water penetrates the soluble dolomite through fissures, dissolving out huge caverns, such as the nearby Echo Caves. However, most are inaccessibly deep underground, where they fill quickly with water during summer rains. Springs in the valley release this water throughout the year, ensuring a strong flow even during the dry winter months.

As a result of high rainfall, steeply sloped terrain allowing water little time to evaporate, and the natural conservation and release of water by the dolomite, the Blyde River receives the highest run-off of any river in southern Africa. Nearly half the moisture falling in the catchment area eventually finds its way into the stream.

About 30 kilometres north of Pilgrim's Rest the riverbed sinks rapidly below the surrounding countryside into a narrow, sheer-sided channel which deepens

21

steadily all the way to Bourke's Luck, where the Treur River enters the Blyde at right-angles from the south-east. In summer the violent uniting of their two floodwaters generates a powerful whirlpool at this spot.

Here the swirling rocks and pebbles have, over thousands of years, drilled out one of the most spectacular assemblies of potholes in Africa. Pieces of rock falling into slight depressions in the riverbed, spun round and round by the current, assisted and replaced by other stones as they wore away to nothing, have gradually enlarged and deepened the original depressions into big cylindrical holes in the solid rock.

Most Bourke's Luck potholes are from two to three metres deep and equally broad, but several are over six metres deep. As the deepest are also the oldest, however, most of them have already broken through their outer walls. Where the hole in one is wider at the bottom than at the top, it breaks through low down into the pothole on the level below it, so that the water draining out the bottom of the first now wells up from the mouth of the second. More commonly the erosion of the outer wall begins at the top and works its way downward. Where the side is only starting to wear away, the water spills over the lip in a small cascade. But where the side has been opened up all the way down to the next level, water crashes down inside and flows on from the pool at the bottom to the next pothole, and the next, and so on into the canyon itself.

It seems fitting that rivers named Blyde,

'joy', and Treur, 'sorrow', should meet at a place called Bourke's Luck. The potholes took the name of an early digger whose good luck it was to pan a fortune in gold nuggets at this spot. The two rivers were named many years earlier. Behind their naming is a tale of people who mourned too soon and were filled with joy when they discovered their mistake.

In 1844 the Voortrekker leader, Hendrik Potgieter, headed a party with four wagons to open a trade route with the Portuguese at Delagoa Bay. As it was already late in the year when they reached the edge of the high plateau, they feared being caught in the Lowveld by the onset of the rainy season and dying of malaria, as others had before them. Leaving the encumbering wagons with the women and children and a few able-bodied men beside a stream, Potgieter and the rest of the men pressed forward on horseback. When they did not return some days after the agreed date, those waiting lost hope of seeing them again and named the stream Treurrivier, in record of their sorrow. They had scarcely begun to retrace their journey, however, when they were overtaken by the returning horsemen at another stream, which they dubbed Blyderivier, to commemorate their joyous reunion.

Below the confluence, the channel of the Blyde broadens like a revelation, and the combined stream pours into the canyon to continue its winding descent through the mountains. High above the forested lower slopes, two great bands of quartzite, separated by a band of shale,

form vertical faces as high as 200 metres, and the eastern sky is blocked out by three peaks whose conical crowns have earned their title, the Three Rondavels. Further to the east rises the flat-topped summit of Marepe. Almost 2 000 metres above sea-level, it is the mighty outer gate-post of the poort through which the Blyde River finally enters the Lowveld to join the Olifants River.

Until recently known as Mariepskop, and before that Maholoholo, 'the very big one', Marepe Mountain was a refuge and stronghold of Pedi and Pulana clansmen who fled to the Lowveld from Mzilikazi. Here they were obliged to defend themselves against the Swazi, who regarded the whole territory as far as the Olifants River as their exclusive domain. Under their leader, Marepe, the fugitives scaled the summit by way of a narrow connecting dyke, and were easily able to beat off their Swazi attackers by raining boulders on them with deadly effect.

Human occupation of this part of the Transvaal Drakensberg goes back a long time. Middle Stone Age implements have been found here. Paintings on cave walls testify to long occupation by Bushman hunters before either black fugitives or white gold diggers came to this valley.

Today the Blyde River Canyon winds through a nature reserve for 57 kilometres. Tarred roads carry busloads of sightseers to vantage points, aluminium footbridges give them easy access to the potholes, and shops and resorts cater to their comfort and recreation. Bushman laughter echoes no more among the krantzes. The cries of battle long ago fell silent on Marepe Mountain. At its foot the Blyde River waters are dammed by a wall 72 metres high across the poort, and the roar of powerboats proclaims that the former home of Man the Hunter is now the playground of Man the Tourist.

To purists wanting all of nature preserved in a pristine state, this seems a travesty. But it reflects the symbiotic tension between conservation and recreation. Conservation is expensive, and there are far fewer committed conservationists than people seeking recreation. They must experience the wonders of nature if they are to support their preservation. They will do so if their needs are met. So the shops and chalets, metal bridges and boating waters are terms of a compromise. It ensures that protea and erica flower each year on higher levels, and that creeper-entwined yellowwood and stinkwood, cabbage tree, cycad, wild fig and mobola plum still crowd the lower slopes of the Blyde River Canyon.

23

24

22

21. Once the rocky defences of Pedi and Pulana refugees from Mzilikazi, the tiered ramparts of Marepe defy approach from the riverbed.   **23.** Twin streams of the Lisbon Falls cascade down the face of the escarpment a few kilometres from Graskop.   **22, 24.** The reduced flow in the rivers during winter reveals the great potholes bored by swirling rocks where in summer the churning floodwaters of the Blyde and Treur rivers meet at Bourke's Luck.

25. Step by step, a narrow ribbon of silver water descends the quartzite cliffs of Swadene. Separating the steep faces, thin belts of vegetation show where fertile soil has accumulated on less abrupt slopes formed by layers of softer shale bedded between tough quartzites.   26. Providing abundant water for grassland, forest and fynbos, moisture in the air crossing the Lowveld from the coast turns to mist and light rain as it rises against the face of the escarpment.   27. Cycads, often confused with palms and tree-ferns, are the most primitive seed-bearing plants in existence, having changed little in the last 50 to 60 million years. Instead of flowers, they produce colourful male and female cones on separate plants, the female cones being fertilized by wind-borne pollen from the male cones. Edible flesh covering the poisonous seed kernels attracts baboons, monkeys and hornbills.   28. A popular flowering plant in South African gardens, agapanthus is endemic to the well-watered slopes above the Blyde River.

TRANSVAAL DOLOMITES
CRYSTAL CAVES AND UNDERGROUND RIVERS

The dolomite responsible for maintaining the strong perennial flow of the Blyde River is a rock formation of far wider significance, underlying many thousands of square kilometres in the Transvaal and northern Cape. As a water-bearing formation, it is unrivalled in southern Africa – a largely subterranean natural wonder of enormous proportions.

One of the rock units of the Transvaal System, it was laid down in the salt water that invaded the whole region some 2 400 million years ago. Unlike other sedimentary rocks, formed from deposits of particles introduced by wind and running water from elsewhere, the dolomite was produced by a chemical reaction. Magnesium carbonate in the water combined with the calcium carbonate in existing rocks composed of corals and shells, replacing it with a double calcium magnesium carbonate. The resulting dolomite contains about 50 per cent calcium carbonate and 25 per cent magnesium carbonate. Because these compounds are soluble in water containing carbon dioxide, springs, caves and sinkholes abound in dolomite country.

As a result of these carbonates being leached out, the dolomite is honeycombed with labyrinthine subterranean caverns and passages which absorb vast amounts of water and conduct it to the sources of rivers and streams flowing from the dolomite. Several large towns in the Transvaal owe their origin to the water supplied by springs in the dolomite. Where the caverns and underground passages have opened and dried out, extensive cave systems are encountered, decorated with stalactites and stalagmites. When the roofs of underground caverns collapse, they produce sinkholes at the surface, such as those that suddenly opened and swallowed buildings and people on the Far West Rand in recent years.

After the dolomite was formed, it was covered to a varying extent by the upper quartzites of the Transvaal System, volcanic outpourings of the Bushveld Igneous Complex and rocks of the Karoo System. The surface drainage pattern was determined by the beds of streams and rivers cut in these later rocks. But when eventually the fast-moving waters sliced through the harder rocks to the underlying dolomite, they immediately began to pass down into it instead of flowing over it. The erosion of the valleys continued underground as subterranean channels usurped the water rights of surface streams, so terminating their existence. Similarly, the rain falling on the exposed dolomite did not make its way over the surface to drain into natural valleys, but quickly disappeared into the ground through cracks and fissures in the dolomite.

Water percolating through crevices gradually enlarges them into vertical shafts that swallow the entire drainage. Underground, the water penetrates into other weaknesses in the bedding planes of the dolomite, leaching out the calcium and magnesium carbonates. Eventually a vast network of inter-connected tunnels, passages, galleries and caverns is hollowed out to become the channels of underground streams and rivers. These continually increase in size and link up with one another. As the water also persistently opens up new vertical shafts deeper underground, further labyrinths are excavated at lower and lower levels and the subterranean flow drains into them, finally abandoning the upper networks and leaving them to dry out. And so the process has been repeated over and over again.

In many places massive quartz veins cut across the dolomite underground. Because quartz is impervious, this seaming dams the subterranean rivers and streams, causing the water level to rise behind them until it breaks through over the top and gushes out at the surface from limestone 'eyes'. Several Transvaal rivers originate from such 'eyes', but the flow may also be reduced or withdrawn quite suddenly, as a result of changes in the underground channels. Blockages may divert water from one channel to another. The steady erosive action of two streams may ultimately break through the dolomite wall separating them. One then captures the waters of the other and redirects them to a different outlet. Many promising human enterprises have foundered because the supply of water they depended upon was removed in this way, and there is archaeological evidence that living sites occupied by early humans for thousands of years were often abandoned for the same reason.

In the western Transvaal the dolomite country is flat, except where impervious bands of hard chert in the dolomite form ragged kopjes and projections. Where the dolomite rock itself is exposed, it is

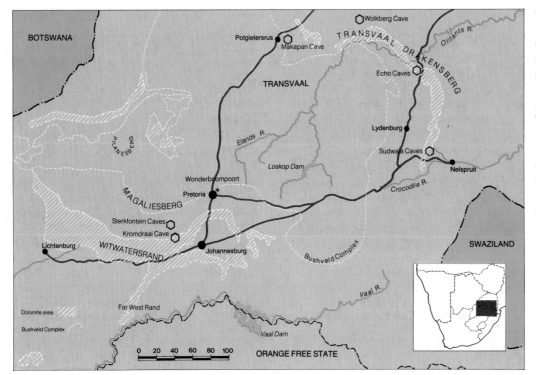

weathered grey or black and fluted and channelled by rain, and finally resembles elephant hide.

Old sinkholes perforate the dolomite country in the northern part of the western Transvaal. North and north-west of Lichtenburg they average 14 to the square kilometre, creating rolling hills. Several are so-called 'wonder holes', through which the waters of underground rivers may be seen many metres below the land surface. The most striking example, however, is in a different dolomite formation in Zimbabwe, where the entrance to the Chinhoyi Caves opens on to the still surface of Sleeping Lake below. These caves are really a series of old sinkholes, linked by underground channels that converge on a larger central sinkhole. Near Lichtenburg, steep-sided valleys end upstream in sheer cliffs as a result of the collapse of the roofs of entire cavernous underground channels.

In the south-western Transvaal erosion is less advanced, so old sinkholes are less common, while new sinkholes continually come into existence. 'Catastrophic' sinkholes occur suddenly, opening up without warning and swallowing whatever happens to be on the surface above them at the time.

Gold mining has accelerated their development on the Far West Rand, where pumping has lowered the water table and so dewatered underground caverns. The water the pumps discharge on the surface percolates down, weakening the roofs of the caverns until they cave in and the loose material they supported disappears into the void below, like sand pouring through an hourglass.

Rivers and streams have intensively dissected the narrow belt of dolomite outcropping on the northern and north-eastern side of the Bushveld Basin near the Great Escarpment. Conical dolomite hills, up to 100 metres high, dominate flat-bottomed valleys. Where the water of long-gone rivers has cut away the bases of these cones, the sides are steeper, and almost vertical dolomite pillars result. The valley sides rise sharply in steps that represent successive erosion surfaces.

Old, dried-out cavern networks opened by sinkholes and hillside erosion form caves throughout the dolomite areas. Like the stepped hillsides, the major cave systems are associated with specific erosion cycles. Where the caves are on more than one level, they were formed by different cycles of erosion, when the water table stood at different levels. Sterkfontein and Makapan caves have only one level, while in the north-eastern and eastern Transvaal, the Wolkberg, Echo and Sudwala caves have three.

The types and combinations of earth and rock deposited in these cave systems

29. *Caused by the collapse of underground caverns in the dolomite, 'catastrophic' sinkholes are particularly prevalent in the south-western Transvaal, where they may occur suddenly in developed and undeveloped areas alike. Although such sinkholes have been appearing for millions of years, mining operations are believed to have increased their frequency in recent times.*

include pieces of rock fallen from the roof, and red earth brought in by percolation from the surface and cemented in standing water. A number of caves must have been completely filled with red earth at some time. The floor later dropped, leaving the red earth stuck to the roof, while the new floor was gradually covered by successive layers of sand and limestone.

It is this lime 'dripstone', deposited after the caves dried out, that forms the stalactites, stalagmites, straw stalactites, and flowstone 'waterfalls' and 'folded curtains'. These are often encrusted with miniature stalactites and crystals, representing a recent phase of minor deposition. Drops of water hanging from fissures in the roof fall, leaving behind minute particles of lime which grow, over a very long time, into carrot-shaped stalactites. Each successive drop travels down a thin tube through the centre to add its little contribution of lime at the tip before falling to the cave floor. They may combine into massive pillars and assemblies like organ pipes. Water dripping from the stalactites also deposits lime on the cave floor. If the drip is slow, a stalagmite may build up from the floor. But if the drip is a fast trickle, it causes too much disturbance where it lands for a stalagmite to form there, and instead spreads a flat limestone sheet over the floor.

Probably the most beautiful of these dolomite caves is the lesser-known Wolkberg Cave, in the northern escarpment area. It is a spectacular sequence of large chambers and passages, underground streams and subterranean lakes, the unbroken surfaces of which mirror dripstone formations rivalling the splendours of the famous Cango Caves in the distant Little Karoo.

Better-known in the escarpment area are the Echo Caves, in a ridge of dolomite hills at the head of the Molapong Valley, north of Lydenburg. The caves derive their name from a dripstone formation that echoes when tapped, and consists of a sequence of connected chambers, the largest of which is 100 metres long and 40 metres high. The caves were probably open for human occupation 53 000 years ago. The Bushman Rock Shelter, a smaller cave in the same valley, has yielded Middle Stone Age deposits between 45 500 and 51 000 years old, and Late Stone Age deposits that are about 10 000 years old. The hiatus in occupation is explained by a long wet period, during which the shelter was too damp to be inhabited.

The most visited underground chambers in the escarpment area are the Sudwala Caves, near Nelspruit. Their entrance is a 12-metre passage leading from a forest midway up the cliff-face of the Mankelekele Mountain, above the valley of a tributary of the Crocodile River. The passage runs into a roughly circular cavern 18 metres high and 66 metres in diameter. In its roof are embedded the saucer-shaped fossils of clusters of algae, representing one of the earliest known forms of life. These occurred in such masses that they were responsible for producing much of the oxygen in the earth's atmosphere, before they were laminated into the dolomite at the time of its formation.

Further chambers are lavishly adorned with bizarre formations of yellowish dripstone, stained red and brown in places by iron and manganese oxides. Unfortunately, as elsewhere, popularizers of the caves have seen fit to give these formations names, such as 'Screaming Monster', 'Weeping Woman' and 'Space Rocket', substituting ready-made analogy for the viewer's direct appreciation of the inherent natural beauty of these phenomena. According to local tradition, the caves continue for 30 kilometres underground, but their full extent has never been determined, and the source of a draught of fresh air wafting through the caves has not been traced. Two and a half kilometres into the mountain mass is an enormous cavern 90 metres long and 45 metres wide, in which the stalactites and stalagmites vary in colour from pure white to shades of blue and green.

Deposits near the entrance indicate that primitive men sheltered here, and oral tradition reveals that two centuries ago Swazi clans took refuge in the caves from marauding Zulu impis. Towards the middle of the last century a Swazi chief, Somcuba, who had been regent during the minority of King Mswazi, was forced to flee when the latter assumed the throne, because he refused to hand over the great herd of cattle he had collected in the king's name while acting as his regent. Eventually, however, he was surprised by a punitive impi sent by the king, and only a few of his followers were able to reach the sanctuary of the caves, led there by a headman called Sudwala, from whom the caves derive their name.

The Makapan and Sterkfontein caves, located in the northern and south-western Transvaal respectively, are rich archaeological sources. Deposits have yielded considerable information about early man and his close relative, *Australopithecus africanus*, believed to have entered southern Africa from East Africa about two and a half million years ago. The first skull of this extinct cousin of man was found in 1924 in the filling of

a similar cave in the dolomite of the Harts River valley, near Taung. Further discoveries followed in caves at Sterkfontein in 1936, Kromdraai in 1938, Makapan in 1947 and Swartkrans in 1948. Since the first find, the fossil remains of 14 individuals have been unearthed at Makapan, and between 25 and 30 at Sterkfontein.

Some 25 kilometres from Potgietersrus, a cluster of caves includes Makapansgat and the Cave of Hearths, so named because within it archaeologists have identified sites at which Early Stone Age men warmed themselves beside their fires.

Makapansgat, directly above the Cave of Hearths, is a relatively new formation, resulting from a collapse of rock into a former extension of the Cave of Hearths, so it has none of the major dripstone and other ancient deposits. In the Cave of Hearths, however, there is a full sequence of deposits, starting with a kind of calc-tufa, which accumulated as calcrete dust

30. *At Chinhoyi, sunlight creates a chiaroscuro of dark water and bright green algae on the still surface of Sleeping Lake, which has formed in a series of dolomite sinkholes linked by underground tunnels.* **31.** *The cluster of tiny white stalactites is a secondary limestone deposit on the puckered dripstone ceiling of the Echo Caves, north of Lydenburg.*
32, 33, 34 *(following page). Bizarre formations of yellowish dripstone, stained by iron and manganese oxides, lavishly adorn chambers in the Sudwala Caves.*

34

blown into the caves during a dry period and was subsequently re-crystallized by water seeping through the roof. The tufa was overlain by red sand that settled on the wet floors. On this red sand surface *Australopithecus* lived, leaving his bones buried in it before the ensuing main period of dripstone formation calcified the surface. Another dry period caused a new deposit of red sand near the entrances, in which Early Stone Age men left their stone implements. Before the entrances, erosion debris was cemented with yet another accumulation of wind-blown red sand, into a breccia that includes the stone implements of the Middle Stone Age occupants and the bones they threw away after their meals.

Makapansgat acquired a place in history as a result of a particularly horrifying episode in the clash over land between the black tribes living in the northern Transvaal and the immigrant Voortrekkers. In October 1854 a hunting party of eight men and ten women and children were slaughtered in a surprise attack by Tlou tribesmen. To escape reprisal, their chief, Makapan, and 2 000

of his people sought sanctuary in the cave. Commandant-general Piet Potgieter and his trekker commando laid siege to the cave in an effort to dislodge them.

Potgieter himself was shot dead when he ventured to the entrance, and his body was retrieved by the later President of the Transvaal Republic, Paul Kruger. After the siege had lasted 25 days, no further shots issued from the cave and the attackers were able to gain entry. Not a living soul remained inside. Some had apparently managed to slip away at various times under cover of darkness, but they left behind the bodies of 1 500 of their clansmen who had died of hunger and thirst in the cave.

After the arrival of white men, almost all the major cave systems in the Transvaal dolomite were plundered by lime-workers who ruthlessly hacked out the dripstone formation to get at tufa for their kilns. Today, however, the formations are protected by law, and the unspoilt portions are preserved as a field of study for scientists and places of wonderment for those who come to gaze upon their beauties.

35

36

35. Minute residues of lime left by dripping water on the ceilings and floors of Echo Caves have accumulated over thousands of years to construct this complex assemblage of stalactite, stalagmite and flowstone. The broken points of several stalactites suggest they were damaged by vandals and souvenir collectors before the caves were given statutory protection. **36.** Embedded in the ceiling of Sudwala Caves, saucer-shaped stromatolites are relics of the earliest known forms of life. They are fossils of algal colonies that flourished in the intertidal zone of Precambrian seas some 2 500 million years ago. So plentiful were the algae at the time that it is thought probable that they produced much of the original free oxygen in the earth's atmosphere. Limy mud, washed over the algae by shallow water, caught in their sticky upper parts and formed a thin layer. The algae grew through it and the process was repeated, slowly building up laminated structures of calcium carbonate that were eventually embodied in the dolomite.

TRANSVAAL MOUNTAINS

ROCKY RIM OF THE BUSHVELD

The great Bushveld Basin of the central Transvaal is rimmed in the east and north-east by the backslopes of the Transvaal Drakensberg. Bounded in the south by the Magaliesberg range, on the northern edge it is overlooked by the red and purple sandstone escarpments of the Waterberg and Soutpansberg. North-west of Rustenburg, the sprawling, circular mass of the Pilanesberg, an extinct volcano almost 30 kilometres in diameter and believed to be the largest of its kind in the world, rises from the level floor of the basin itself.

North of the Witwatersrand, the downward slope towards the Bushveld Basin is interrupted around Pretoria by a series of rocky ridges, a landscape named the Bankeveld, from the Afrikaans word *bank*, meaning 'bench' or 'ridge'. The first of these, Kalkheuwel, is an outcrop of resistant chert in the Transvaal dolomite. The remaining three represent the alternate shales and quartzites in the uppermost series of the Transvaal System. Here erosion has scoured out valleys in the softer shales, 300 metres deep and up to 13 kilometres wide, leaving the hard quartzites of the Timeball Hill, Daspoort and Magaliesberg ranges between them.

The Magaliesberg range, starting west of Rustenburg and petering out well to the east of Pretoria, is the last and most prominent of these ridges. Its bold, south-facing escarpment drops abruptly into the *moot*, or 'moat', as the Voortrekkers named the broad valley in which they laid the foundations for the new capital of their Republic. On the northern side it slopes more gently down into the Bushveld Basin.

It was in the northern foothills of the Magaliesberg that the sable antelope was first recorded and described in 1836 by Captain William Cornwallis Harris. In his

37

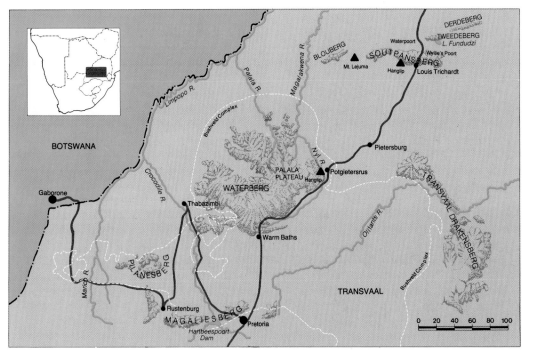

day the range was known as the Cashan Mountains, a corruption of Kgaswane, the name of the chief of the Tlokwa tribe living north of the range before Mzilikazi's Ndebele drove them out. Later, when the Voortrekkers arrived in this area, they found fugitives from the Ndebele hiding in the mountains with their chieftain, Mogale, whom the trekkers associated with the range in giving it its present name.

Harris, by his own account a blood-thirsty hunter, paused in his 'sport' to admire the 'stupendous depth and formidable character of the ravines and chasms, which had been scooped out by mighty torrents of water that roll down during the rainy season. . .' In the valleys he found 'a perfect panorama of game', which included roan and sable antelope, white rhino, buffalo and the animal he had come specifically to hunt, the elephant. Upon entering one valley, he records, 'the whole face of the landscape was actually covered with wild elephants. . . no fewer than 300 within the scope of our vision. Every height and green knoll was dotted over with groups of them, whilst the bottom of the glen exhibited a dense and sable [meaning black] living mass. . .' Considering his occupation, it is not surprising that he also saw 'myriads' of vultures in the Magaliesberg.

37, 38. *Cleft by ravines, the quartzite scarps of the Magaliesberg form the northern bulwark of the protected valley in which Voortrekkers founded the city of Pretoria. In wooded gorges, such as Cedarberg Kloof (above), and valleys, leopard still hunt within sight of city lights.*

Since Harris's time, others like him and farmers who settled in the Magaliesberg have caused the big game to disappear. But colonies of endangered Cape vultures still nest on the lofty cliffs at Skeerpoort and Roberts Farm. Since 1973 these colonies have been intensively monitored by a study group of the Endangered Wildlife Trust. They have noted a remarkable decline in the breeding successes and attribute this mainly to the fact that agriculture has deprived the vultures of the calcium they used to obtain from the bones of wild animals in the veld. This deficiency in the diet of the parent birds causes them to produce eggs with inadequate protective shells, while 15 to 20 per cent of the chicks that do hatch suffer from skeletal abnormality owing to insufficient bone fragments being fed to them by their parents. As a result of these discoveries, unique 'vulture restaurants' have been established, at which the birds may correct the deficiency by dining on the carcasses of farm animals that would otherwise have been buried or burnt.

Many smaller and more secretive animal species still live in the Magaliesberg, however. Small parties of graceful, woolly-coated rhebuck may be seen grazing on grassy slopes and flat summit areas. Klipspringer appear briefly on rocks, duiker hide in thickly wooded gorges and brown hyena move unseen in broken valleys, while jackal and leopard still hunt here within sight of the lights of Pretoria.

Where the suburbs of Pretoria encroach on the Magaliesberg at Wonderboom-poort, there is an amazing growth of the so-called wonderboom fig (*Ficus salicifolia*), which has given its name to the poort and the suburb. Here one tree, estimated to be 1 000 years old, has taken over a huge area. Wherever its lax, spreading branches have touched the ground, they have put down roots from which new trunks have grown. Their branches in turn have repeatedly continued the process to create a forest from a single tree.

While the rocks of the Magaliesberg belong to the last phase of the Transvaal System, those that built the Waterberg, in the north-western Transvaal province, belong to an entirely new system, named the Waterberg System after the range.

Bordered in the north, and partly in the west, by the Limpopo River, the Waterberg range runs roughly from south-west to north-east, from Thabazimbi to Potgietersrus. Here the elevated table-land of the Palala Plateau breaks off 600 metres above the surrounding country, with bold red sandstone cliffs forming escarpments on three sides. The highest point, lying 2 085 metres above sea-level, is at the Thabazimbi end, while Hanglip is poised at 1 793 metres, 32 kilometres from Potgietersrus.

In the northern Transvaal the red sandstones and underlying coarse conglomerates of the Waterberg System cover an area of about 18 000 square kilometres, the Palala Plateau constituting the largest part. Here the sediments were deposited on a surface of pink Bushveld Complex granite and of Transvaal System rocks adjoining the granite on the northern side. The coarser sediments were deposited in inland depressions filled with shallow water. The colour of the sandstone particles, comparable to the red Kalahari sands of today, indicates that they must have accumulated under desert conditions, otherwise the thin layer of iron oxide coating each grain would have been removed by the chemical action of decomposing vegetation under humid conditions.

The first white settlers trekking across the dry Bushveld in the middle of the last century named the range the Waterberg, in recognition of the countless brooks, streams of refreshing drinking water and iron-rich mineral springs on the mountainside. The choice was apt, for the Waterberg is the source of several major tributaries of the Limpopo, which include: the Palala, a corruption of the Northern Sotho word *lephalale*, meaning 'overflowing'; the Dobodzi, named after a Venda clan in the area; and the Nylrivier, formerly called Magalakwena, or 'angry crocodile'.

How the 'angry crocodile' became the 'Nile' is rooted in the mistaken ideas of men whose only knowledge of geography came from the pictorial maps at the backs of their Bibles. They were a group of Voortrekkers under General Johan Adam Enslin, who set off by ox-wagon in the 1830s on a pilgrimage to Egypt and the Holy Land. Arriving after several weeks at a north-flowing river, and seeing nearby a kopje that imagination transformed into a ruined pyramid, they decided that this was the Nile. Although they discovered their mistake as soon as they followed it to its junction with the Limpopo, the Magalakwena has been known as the Nylrivier or Nylstroom ever since.

To the north-east of the Waterberg, the Soutpansberg range, running almost

39. *In the Waterberg range, red sandstone builds the krantzes of 1 793-metre Hanglip. On the summits beyond extend the plains of the Palala Plateau, home of many tributaries of the Limpopo River.* **40.** *Sinuous, deeply incised watercourses, tangled in vegetation, have given the name 'The Maze' to the summit area of the Blouberg, an isolated mountain mass to the north-east of the Palala Plateau.*

due cast from the Nylrivier for about 150 kilometres, is composed of the same rock formations. But here the sandstones are paler, more quartzitic and the sediments originally accumulated on a surface of old Basement granite previously denuded of its younger rock covering. Later faulting of the new sedimentary rocks rearranged them in three parallel ridges with steep south-facing escarpments and gentler northern slopes falling away gradually into the Lowveld of the Limpopo Valley. The most southerly of these ridges is the Soutpansberg proper, while the other two are known as Tweedeberg and Derdeberg.

Ranging from 18 to 32 kilometres in breadth, the Soutpansberg is generally over 1 500 metres above sea-level, with the highest point, also called Hanglip, peaking at 2 550 metres about five kilometres north of Louis Trichardt. At the western end Lejuma Peak attains 1 743 metres.

Within the mountains, streams have carved deep, narrow valleys, such as Wyllie's Poort, through which the main north road to Zimbabwe now passes, and Waterpoort, where the railway line carves its precipitous route along a deep gorge with sheer 300-metre sides.

As elsewhere in southern Africa, these well-watered mountainlands and their rolling foothills, thickly forested with wild figs and stinkwoods, were inhabited from Stone Age times by Bushmen. At some later stage, the area was occupied by people of unknown origin called the Ngoma. Then, over three centuries ago, they were replaced by people who came from Zimbabwe across the Limpopo and who may have begun their southward migration in the region west of Lake Malawi. These people brought with them a magic drum said to cause all their enemies to fall down in a deep sleep, totally at their mercy. They called their new home Venda, meaning 'pleasant land', the name by which they too are known today.

According to Venda beliefs, a lake called Fundudzi, in the Mutale valley of the Soutpansberg, is inhabited by fearsome one-eyed beings, to whom the Venda must pay their respects when visiting the lake by bending forward, with their backs to the lake, and viewing it between their legs. Also said to live in the depths of Fundudzi is the python god of fertility. To ensure a good harvest, he must be ceremonially propitiated each year with a gourd of the best beer, poured into the waters by a member of the chiefly lineage. Nubile maidens assemble annually to dance the ritual python

41. *Its sculpted rocks reminiscent of shapes weathered in sandstones of the Cedarberg, this locality in the Magaliesberg has borrowed the name of the western Cape mountain range.*

dance, which ensures that their marriages will be fruitful.

The Soutpansberg was so named by the followers of a frontier maverick, Coenraad Buys, who, after a turbulent life as an outlaw and producing a horde of children by women of various tribes, finally settled near a large salt pan in the area in the 1830s. The Voortrekkers under Hendrik Potgieter, who followed Buys into the Soutpansberg in 1848, established a small republic here. Dependent on the ivory trade for its prosperity, it remained an independent community until 1858, when the Soutpansberg people formed a united republic with Potchefstroom.

Created by volcanic eruptions thrusting up through the rock of the Bushveld Complex some 1 290 million years ago, the present-day Pilanesberg was buried many millions of years later beneath Karoo strata. The erosion of the softer rock cover and the levelling of the surrounding plain afterwards exhumed the old volcano, more widely known today because of its proximity to the gambling tables of Bophuthatswana, and the diversion provided by the 60 000-hectare game reserve in its extinct crater.

The huge volcanic plug of the Pilanesberg rises over 600 metres above the flat country. Its distinctive chain of concentric hills extends some 518 square kilometres as a more or less circular tract of mountainous land. The volcanic composition is of a type known to geologists as 'alkaline', and with its concentric pattern, the Pilanesberg is described as an 'alkaline ring complex'. Generally such complexes are very much smaller and the remarkable size of the Pilanesberg is rivalled only in Russia.

Initially, a number of small volcanoes developed at a structural weakness where different rocks of the Bushveld Complex met, and a tough crust of 'alkaline' volcanic rock formed. Continued outpouring relieved the pressure of molten material beneath this crust, causing the thick central plug to subside under its own weight and allowing molten rock to well up around the plug, ringing it with dykes.

The 'ring dykes' of the Pilanesberg are related to a swarm of dykes which extends from Botswana southward to Potchefstroom in the west and Springs in the east. The volcanism that produced them was the last major geological event of the Precambrian in the Transvaal. A period of denudation followed lasting a few hundred million years, during which the foundations were laid for the mountains of the western and southern parts of the subcontinent.

42. Scarcely more than a narrow defile cut by the Sand River, Wyllie's Poort provides a breach in the Soutpansberg for the main road north through Africa. **43.** Early Voortrekkers gave the Waterberg its name, grateful for the fresh drinking water supplied by the numerous streams and pools of the range. **44.** Well-watered meadows green the lower slopes of prominent hills leading down towards the Transvaal Drakensberg from the eastern end of the Soutpansberg.

THE ORANGE RIVER

RIVER OF DIAMONDS

Almost a century before it was first seen by Europeans the Orange River was called the Vigiti Magna by the Dutch at the Cape. From vague Khoikhoi accounts they wishfully deduced it to be the large river depicted on old maps, flowing past a fabulously wealthy city of that name, gateway to the treasure house of the Kingdom of Monomotapa. The truth was more prosaic, its riches of a different kind, evaluated in terms of grazing land and irrigable floodplains. Only in the present century was the treasure house of the Orange unlocked by the discovery of vast accumulations of diamonds deposited by the river at the coast.

From its confluence with the Vaal to its Atlantic finale the Orange River is still spoken of as Grootrivier, 'great river' It has been known as such since the beginning of the last century to Griqua, Baster and Dutch pioneers and their descendants, although in 1799 it was formally named the Oranje, in honour of the Prince of Orange, by Colonel Robert Gordon of the Dutch East India Company. But Grootrivier is closer to the indigenous tradition, being a direct translation of Kygariep. The Korana formerly gave this name to the river below the confluence, to distinguish it from the Upper Orange, the Nugariep, meaning 'black river', and the Vaal, a translation of Heigariep, meaning 'grey river'. Much longer than any other river south of the Zambezi, the Orange has the strongest claim to greatness.

Rising near the summit of 3 300-metre Mont-aux-Sources, the Orange River flows more than 2 000 kilometres across the subcontinent to the Atlantic. Beginning where the Lesotho highlands are snow-covered all winter, and the rainfall is from 1 000 to 2 000 millimetres a year, it descends through increasingly

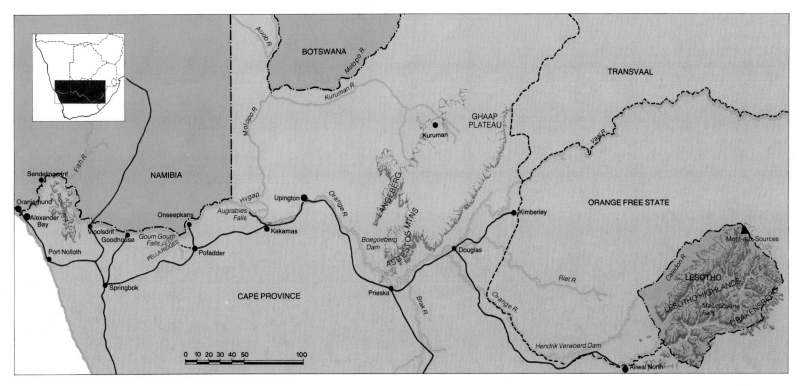

arid regions of the interior, ending in the sun-baked Richtersveld, where most years there is no rain at all.

As it journeys seaward the Orange River traverses all the major rock formations laid down in the interior after the rocks that built the Transvaal mountains came into being. From its source on the most recent of these formations, the basalt upper ramparts of the Drakensberg, the river cuts its way through earlier sedimentary series of the Karoo System and outliers of Transvaal rock, ultimately carving deep gorges and canyons in far older granites and gneisses, and in schists and quartzites believed to be as ancient as the oldest rocks in the Barberton Mountainland. The immense volume of soil removed from the interior through the ages by the Orange River and its tributaries has been sorted by coastal waters into the sand of the great 'dune sea' in the Namib Desert, and the diamond-rich gravels deposited on terraces along the coast.

Almost 400 kilometres from its mouth the Orange River gives its most spectacular display. Foaming waters drumming through a narrow channel plunge 146 metres over Augrabies Falls. Higher than both Victoria Falls and

45. *Orange River treasure trove. For millions of years, diamonds swept into the Atlantic by the river have been deposited on marine terraces by ocean currents, creating on the west coast the richest alluvial diamond fields in the world.* **46.** *High in the mountains of Lesotho, one of the Orange River's headstreams, the Malutsinyane, plunges 192 metres over the falls of the same name.*

Niagara, though very much narrower, Augrabies Falls is ranked among the world's six major waterfalls.

The present catchment of the Orange is well over a million square kilometres, but its floodwaters come from less than half that area on the highlands drained by the Upper Orange and the Vaal. It is a river of extreme moods. In winter, when the high mountain grasslands of Lesotho are thickly covered with snow, little water is released into the headstreams, the flow dwindles, even ceasing altogether, and the great Orange is reduced to a chain of pools in the riverbed. But when the snows melt in September, the flow is quickly restored, and from the first summer rains on the highlands in November the river rises steadily. In March the flow is suddenly swollen by late-summer rains to some four times its strength of the month before. Then, transformed into a heaving flood of brown water, the Orange spreads over broad floodplains where the banks are low, rising perhaps 30 metres where the entire stream is funnelled into narrow, steep-sided gorges, and carrying with it all the buoyant debris gathered on the way. Uprooted trees, their crowns still bright with foliage, sail past, and the bloated carcasses of drowned animals are hurried on to feed the sharks waiting in the stained waters where the river debouches into the sea.

Three rivers that gather their waters on the basalt crest of the Drakensberg near Mont-aux-Sources afterwards converge and form the Upper Orange. Descending rapidly through Lesotho, they bound over numerous waterfalls, among them the

192-metre Malutsinyane Falls, on the tributary of the same name, passing between yellow sandstone precipices capped with dark basalt cliffs. The Malutsinyane and the headstream of the Orange itself flow southward and combine while still inside Lesotho, thereafter taking a south-westerly course to Aliwal North. The Caledon River first runs north-west for a short distance before turning south-west along the Lesotho border, eventually joining up with the Orange in the Hendrik Verwoerd Dam west of Aliwal North.

Below the dam, the Orange continues in a deep valley, where occasional isolated basins have provided sites for further large dams. Flowing north-west through increasingly arid country, it encounters the natural barrier of the Ghaap Plateau, marked by the limestone cliffs of the Campbell Rand. Forced to alter direction sharply, the Orange adopts the south-westerly course of the Vaal at their junction near Douglas.

A short distance below this confluence the Orange encounters older rocks, stripped of their Karoo rock cover. Eleven kilometres downstream it cuts the Mazelfontein gorge, 90 metres deep and 300 metres wide, through an outlier of old Ventersdorp lava. An even more imposing gorge has been incised 15 kilometres further on. Some 120 metres deep, it is gouged for eight kilometres through the dolomitic limestones at the southernmost extremity of the Ghaap Plateau. Turning north-west at Prieska, the river's course is hewn through tough banded ironstones of the Asbestos Mountains, weathered to steep slopes and deep valleys. Some 110 kilometres downstream it slices the tip of the Langeberg range, forming rapids on old quartzites for eight kilometres below the Boegoeberg Dam. Emerging once more into flat, open country, its freedom to wander from side to side has produced numerous alluvial terraces, conspicuous as strips of greenery in the dry landscape that extends away from the river on either side.

From above Upington, in a generally westerly direction almost all the way to the sea, the Orange River incises its bed in old grey and red granites and gneisses, interrupted in a few places by quartzites, schists and other metamorphic rocks formed from even older sedimentary and volcanic material. And as the nature of its bed changes, the whole character of the river itself alters dramatically. Running parallel to the folds in the rock, it excavates deeply between the harder parts of the gneiss, forming 'river ranges', broken here and there by tributary streams, and worn down to low ridges where the rock is less resistant. Rapids form where it flows over bands of harder rock, and well-defined gorges are carved where it cuts across the folds.

For the first 110 kilometres below Upington the Orange River is braided into several streams by hundreds of small islands. Cannon Island, 13 kilometres long and two and a half kilometres wide, and the slightly larger Paarden Island below Kakamas, are more prominent. Narrower channels at a slightly higher level fill with water when the river rises, cutting up larger islands into groups of smaller ones. The combined width of channels and islands sometimes broadens

47

49

to nearly seven kilometres, and in places the river is flanked by extensive terraces on both banks. Uneven erosion of the gneisses led to silt being deposited on the downstream sides of harder rock fragments projecting up from the riverbed. Each successive flood added to the deposits, until they were raised higher than the normal flood levels. Wind-blown sand and a dense growth of vegetation completed the islands' establishment.

During the earlier part of the last century, this island-infested stretch of the Orange River was a favourite haunt of men like Jager Afrikaner, Jan Bloem, Stephanus, Danser and Stuurman. Bandits, fugitives from colonial justice and outlaws of all kinds, they banded together to plunder tribes to the north and east, and settlers from the south who were slowly moving closer to the Orange in quest of pasture. When the authorities sent commandos to deal with them, the outlaws simply withdrew into the thick bush on the maze of islands, from the safety of which they hurled bullets at their attackers on the exposed approaches until the siege was abandoned.

Islands crowd the river to the brink of the Augrabies Falls, where they split the flow into many minor and three major channels: the western Os Island channel, the middle Klaas Island channel and the eastern Groot Island channel. This last at one time continued north of Waterval Island to rejoin the mainstream a few kilometres further west. But the other channels deepened faster and drew off water at the eastern end of Waterval Island, so that today the old channel, with its own deep gorge and 'Dry Falls', rarely contains any water.

The middle and eastern streams, carrying the most water, come together at the northern end of Klaas Island. Almost immediately the combined flow plunges 24 metres down a series of rapids, and then cascades over a virtually sheer drop of 122 metres, broken 46 metres from the top by a ledge containing a large pothole. Finally the fall crashes to a huge plunge-pool, over 45 metres deep, at the bottom of a narrow gorge between smooth, vertical cliffs of brownish-red gneiss.

Augrabies is a corruption of the Khoikhoi name for the falls, but its original form is uncertain. It has been translated variously as: 'rocky waterfall', 'noisy place', 'place that drones', 'thundering water' and 'dangerous cliffs'. All seem appropriate. There is something disquietingly menacing in the perpetual roar of the yellow water bursting through the gap at the head of the falls, while a fine spray continually renews the slippery film on the smooth, rounded upper edge of the cliffs, more than 120 metres above the maelstrom in the gorge.

Although the combined width of the channels and islands above the falls is a little over three kilometres, almost the entire flow converges on the narrow gap of the main fall. Scarcely more than a trickle towards the end of winter, in late summer the river above the falls swells to double its normal width. The smaller channels suddenly brim and gush, and there may be as many as 19 separate waterfalls pouring into the gorge from both sides at one time.

From the bottom of the main fall, the Orange River zigzags 18 kilometres through a narrow gorge cut in grey gneiss,

47. *One of the broader reaches of the Orange River between Upington and Augrabies Falls, flanked on both banks by extensive alluvial terraces.* **48.** *The main streams of the braided river combine at the head of Augrabies Falls and plunge 146 metres into the maelstrom at the bottom of the gorge.* **49.** *Slanting sunlight imparts a roseate glow to the grey gneiss in which the river has hacked a deep, ragged gorge for 18 kilometres below the falls.*

forming rapids where it passes through ridges of red granite lying across its course. About a kilometre above the Hygap confluence it emerges into a widening valley, in which rocky outcrops are interspersed with long sandy stretches on either side.

The Hygap, now a fossil watercourse, was once a major tributary of the Orange, carrying the combined waters of the Molopo, Kuruman, Auob and Fish rivers. It is probable that at one stage the Limpopo, then flowing west instead of east, and the Upper Zambezi, continuing south instead of turning east, joined the Molopo and entered the Orange through

Flowing from left to right (50), the Orange River at Vioolsdrif passes under the road bridge linking Namaqualand to Namibia. East of the bridge, the broad floodplain on the southern bank is planted with sultana vines. West of the bridge, the cultivated floodplain is on the Namibian bank, facing the precipitous escarpment of the Neint Nababeep Plateau, which (51) rises directly from the riverbed.

this channel. After the Zambezi, Limpopo and Fish found other routes to the sea, the flow was insufficient to keep the channel open. A few kilometres up the Hygap are what were once two mighty waterfalls, 150 metres high, now long silent and carrying no more than occasional trickles produced by rare local showers.

Below Onseepkans the Orange cuts deeper into the granite and schist surface, passing further downstream at the foot of the high Pella ridges, shaped in ancient quartzite and schist. From Pella Drift to Goum Goum Falls the river runs in a true gorge between nearly continuous 'river ranges'. Then it again widens, flowing across a rock-surfaced plain with large accumulations of sand. The high ground here paralleling the river at a distance of six to eight kilometres turns in towards the channel near Goodhouse, from where the river is once again confined in a steep-sided gorge over 300 metres deep. Near Vioolsdrif the ground rises gently from the river on the northern side, but for

about eight kilometres on the southern side it is flanked by the precipitous north-facing escarpment of the Neint Nababeep Plateau. After passing through the gorges of the last great loop that curves around the Richtersveld, the Orange River emerges to cross the coastal plain on its last lap to the sea. Here it ends, behind a wave-built sand bar normally broken only by a narrow channel when there is sufficient water in the river to flow out at low tide.

Early explorers and fortune-seekers never found the gold of Vigiti Magna, although the diamonds the Orange deposited at its mouth have since yielded greater riches than ever they dreamed of. But the real wealth of the Orange River is its life-giving waters, which have enabled men to turn terraces and floodplains along its course into oases of sultana vineyards and date palms. And in recent decades these waters have been stored in dams and redirected by feats of engineering to make deserts bloom.

50

THE RICHTERSVELD

HEITSI EIBIB'S DOMAIN

It seems ironic that Rhenish missionaries chose to name the southern extremity of the Namib Desert after their old teacher at the mission seminary in Germany, the Reverend W. Richter. Had his lectures truly been all that barren and dry? The 'honour' might easily have been a former student's idea of a prank, for no place in southern Africa is more savagely bleak than the Richtersveld, where rain almost never falls, and boulders burst in the heat of midsummer.

Lying inland from the coast between the mouth of the Orange River and Port Nolloth, the area broadly called the Richtersveld encompasses approximately 8 000 square kilometres. More than half is coastal plain and sandveld, to the east of which lies the true Richtersveld: nearly 3 000 square kilometres of tortured desert mountainland occupying the big loop in the lower course of the Orange River. It presents a scene of desolation matched only north of the Orange, in the arid mountainous country adjoining the lower reaches of the Fish River, and in the great Namib Desert itself.

On a reconnaissance map of the Richtersveld published 'for official use only' by the British War Office in 1907, the forbidding complexity of the terrain is reflected in the annotation provided by the army officers who did the arduous leg-work. In several places their exasperation is recorded tersely: 'Dangerous'; 'Pathless and intricate'; 'Riding impossible'; 'Precipitous and inaccessible'; 'Impassable mountain barrier'; and the definitive 'Waterless'. Elsewhere they are more descriptive: 'Very rocky hills with narrow stony valleys between'; 'Lofty mountains, very broken in outline, and mostly covered with rocks and stones'. There are some places too where they seem ready to admit defeat: 'Very puzzling mountains. Only passable on foot. Native guides essential'; 'Practically impassable for white troops'. Occasionally their comments are ambivalent, even mildly optimistic: 'Waterless country, but rocky hills offering great cover'; 'Great facility for ambush'. Or were they merely being ironical, adding to themselves, 'if anyone else's army is ever crazy enough to come this way'?

The topographical diversity of the Richtersveld mirrors its geological complexity. The oldest rocks are volcanics and sediments dating back more than 2 000 million years. Through the ages they have been intruded by gneisses and granites, veined by dolerite and quartz and transformed by the heat of

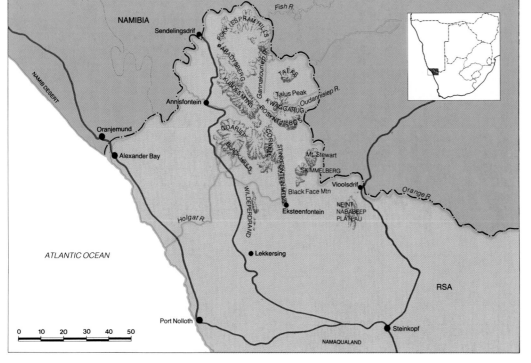

molten rock into slates, marbles and schists. White-hot lavas have spread over them, the sea has submerged them and thick layers of sandstone and quartzite, limestone, conglomerate and silt have mantled them. Repeatedly all these rocks have been shattered and contorted, broken, folded and compressed by upheavals in the earth's crust. Nine times mighty glaciers have scoured their paths across the Richtersveld, and two great ice-sheets, moving in different directions, once met here.

Amid this chaotic assembly of barren rock and stone, Heitsi Eibib, the feared supernatural hero of Nama mythology, was once believed to reside in a limestone sinkhole 50 metres deep. In his absence it became the lair of a giant river snake that claimed the lives of all who ventured too near.

The bare mountainsides are deeply scarred by old watercourses, draining into the Orange River on one hand, and

towards the Atlantic on the other. But
they are silent reminders of bygone ages,
when there was water enough to cut them.
Today a scant rainfall, averaging less than
130 millimetres a year and often less than
20 millimetres, scarcely moistens the bare
slopes. On very rare occasions, thunder
clouds wandering beyond their normal
range bump their heads on mountain
peaks, and more rain falls in an hour than
may normally fall in several years. Then
flash floods, rolling huge boulders before
them, convert the old river channels into
ephemeral torrents. But even when this
happens, the streams flowing towards the
Atlantic peter out in the sand of the
coastal plain. Only the largest, the Holgat
River, has been known to reach the sea,
and then only once or twice in historical
times. There is no permanent running
water in the Richtersveld, save a trickle in
the upper part of the Gannakouriep River,
which quickly drains away into the sandy
riverbed.

In this region of harsh, untamed beauty,
probably the most impressive feature is
the raw cleft hacked in the naked rock by
the Orange River where it loops around
the mountainous tract of the Richtersveld.
Entering the area west of Vioolsdrif,
through a gorge it has cut back into the
rock-strewn flats of the Neint Nababeep
Plateau, the river opens out into a small
basin, bordered by wide, gravel-covered
terraces. But soon the brown waters race
again through a steep-sided gorge almost
600 metres deep. For nearly 40 kilometres
the river twists and turns through a
wild, granite-walled canyon, to slice a
spectacular gap towards the end through
the hard quartzites of the Rosyntjiebos
Mountains, towering 900 metres. From
this point the Orange passes through
small basins and lesser gorges, emerging
eventually from the rapids above the old
missionary crossing at Sendelingsdrif,
and flows on between banks that become
flat and featureless.

52. *Its escarpment rising abruptly from the
southern bank of the Orange River at
Vioolsdrif, the Neint Nababeep Plateau leads
on westward into the tortured desert
mountainland of the Richtersveld.*

The rocky backbone within the bight of
the Orange River is formed by several
interconnected ranges, running from east
of Lekkersing, in the south, northward to
the Pokkiespram Hills east of Swartpoort.
Steep and scarp-like on the eastern side,
the western slopes are more gradual and
deeply incised by the gorges of tributaries
of the Holgat River. Their crags are
carved from light grey and pale pink
conglomerates, sandstones and quartzites
laid on the surface of the older granites,
gneisses and metamorphosed ancient
sediments.

Between Lekkersing and Eksteenfontein
the crestline tops 957 metres on Dun's
Mountain, paralleled to the west by
Wildeperdrand. North of Eksteenfontein

the main crestline continues along the summits of the Stinkfontein, Cornell's and Kuboes ranges, rising to a highest point of 1 378 metres on Cornell's Mountain. To Nama inhabitants these ranges are collectively known as Xoggän TcUib, the 'jagged mountains'.

East of the main crestline, quartzites and schists of the most ancient system form an offshoot. Commencing at Mount Erebus, they build the ragged, saw-toothed ridge of the Rosyntjiebos Mountains, including the Seven Sisters and bare peaks with uninviting names, like Mount Terror, Gorgon's Head and Devil's Tooth.

Beyond Mount Erebus the deep gorge of the Gannakouriep River dissects the main range, which continues in a north-westerly direction, becoming less prominent in the landscape, until in the hills near Swartpoort it fails altogether.

North of the Rosyntjiebos Mountains, between the Gannakouriep and the Orange, is the gash of the Oudannisiep gorge and the almost perfectly symmetrical concave of the Springbokvlakte. Here the wide, sandy plain is scattered with many solitary hills, more numerous on its southern side, where in places they combine to make high peaks and ridges such as Talus Peak and Kwaggarug. On the plain's northern

margin the Tatas Mountains rise abruptly, formed by great piles of boulders from a pluton of younger granite.

West of the main crestline, a far larger pluton, covering 690 square kilometres, provides the granite mass of the almost circular Goariep Mountains, which rise steeply from the sandy plains of the Annisvlakte in the north, and the Geigasvlakte in the south. The latter extend southward to the Holgat River, eastward to the Black Hills, and westward until the plain runs into a field of high red sand dunes.

Outlying eminences, separated by broken stony tracts, flank the major ranges. They include mountain-sized masses, such as Paradysberg, Skimmelberg, Black Face Mountain, Mount Stewart and Rooiberg, as well as countless small unnamed kopjes, hills and ridges.

Shadeless, the plains shimmer silently in the blaze of the midday sun, and the rocky gorges are like furnaces. Desiccating heat dominates. Then late-afternoon breezes from the sea begin stirring among the rocks, temperatures suddenly fall, and the mountain ranges become serried bands of purple and terra-cotta, red and gold and black. The heat is blown away, but the dryness lingers on through the night.

What little rain the Richtersveld receives falls chiefly in winter as soft drizzle, the result of moist north-westerly winds thrust up into colder levels of the atmosphere by the mountains, beyond which little moisture ever passes. So the western slopes of the main ranges are moderately well covered with assorted shrubs. In the broken veld to the east the only plants are succulents able to absorb moisture from occasional mists and store it for future use. Many species grow here and nowhere else. They include tiny 'stone plants', virtually indistinguishable from the pebbles they grow among, and a large variety of small, fleshy-leaved plants nestling in protected niches among the rocks. On stony hillsides the unique halfmens plants bow their heads towards the north to prevent direct sunlight from damaging the growing shoots at the tips of their tapered, spiny stems. Tree aloes, such as the kokerboom and its rarer look-alike, the basterkokerboom, strike commanding poses overlooking boulder legions.

Woody trees, such as the camel thorn, wild ebony and abikwageelhout, survive only on the banks of the Orange River and some of its larger tributaries. Opportunistic annual grasses may spring up after showers on the sandy plains. Plant species that survive only as seed in

the ground through years of drought complete an entire life-cycle in the space of a few weeks following rain, and the plains are covered with a magnificent floral mosaic. For the Richtersveld is part of Namaqualand, famed for the spring displays of 'daisies' which are regarded by thousands of seasonal visitors as one of the wonders of southern Africa.

The succulents sustain the chain of animal life in these dry parts. Dassies, steenbok and klipspringer eke vital moisture from their diet of juicy leaves, bulbs and roots, while leopard and rooikat, suricate, jackal and hyena slake their thirst with the blood and body fluids of their prey. Even the Bushman inhabitants of former times could hunt in the mountains, far from their regular supplies, because they knew how to supplement the little water they carried with moisture from plants and animals. But the people who settled here to live off the produce of their flocks and herds needed far more copious sources of water to survive.

Natural seeps and springs, though not numerous, are more common in the Richtersveld than is generally supposed. In the older rocks they are mostly too saline to be potable, sweet waters coming principally from the younger quartzites of the main ranges. Fairly strong flows spring from these rocks at Lekkersing, Eksteenfontein and six other points in the south, as well as at Nanoas and Paradys in the far north. Good water also wells up where these quartzites and younger granite meet at Kuboes, while at Annisfontein it comes from a natural underground reservoir formed by a dyke in the younger granite.

It was at these springs that the Nama herdsmen who gave their name to Namaqualand settled with their goats long before the first Europeans arrived at the Cape. And here their descendants still herd their goats today, together with other men of colour whose forefathers braved the hardship of a long trek into the wastelands in quest of independence from a society in which they were permanently disadvantaged.

Today there are schools and churches and water pumps in the Richtersveld, but the rhythms of daily life seem little changed. Yet clearly they are changing. Still too remote to attract tourists, the area falls increasingly within the sphere of geologists and mining men. The long silences are suddenly pierced by the distant whine of a supply truck on its way to the alluvial diamond diggings on the adjoining coast at Alexander Bay. Progress has come to the domain of Heitsi Eibib.

55

53. *A parasite on the roots of bushy plants, the vivid skilpadblom was known as the inkblom in early colonial times because the flowers, which turn black when dry, were used to make ink.* **54.** *The strange halfmens (half human), a spiny succulent tree which from a distance can easily be mistaken for a person, is endemic to the rocky hillsides of the Richtersveld.* **55.** *The succulent leaves of these representatives of the Crassula and Lithops (stone plant) genera equip them for survival in the arid climate of the Richtersveld.* **56.** *After good winter showers a plain bursts into flower with an ephemeral orange carpet of Dimorphotheca daisies.*

56

THE FISH RIVER CANYON

CAPTURED WATERS

North of where the great Orange River loops around the Richtersveld, the desert plateau west of the Klein Karas Mountains is bisected by the Fish River Canyon. Rising almost imperceptibly westwards, the plain is strewn with the sun-shattered debris of pale quartzite surface rock: a litter of sharp-edged fragments, and sand pockets in which the hardy, succulent melkbos roots. Twisted lines of stunted thorn bush define the beds of infrequent streams. The angular branches of an occasional solitary kokerboom are tipped with rosettes of fine-toothed, fleshy leaves, backlit by a pale, cloudless sky. The plain spans out, seemingly uninterrupted. Suddenly the ground falls steeply away, dropping some 140 metres in tiered scarps of alternating quartzites and sandstones to the black limestone floor of a huge trough, some eight to 16 kilometres wide. In this sunken floor the Fish River has hacked the ragged gash of the lower canyon to 600 metres below the edge of the plateau.

On the far side, the limestone of the trough floor sweeps upward, forming the surface of the western scarp, 180 metres high, and deeply dissected by tributary erosion. In places it is topped with layers of easily split sandstone and shale, but for the most part these have been weathered away. Out of sight beyond the bounding scarp, the stony plateau continues, lowering gently westward.

Even to an untrained eye it is fairly obvious that the forces that produced the broad, flat-bottomed trough of the upper canyon cannot have been identical to those that incised the narrow zigzag cleft

57. *Nearing the end of its tortuous canyon, the Fish River zigzags towards the Orange. Here the narrow, flat surfaces topping the higher interfluves are all that the river, in its wild meandering, has left of the original plateau.*

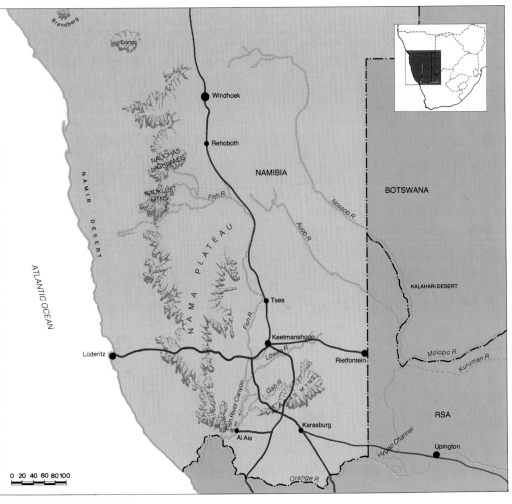

58

58. *The kokerboom, or quiver tree, is a common sight on the plateau above the Fish River Canyon. A tree-like aloe, with tapering stem a metre or more thick at the base, it derives its name from the fact, noted by Simon van der Stel in 1685, that Namaqualand Bushmen hollowed out its fleshy limbs to make quivers for their arrows.* **59.** *Before the Fish River reaches the hot-water springs at Ai-Ais, the flanking slopes lose their Nama rock capping. The sunset-lighted peaks mirrored in the water are composed of Basement gneiss and granite.*

of the lower canyon. The second is clearly the work of powerful floodwaters dragging boulders and smaller pieces of abrasive rock over the channel bed; the first the result of massive surface distortion, at a time when the whole subcontinent was being raised to a new level. The continuation of the limestone surface from the floor of the trough up the western slope indicates that the scarp on that side was created initially by a fold. On the eastern flank, however, the sequence of rocks exposed beneath the limestone in the sides of the lower canyon is repeated in the face of the upper scarp. Therefore, the scarp on this side was created not by a fold, but by a break, or fault, causing vertical displacement of the rock.

Tilting slightly below the horizontal south to north, the weathered surface of the upper canyon floor resembles the adjoining plateau, except that it lacks

almost any vegetation, and the limestone has broken down into smaller fragments than the quartzite on the plain above. Only a few small sandstone hills break the even surface. The barely discernible drainage lines traced on the baked plain by local rainfall run-off trend northwards, following the tilt, as they converge on the lower canyon. But the short-lived, violent rainstorms that may break here during a brief period of three or four weeks in late summer are more inclined to produce sudden sheet floods than establish streambeds.

The tortuous lower canyon of the Fish River hugs the eastern side of the trough, and its deeply incised meanders frequently undercut the upper plateau. As a result, little of the trough surface remains east of the river, except where the isolated ridges of narrow spurs run out from the foot of the eastern scarp to form the cores of meander loops.

Viewed from the eastern edge of the plateau, the underlying geology of the area is graphically delineated in the opposite slope of the lower canyon. The lip cut in the resistant black limestone of the trough floor, which forms a horizontal band about 10 metres thick, is notched in places by the small seasonal streams draining the trough. Beneath the limestone, a layer of very hard quartzite, 15 metres thick, is followed downward by a succession of hard quartzites, softer micaceous sandstones and grits, to a total thickness of 150 metres. Collectively, these sedimentary rocks of the Nama System form the near-vertical krantzes, in which sand-blasting has picked out the harder elements as prominent ledges. The massive plinth of Basement gneiss and granite descends less abruptly to the riverbed, its slopes littered with rock fragments fallen from above. In the continually altering play of light, the rocks change from black to grey to blue, brown to pink to gold. Far below glimpses of sunlight flash from the surfaces of deep, clear pools.

The Fish River's headwater streams rise in the Naukluft Mountains and on the Nauchas highlands, in western Rehoboth, whence it flows some 800 kilometres before finally discharging into the Orange River. Only about 65 kilometres of its course lie in the canyon tract; barely half that distance, taking a straight line across the meanders between the start of the canyon proper, below Hell's Corner, and where the Nama rocks of the plateau end near Gochas Drift. But the first river that flowed through this tract was not the Fish River of today.

There was a time when the Fish River

avoided its south-west turn near Tses and continued south-east. The line of large salt pans near Rietfontein, in the south-western Kalahari, lies on the course it then took to join the combined waters of the Auob, Nossob, Kuruman and Molopo rivers before they entered the now-dry valley of the Hygap. This then channelled them into the Orange near the Augrabies Falls, over 300 kilometres east of where the Fish now enters the Orange.

According to the record engraved in the Nama plateau, the canyon tract was occupied initially by two rivers drawing their waters from local drainage. One flowed northward, following the gentle dip of the trough floor and exiting through the valley of the present Löwen River into the then lower course of the Fish River. The other, a steeply graded, smaller tributary of the Orange, cut back north into the plateau until it began tapping the headwaters of the former and reversed the direction of drainage. Eventually it cut back to where it captured the Fish near Tses and redirected its waters through its present lower course.

North of Tses the Fish River flows in a shallow channel; to the south it incises progressively deeper into the plateau. By the time it is joined by the Gab River, the bed of the Fish is 45 metres below the surface of the plain. A few kilometres further downstream it plunges over two major waterfalls and enters the gorge tract. At first the canyon walls consist only of layered sedimentary rocks. At Hell's Corner, however, the sinuous meanders begin, and the river cuts deeper and deeper into the underlying Basement rocks, to an eventual depth of almost 200 metres below the sediments, and 600 metres lower than the plateau. From the abrupt end of the sedimentary rocks and the plateau above Gochas Drift the river flows on to its confluence with the Orange through mountainous country gouged in Basement granite and gneiss that have lost their sedimentary cover.

In spate, fast-flowing waters steepen the walls of the canyon on the outer sides of bends by undercutting. The overhanging rock caves into the gorge, leaving freshly exposed rock in the collapsed face. The upstream sides of the spurs reaching out into the loops of the meanders are similarly eroded, and the river eventually breaks through to the other side of a spur, taking a short-cut that leaves the old meander loop without water. In various stages this occurs throughout the canyon, but most impressively at Hell's Corner, where a meander loop, cut when the floor of the canyon was higher than today, lies high and dry about 30 metres above the present riverbed.

For most of the year the floor of the canyon is a series of pools, linked by smooth, flat rock surfaces submerged in a few centimetres of slowly moving water, or by stretches covered with jumbled masses of rounded boulders. These stretches become foaming rapids when the river is in flood. Sand, produced by the disintegration of the rock faces above, is blown up into banks fringed with tall reeds, diverting the stream from one side of the canyon floor to the other.

When the sun is high, groups of Hartmann's zebra and kudu families drowse in the shade of camel thorns and ebony trees on sandy terraces above flood-level. In the oven-like depths of the canyon, heat radiated by the rocks silences even the birds and the cicadas. Occasionally the wild cry of a fish eagle making off with a plump barbel or yellow-fish snatched from the surface of a pool rends the stillness; or the suspended haystack of a sociable weaver nest in a camel thorn may suddenly burst into pandemonium as its multitude of inhabitants catch sight of a Cape cobra weaving through the branches. At night, the hoarse cough of a leopard in a ravine may be followed by the alarmed shouts of baboons, or the yell of a black-backed jackal in the darkness beyond the firelight.

Day and night, in late summer, the long silences of this place are lost in the roar of floodwaters gathered from distant catchments to rage through the gorge. Filling the air with the rumble and rattle of boulders in transit, they scour out the accumulated scree from the floor in the great annual display of immense power that has created the canyon.

THE NAMIB DESERT

A SEA OF SAND

The one true desert on the continent south of the Sahara, the Namib covers some 270 000 square kilometres. In an arid band 80 to 145 kilometres wide, between the Atlantic Ocean and the western escarpment, it runs for a distance of over 2 000 kilometres, from near Mocamedes in Angola to south of Port Nolloth in Namaqualand.

The name is of Nama origin but uncertain meaning. However, the part the Namib Desert played in discouraging and delaying colonial penetration from the coast to the South West African interior until late in the nineteenth century has given the Namib a new meaning. In the minds of inhabitants of South West Africa it has symbolic significance; hence they have renamed their country Namibia.

That the Namib presented such a daunting barrier to would-be colonists is readily appreciated. In the central portion, over 400 kilometres of bleak coastline is backed by a vast 'dune sea', in which rank upon rank of sand ridges, often more than 100 metres high, parallel the coast to a depth of 90 kilometres inland. Where the dunes rise above 250 metres, they are probably the highest in the world.

The coastal strip, receiving less than 20 millimetres of rain a year, is almost devoid of vegetation, and yet is continually shrouded in fogs, making it one of the most humid places on earth.

Whether or not the oldest coastal desert in the world, as some claim, it does have the distinction of being the only coastal desert with a fauna adapted to living on the unvegetated dunes, relying on the fog for moisture and the wind for food.

Today, as when it was formed, the Namib is swept by dry air masses brought by anti-cyclones. These winds also drive the surface water from the continental shelf, causing cold water from the depths of the Atlantic to well up at the edge of the shelf and take its place. This further chills

the already cold Antarctic water swept northwards up the west coast by the Benguela Current, and very little moisture is carried inland by onshore breezes. Winds passing over the cold coastal waters are cooled by them, and with the drop in temperature the moisture in the air condenses as fog, but this usually penetrates only a few kilometres inland. Fogs are common in all seasons on the coast, where the humidity reaches 100 per cent on 340 days a year, and seldom falls below 90 per cent. Yet despite the high humidity, rain seldom falls, as the fog layer is too shallow to hold enough total moisture to produce rain.

Summer and winter, day breaks slowly as the light filters through the pall of fog. The rays that pierce the gloom warm the sand sufficiently by mid-morning for it to radiate enough heat to warm the air, causing the fog to dissipate in the steadily increasing breeze off the sea. The sand becomes softer as it relinquishes the dampness absorbed during the night, and particles are blown about by the wind. If it blows strongly enough, the dune crests 'smoke' like volcanoes. But in the late afternoon the air again becomes cooler, and the fog returns.

Further inland, however, the air is extremely dry. Fog is very rare and the sky almost always clear. The wind from the sea is warmed as it passes over the sun-heated sand, accounting for more distinct seasonal differences in the eastern Namib, near the foot of the escarpment. Here the summer humidity is only 20 to 30 per cent. Winters are drier and colder, with minimum temperatures averaging 4,5 degrees, and maximums around 21 degrees, while average summer minimums and maximums are 18 and 30 degrees. In the depths of river canyons in the rocky parts of the inland Namib it is often very much hotter.

Curiously, the hottest days of all are in winter, when the east wind blows.

Beneath clear night skies, the dry highlands beyond the escarpment rapidly lose heat after sunset. The air cools faster than at the coast, and during the night the mass of cold air starts sliding down the western slopes of the highlands towards the sea. Compression from the 1 800-metre descent converts the bitterly cold air into a furnace blast, dry and dusty. But the east wind frequently stops short of the actual coast and glides over the top of the cold, foggy air near the shore.

The little rain that does occasionally reach the coastal Namib comes from the scant moisture remaining in late summer's easterly and north-easterly winds after they have crossed the continent.

In the eastern Namib, occasional thunder showers support several species of mesembryanthemum, the unique *Welwitschia mirabilis* and the bushy succulent, Bushman's candle, which secretes highly inflammable resin. In

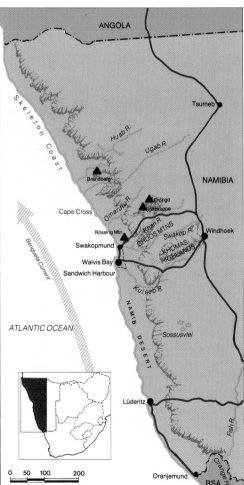

60. *Great sand ridges of the 'dune sea' define the desert skyline of the Namib between Lüderitz and Swakopmund. Generally 65 to 100 metres high, they attain 250 metres in places. Although superficially their features are continually changing, the massive ridges themselves may have been in their present positions for thousands of years.*

61

marginal areas, spiny euphorbia, stone plants, milkweed, kokerboom and the squat, thick-trunked grape tree, with its vine-like fruit and flowers, survive on sporadic watering. Further east these give way to acacia grasslands. But in the west, the shifting sands are generally quite bare, with only rare patches of hardy dune grass here and there in protected hollows.

Some 20 million years ago, the region between the escarpment and the sea was traversed by several rivers, each flanked by dense riverine woodland, and the land between them was covered with open savanna. The sea was warmer, so the climate was hotter and moister than today, until 10 to 14 million years ago when the East Antarctic ice-sheet developed, leading to a sharp drop in sea temperature.

Dry climates were eventually fully established about six million years ago, and intensified some four million years later. Although the trend since has been towards more arid climates, there have been short, wetter spells in the past two million years when rivers again flowed to the sea between Lüderitz and Walvis Bay. Their dry former estuaries truncated by the 'dune sea', they now end in vleis behind the dunes, as at Sossusvlei.

Incredible as it may seem, the vast accumulation of sand in the 'dune sea' has been transported from places as distant as the Drakensberg and dumped off the west coast, chiefly by the Orange River. The current then carried it up the coast and cast it ashore for the wind to blow inland. This may be clearly seen south of Lüderitz, where the Nama rocks have been intensely folded and relentless sea winds have blasted away the soft shales in the folds, producing numerous shallow troughs running south to north in a landscape of bare dolomite and quartzite outcrops. Where portions of these troughs have been drowned by the sea, they form bays and inlets. Sand thrown up on the northern shores of these south-facing bays dries out at low tide and is blown inland to form long dune chains and occasional huge, isolated, crescent-shaped barchan dunes. The wind drives all these northward, continually adding to the 'dune sea'.

There are several areas covered by dunes on the northern Skeleton Coast and between the Kunene and Curoca rivers in Angola. But none is comparable to the 'dune sea' occupying almost the entire width of the Namib. From the coast to the escarpment, between Lüderitz and Walvis Bay, it covers an area of some 34 000 square kilometres.

Pierced in places by lone rocky inselbergs, the great mantle of sand – yellow near the coast, but reddening towards the interior – builds parallel lines of dune ridges. One to three kilometres apart and up to 50 kilometres long, they rise 65 to 100 metres, soaring more than 250 metres at Sossusvlei. As dunes of this type run in the same direction as the winds that formed them, it is assumed that these ridges must be relics from when south-easterly winds were prevalent. Low barchan dunes, their crescent horns reaching ahead as the wind slowly drives them forward, are fashioned by south-westerly winds on the flanks of the older dune ridges.

Although in places there are dunes right down to the shoreline, the immediate coastal strip is generally low-lying sand, backed at a short distance by massive dune ridges. Sand accumulating on the southern side of an isolated rocky point or low headland here eventually spills round its tip and builds out a narrow sandspit parallel to the coast, forming an elongated bay, as at Walvis Bay. At Sandwich Harbour, however, the sandspit has closed the gap with the coast and converted a bay into a lagoon, which is maintained by the sea occasionally breaching the sand bar. Where such

prevents evaporation, so that moisture absorbed from fog humidity may be retained for years about 20 centimetres below the surface.

Dune-dwelling species form a hierarchy ordered by food and moisture chains. Organic material blown into the area is mixed with the shifting sands as a permanent store of food for beetles, fishtails and termites. They are equipped either to absorb moisture directly from the fog or to manufacture their own water from a dry diet by oxidation. In turn, they furnish food and moisture for the spiders, scorpions, solifuges, crickets, flies, lizards, snakes and moles that prey upon them.

The physical adaptations of some dune dwellers are plain to see. The Namib sand runner has unusually long spidery legs, enabling it to run about on the surface in daytime, its body raised well above the hot sand, while short-legged beetles are usually nocturnal. The eyes of the venomous little sand viper are on top of its head, allowing it to take refuge in the sand during the day, with only its eyes and the tip of its tail showing.

No other coastal desert in the world has a fauna adapted to unvegetated dunes. It is believed that the Namib was given a headstart in acquiring one by an ancient connection with the Sahara some 50 million years ago, when the earth's climate was generally warmer and drier. Gemsbok, the dominant large antelope of the 'dry west', and several species of small mammals, reptiles and insects that inhabit the Namib today have vanished from the better-watered interior, but are still found in arid parts of north-east Africa, from which originally the ancestors of the Namib animals came.

The 'dune sea' ends abruptly in the north where further advance of the sand is checked by the deeply incised bed of the Kuiseb River. However, in the lower 'delta' region, dunes cross the Kuiseb in a narrow coastal strip and are finally halted by the Swakop River. The rock and gravel surface of the 'Plain' Namib begins on the northern bank of the Kuiseb. Sand blown into the dry riverbed is flushed out when the river flows briefly in late summer and collects in the inland 'delta'. Once every 10 years, on average, when the Kuiseb

61. *This 'oasis' of sparse greenery is at Sossusvlei, where the sporadic Tsauchab River ends in a shallow vlei behind some of the highest dunes in the world.* **62.** *Remnants of a granite pluton, the bare peaks of the Spitzkoppe rise amid their own debris from the stony Namib plain near Usakos.*

lagoons are not periodically refreshed by the sea, as at Cape Cross, they slowly fill with salt and wind-blown sand, and become salt pans.

The 'dune sea' is not as sterile as its barren appearance suggests, and in fact supports a fair variety of vertebrate and invertebrate creatures. These are not only able to survive without active vegetation and regular rainfall, but are also adapted specifically to the dune environment, and cannot live anywhere else.

Grains of Namib sand have the typically rounded 'desert' shape produced by wind abrasion. Their shape and loose arrangement leave tiny spaces and channels between the grains, which permit the circulation of oxygen beneath the surface. Ventilation is maintained by daily fluctuation of air pressure and difference between climates above and below ground. The presence of air space between the grains also greatly reduces the pressure of sand inside the dunes. This makes it easier for small creatures, whose organs of movement are adapted specifically for the purpose, to penetrate it and move about beneath the surface, shielded from the climatic extremes they would be exposed to above ground. The poor conductivity of the sand maintains fairly constant temperatures at depth and

62

flows all the way to the coast, the
accumulated sand – an estimated
16 million cubic metres in 1964 – is
returned to the sea.

Rising on the highland plateau west of
Windhoek, the Kuiseb is the first river
north of the Orange to cross the Namib.
The last 140 kilometres of its course form
an extended oasis between the 'dune sea'
and the gravel plains. Although it flows
only a few days a year, plentiful
underground water in the riverbed
maintains riverine forests of huge ana
trees, camel thorn, haak-en-steek and
sweet thorn. Pools remaining after floods
attract game, and the vegetation offers a
reserve of food for a number of desert
animals when supplies fail elsewhere, as
well as providing permanent sustenance
for birds and resident mammals such as
gemsbok, klipspringer and baboon. The
underground resources have also made
human habitation possible, and the so-
called 'Topnaar Hottentots' have lived
along the lower Kuiseb for centuries,
digging wells in the riverbed for
themselves and their goats.

The escarpment bordering this part of
the Namib is formed by the old schists of
the Damara System that built the Khomas
Highlands. At the western edge of the
highlands the escarpment drops more
than 600 metres to where the Namib plain
begins 1 100 metres above sea-level,
140 kilometres from the coast. At the
north-western corner of the Khomas
Highlands, however, erosion by the
Swakop, Khan, Omaruru and Ugab rivers
has removed the escarpment from the
landscape, until it reappears north of the
Huab River.

The rivers have reduced this part of the
Namib to an extensive plain, surfaced in
places with more recently formed
calcrete, but generally covered with a
thick accumulation of rubble and sand
weathered from the rock that previously
overlaid it. The more resistant remnants
of the old superstructure project above the
plain as mountainous tracts, rocky ridges
and inselbergs. Remarkable amongst these
are the Spitzkoppe, Erongo Mountains,
Rössing Mountain, Chuos Mountain and
the great circular granite dome of the
2 683-metre Brandberg, 40 kilometres
in diameter, which rises 1 900 metres
above the surrounding plain. Canyons
and valleys 300 metres deep, cut through
the mountainous tracts by the rivers and
their many smaller tributaries, create a
badland landscape.

North of Swakopmund, the continually
changing configuration of the beach and
undersea sandbanks has made this one of
the most treacherous coastlines in the

63. *A forest giant that fell in deep mud some 200 million years ago is now desert stone, among others like it in the Petrified Forest at Khorixas, north of the Brandberg. Minerals in solution penetrated the wood and gradually replaced it, replicating its cell structure in minute detail and literally turning it to stone. Rooting beside it is a 'living fossil', the celebrated Welwitschia mirabilis, described by Charles Darwin as the 'platypus' of the plant world. Growing nowhere but in the coastal strip from the Kuiseb to Moçamedes, the welwitschia has no surviving relatives and is an entire plant family in a single species. This youthful specimen is 50 to 100 years old, but the ages of some larger individuals are estimated at more than 2 000 years.*
64. *Roof of the Namib, the granite dome of the Brandberg rises 1 900 metres above the surrounding plain.* **65, 66.** *Uncluttered by vegetation, the bare sands of the Namib leave exposed the mineral treasures of the earth, like the apparently petrified 'desert rose', in reality a bizarre formation of gypsum crystals. Quartz, the most abundant of the earth's minerals, can be clearly seen in crystalline form.*

world. Graveyard of countless ships, from the earliest days of maritime exploration to the present, it has earned the ominous name, Skeleton Coast. Usually fairly gradual, the changes are sometimes spectacular, as in the rainy season of 1933-34 when, after five years of drought in the interior, the Swakop River flowed for four months. It carried such an enormous volume of sand and debris to the coast that for several kilometres north of the river mouth the beach was extended almost two kilometres out into the sea, leaving the old landing jetty at Swakopmund stranded a kilometre and a half inland.

Of all the natural areas on the subcontinent, the Namib is probably the one man is least able to damage permanently. The largest assembly of earth-moving machinery on earth is used to strip the beaches to bedrock for the immense wealth of diamonds beneath the sand, but eventually wind, sea and sand will smooth over the depredations as if they had never been.

68

67. *Backdropped by the red sands at Sossusvlei, an ostrich hurries off over the gravel plain at the approach of a vehicle.* **68.** *Pitted by desert winds, Vingerklip, 'finger rock', is the most prominent of unusual rock formations in the Ugab valley, near Outjo.* **69.** *Ragged rock ridges and inselbergs compose a desolate scene in the country flanking the Swakop River.* **70.** *A ridge of black dolomite jutting out into the Atlantic forms the giant stone arch of Bogenfels. Seventy metres high, the bands of softer rock below have been removed by wave action, leaving the hard uppermost band resting on a supporting column.*

67

69

LANGEBAAN LAGOON

'WATERING PLACE OF SALDANHA'

If, three and a half centuries ago, there had been adequate fresh water at Saldanha Bay, European settlement would have commenced there, beside the best natural harbour on the South African coast. Instead, Table Bay was selected, where a perennial stream of crystal water from the mountain flowed into the sea. And Table Bay would perhaps have been called Saldanha Bay today, if the name Aguada de Saldanha, 'watering place of Saldanha', given it by Antonio de Saldanha in 1503, had not been mistakenly transferred 98 years later to the bay further north now bearing his name, although never his watering place.

Early mariners frequently took advantage of the safe anchorage at Saldanha Bay. Those whose recorded impressions have survived wrote warmly about its virtues as a harbour, the abundance of fish and seals, the convenient tidal flats of the lagoon where they could careen their ships for repairs, and the easy trade in hoop iron for fresh meat they did with locals on the beach. But they all lamented the lack of drinking water. With a geologist's understanding of landscape, however, they might have noted wryly that they had arrived there a few million years too late, for once the bay was indeed part of a deep valley in which a broad river flowed.

71

Like the dome of Paarl Rock and the foundations of Table Mountain, the rocky heads that post the entrance to Saldanha Bay and the bleak islands lying within have been shaped from one of many relatively young granite plutons formed some 600 million years ago in the south-western Cape. These crystallized beneath older Malmesbury rocks, of which they were subsequently denuded.

At Saldanha Bay the Cape Granite and associated quartz porphyry have been hacked down by the salt-sharpened edge of Atlantic gales, and the relief is fairly low. Malgaskop, on the northern side, and South Head, nine kilometres away across the entrance, are both only slightly more than 110 metres high, while the tallest eminences, Vlaeberg and Konstabelkop,

facing inland over the sheltered waters of Langebaan Lagoon, are both lower than 200 metres.

On the southern side, granite forms the clubhead at the end of the narrow, sand-covered peninsula separating the lagoon from open sea. Along the eastern shore the granite outcrops for a few kilometres on either side of Langebaan, extending about 12 kilometres inland. Outliers of this mass are masked by a series of sandy hills – Kleinberg, Anyskop and Die Kop – that trend north-east past Langebaanweg, between Langebaan and the mouth of the Berg River, on the eastern side of St Helena Bay. North of the entrance to Saldanha Bay, Cape Granite is exposed in the headlands and over much of the area west of a line from Hoedjies Point to the middle of the St Helena Bay shore.

The granite is largely responsible for the general configuration of the present coastline in the Saldanha Bay area, having furnished the matrix for later events. The blanketing sands that today provide the setting for the jewel of the scenery – the turquoise waters of Langebaan Lagoon – accumulated much later. Indeed, man's ancestors were living here long before there was a lagoon.

Originally, the precursor of the Berg River did not flow north into St Helena Bay. Passing near to Langebaanweg, it

emptied into a deep valley leading south-west through Saldanha Bay, continuing in that direction some 70 kilometres beyond the Heads before reaching the sea.

Four or five million years ago the sea flooded the low-lying area between Saldanha Bay and St Helena Bay, cutting off the western granite outcrop as an island. Protected by it from the ravages of the open sea, the mainland coastline ran past Langebaanweg, where the Berg River then flowed into the ocean. Phosphate rocks, derived from seabird guano formed here on land and in shallow sheltered water at that time, have since given access to a fossil record of the period.

This fossil store adds a further dimension to the fascination of Saldanha Bay. It is the most prolific source of fossils from this period thus far uncovered anywhere in Africa, the only other important occurrence of equivalent age being thousands of kilometres away in Kenya. The earliest fossils are of small marine invertebrates and of sharks, rays, skates, fish, whales, seals and seabirds whose remains were embedded in the phosphate rock that formed underwater. But an amazing variety of land animals were also attracted to the vicinity by the river, which was flanked by trees and grassland. Apart from freshwater fish, giant otters and other creatures dependent directly on the riverine habitat, there were some 70 different species of mammals alone. All now extinct, some were evolutionary ancestors of animals still found in Africa, while others evolved into species endemic to other continents today.

Here the first fossil evidence of bears in sub-Saharan Africa is provided by bone fragments from a 500-kilogram relative of the giant panda, today found only in China. Sharing his habitat then were short-necked giraffes with long horns, three-toed horses and two species of sabre-toothed cats, superceded by leopards and lions. There were also six species of hyena, one of them an early ancestor of the spotted hyena, and a rhinoceros from which the white rhino is descended. Living with them were a

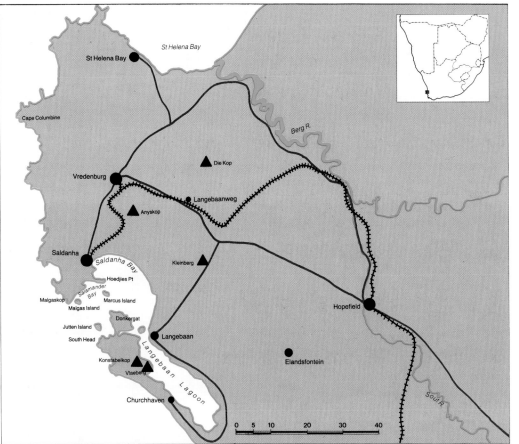

variety of other creatures, from tiny mice to early relatives of the elephant, including the so-called 'true elephant', an ancestor of the woolly mammoth.

Later uplift of the subcontinent raised the floor of the strait above sea-level, reuniting the island with the mainland, and eventually the Berg River opened a new outlet to the sea at St Helena Bay. Proof of early human residence in the area is provided by the crude stone implements abandoned there perhaps two million years ago by an ancestral species of man. The sands at Elandsfontein have yielded stone implements of this and later ages, and skull fragments of an early Middle Stone Age type who lived here about 40 000 years ago. This 'Saldanha Man' was once thought to have been a near relative of the extinct Neanderthal, but is now considered a variant of our own species, *Homo sapiens*.

At least twice, subsequent fluctuations of the polar ice-caps caused the sea to rise again temporarily over parts of the land surface. Thereafter, arid conditions deprived the land of vegetation, and wind-blown sands covered much of the landscape with dunes. About 6 500 years ago the sea rose above its present level for the last time, drowning the dune fields, and scouring out the hollow that later became Langebaan Lagoon when the water receded and the present sea-level was stabilized in about 200 AD.

Since then, weathering of the granite

outcrops has constantly supplied new sediments, which wave action in Saldanha Bay concentrates in its sheltered northern recesses, and behind the protective mass of Schier Island on the southern side. Here the interaction between the waves in the bay and the strong tidal ebb through the outflow channels of the lagoon has produced a well-defined tidal delta of fine sand.

The environment of the 16-kilometre lagoon is controlled by tidal currents. At the northern end the ebb tides run strongest, maintaining tidal channels and sub-tidal sand bars. Further south, narrow tidal channels and broad intertidal flats predominate, while at the south-eastern extremity the lagoon tails off into salt marshes and a cluster of small salt pans.

The vegetation on the sand dunes, coastal shelf and granite hillsides adjoining the bay and lagoon is fairly open, clumpy scrub that is adapted to the dry, sandy conditions of the west coast Strandveld. Reeds, rushes, 'Cape grasses', ericas, galenia bush and certain varieties of pelargonium give this type of vegetation some affinity with the fynbos of the Cape Floral Kingdom neighbouring it to the south and east. However, a preponderance of fleshy-leaved shrubs, such as melkbos, thick-stemmed crassulas, mesembryanthemums, gouty geranium and other succulent varieties of pelargonium, give it more in common with the Succulent Karoo-type vegetation

71. *The most distinguished of the wading birds visiting the tidal mudflats of Langebaan Lagoon, flamingoes sometimes gather by the thousand in the shallows to feed on small intertidal creatures.* 72. *Southward from Saldanha Bay the lagoon extends for 16 kilometres, disappearing in the haze along the opposite shore, beyond a flock of flamingoes foraging on a shallow sandbank. Accumulations of seabird droppings whitewash the tops of lichen-tinted granite boulders.*

73

of Namaqualand that borders the Strandveld in the north.

In the salt marshes the plant population is far more cosmopolitan. In addition to the bulrushes, sedges, water grasses and reeds common to marshes in the Cape, are salt-resistant species of *Spartina* grass, *Juncus* rush, *Salicornia* and paper-flowered *Limonium*, or sea lavender, which have an even wider distribution in similar environments elsewhere.

Seabirds and waders feeding along the water's edge are conspicuously the most prevalent forms of wildlife on the shores of bay and lagoon. The barren granite islands within the entrance to the bay are important breeding grounds of many seabird species. Aptly named Malgas

Island, off the northern headland, harbours a colony of 20 000 Cape gannets, or *malgas*. To the south, Jutten Island has a large population of jackass penguins, and is a breeding ground for sacred ibis, cormorants and Hartlaub's and black-backed gulls. Marcus Island, in the middle, has 10 000 jackass penguins, a similar number of Cape cormorants, several hundred crowned and bank cormorants, and large populations of oystercatchers, gulls and swift terns. Out over the water, gannet clouds bombard pilchard shoals; a continual rain of streamlined white bodies plummet dart-like from on high to seize wriggling morsels beneath the surface. Nightly, at low tide, black oystercatchers forage

noisily for titbits among rocks covered by sea at other times, prising off mussels with their strong orange beaks.

Extensive mudflats exposed in the lagoon when the tide is out are rich in small crustaceans and other little invertebrates that depend for nourishment on organic material washed from the reedbeds and salt marshes. The abundance of these tiny creatures attracts more wading birds to feed than anywhere else in South Africa. In winter there are about 30 000 resident waders on the mudflats, but in summer their number swells to three times as many with the arrival of migrants from their breeding grounds in northern Europe and Asia. At times there may be several thousand flamingoes feeding among them on the mudflats, but curlew sandpipers make up about 75 per cent of the total. Numbers peak towards autumn, when birds mass here to top up their energy reserves for the 10 000-kilometre return flight.

With their sheep, the Khoikhoi, whom the early Portuguese navigators met in the vicinity of bay and lagoon, pursued the shifting herdsman's way of life suited to the dry conditions of the Strandveld. But the way of European settlers, who needed arable land, regular rainfall and a constant supply of water, was not easily adaptable, and for want of these an attempt by a French party to found a colony here in 1632 was short-lived.

After establishing themselves at the Cape 20 years later, the Dutch frequently sent ships to Saldanha Bay for seal skins, fish, birds' eggs, salted seabirds for feeding their slaves, and to obtain ivory, rhino horn and sheep by trading with the Khoikhoi on Skaapeiland, at the entrance to the lagoon. But regarding the prospect of actual settlement, the official view was that the Dutch East India Company 'can do nothing at all with the place, for it seems that there is no land in the whole world so barren and unblessed . . .'

Strategic considerations later obliged the Dutch to set up a military observation post at the foot of Konstabelkop, maintained throughout the eighteenth century, when the French, English and Dutch fleets were involved in wars, and naval engagements were fought in the bay. As far as civilian settlement was concerned, however, the aridity and scarcity of water continued to discourage all but a handful from occupying land facing the lagoon. Serious proposals by Dutch, and later English, officials to divert the Berg River into Saldanha Bay were never taken up.

Whalers, sealers and fishermen were nevertheless continually drawn to the

74

area and were responsible for the growth of Langebaan village in the 1870s and the development of a smaller settlement at Churchhaven. By this time there were only nine houses at Hoedjies Bay, but the growth of the fishing industry and shipping services, the establishment of the first canning factory and efforts to mine the phosphate deposits at Langebaanweg increased the population to 600 in the next 30 years. Whaling stations opened at Donkergat in 1909, at Salamander Bay two years later, and a railway link between Hopefield and Hoedjies Bay was completed soon afterwards.

Major development at Saldanha Bay only began in earnest during World War II, however, when strategic considerations dictated extensions to the harbour facilities and the piping of water from the Berg River. A South African Air Force base was built at Langebaanweg in 1942, and twelve years later the Naval Gymnasium opened at Saldanha. Although the whaling stations finally closed down in 1967, the fishing and canning industries had by then expanded considerably, and new enterprises had grown up around the phosphate industry. The basis for the total transformation of the area was laid in 1973, when the Cabinet approved Iron and Steel Corporation plans to develop Saldanha Bay as a deep-sea harbour – bigger than all the country's major ports put together – for the express purpose of exporting some 60 million tonnes of iron ore annually.

From the outset, conservationists have been concerned about the long-term impact of these developments on the island seabird breeding colonies and on Langebaan Lagoon. The waters of bay and lagoon are completely interdependent, and any chemical or oil pollution of Saldanha Bay will inevitably also contaminate Langebaan Lagoon, destroying the intertidal organisms of the mudflats and salt marshes, and with them the whole dependent web of life.

The granite rock of the protected coves and inlets that hosted economic development has endured 600 million years. The lagoon, barely 2 000 years old, is a more ephemeral natural wonder, which in the natural course will be erased by sand or sea within a millennium or two. Meanwhile, it is there to be enjoyed for as long as conservationists can negotiate meaningful compromises with the imperatives of development. But long after the lagoon has disappeared, when even the last traces of human residence here may have corroded away, the granite will endure, seemingly unchanged.

75

73. Enlivened by the golden blooms of the seegousblom, the Strandveld vegetation has some affinity with fynbos, but a preponderance of fleshy-leaved plants gives it more in common with the Succulent Karoo vegetation of Namaqualand.   **74.** A large colony of Cape gannets lives on Malgas Island off the northern headland, nesting on the ground in a compact mass.
75. The barren granite of Marcus Island, in the middle of Saldanha Bay, is the breeding ground of 10 000 jackass penguins.

PAARL ROCK
PEARL OF THE BOLAND

In 1657 a Dutch expedition, returning from a vain attempt to find the fabled city of Vigiti Magna, entered an unexplored valley less than two days' journey from their base at Table Bay. East of them rose the wall of blue mountains facing Table Mountain across the Cape Flats. To the west they looked up at the bare, grey granite domes of Paarl Mountain sparkling with dew, like enormous precious stones.

The glistening domes made a similar impression on the farmers who settled in the valley beneath them some 30 years later. The most easterly of the domes they named Paarl, Dutch for 'pearl', and the dome behind it they called Diamandt. The first name stuck, but 'Diamandt' was later dropped in favour of Gordon's Rock, honouring Colonel Robert Gordon, the man who named the Orange River and commanded the Dutch forces against the English at the Battle of Muizenberg. For some unrecorded reason, probably traceable to the French Huguenots, who were among the first to plant their vineyards in the fertile valley, the third large dome came to be known as Bretagne (Brittany) Rock.

Fourteen kilometres long and six and a half wide, covering 33 square kilometres, Paarl Mountain is the most southerly and impressive remnant of a series of Cape Granite plutons. This almost continuous range of hills stretches from St Helena Bay to the Drakenstein Valley, varying in height between 300 and 450 metres. Paarl Mountain, 729 metres at its highest point, is therefore a prominent landmark.

When the plutons were formed about 600 million years ago, they lay beneath, and were embodied in, an immense mass of older Malmesbury rock. As erosion gradually levelled and lowered the surface of the older rock, the tops of the plutons were exposed and became part of the surface. More than 150 million years later the whole of this surface was covered over by upward of 1 000 metres of sedimentary rock. In the south-western Cape this subsequently weathered away completely in the middle, over the Cape Flats and further north, but on either side partially survived as the bold upper faces of Table Mountain, away to the west, and Groot Drakenstein, on the other side of the Drakenstein Valley.

On the slopes of Groot Drakenstein the granite and sandstone meet about 200 metres higher than the summit of Paarl Mountain. Looking eastward across the valley, one gains a vivid impression of what an enormous volume of rock had to be weathered away before erosion could even begin to carve the outlines of Paarl Mountain from the granite.

The shape that was to emerge, however, had been determined to a significant extent long before all the rock covering the granite was removed. The steady relief of pressure as the burden of such a vast mass of rock gradually lessened, produced an opposite reaction in the granite. It responded by expanding, and not being a plastic material, it cracked, incurring multiple fractures. Water percolating from the surface and forming corrosive solutions with chemicals, penetrated the rock through these fissures to hundreds of metres below the surface, causing the granite to decay along the cracks.

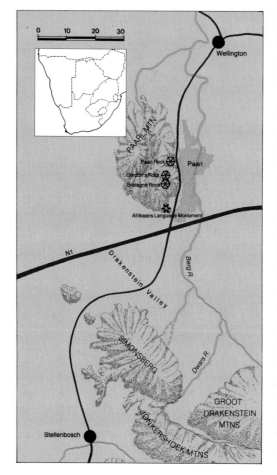

When the once-monolithic pluton became exposed directly to weathering by rain and wind and the alternation of high and low temperatures at the surface, the granite began to crumble where it was decayed, breaking up into angular blocks which slowly rounded at the edges and corners. Where the original cracks were very far apart, they formed the huge domes themselves; where they were closer, the granite blocks were fashioned into the rounded boulders now strewn about the mountain. The weathering processes are typical of granite areas: the 'onion skin' type; and the fine flaking of the whole surface, which generally does not alter the shape of the rock, but gradually reduces its size, scaling it down.

Places of refuge for deserters and runaway slaves in Dutch East India Company times, many of the caves in the Paarl Mountain granite are the result initially of chemical action. Chemicals drawn from the centre of the rock harden at the surface at the expense of the core, and when rainwater penetrates through into the core the softer rock is hollowed out. These cavities are then enlarged both backwards and upwards by the process of flaking, and may eventually become large caves.

Paarl Rock gave its name to the thriving town that grew to be, after Cape Town, the largest in the western Cape – the 'Pearl of the Boland', set in the lush winelands of the Drakenstein Valley. Here, too, the soil was fertile for nationalist causes. Paarl Rock became a symbol of the movement of farmers, professional men and clerics who in 1875 founded the 'Genootskap van Regte Afrikaners' to campaign for official recognition of their language. A century later the inheritors of their tradition chose Paarl Mountain as the site for the Afrikaans Language Monument. Although conservationists argued that the mountain made a preferable monument in its natural state, cultural and political considerations prevailed. So from the valley today one may look up at the mountain and see, according to one's predisposition, a symbol of a human struggle, or, viewing only the great, gleaming granite domes, a monument to events that took place in the south-western Cape 600 million years ago.

76

78

76, 77, 78. The prominent domes on Paarl Mountain display the typical shapes of rock formations in granite areas. So-called 'onion-skin' weathering has shaped the smooth curves of the domes themselves, and sometimes left broken remnants of the former 'skin' still in place after the rest has slid off. Fine surface-flaking also gradually reduces the bulk, if not the shape, of domes and boulders. Chambers hollowed inside the rock by chemical and physical processes are sometimes exposed by the erosion of the outer rock above, leaving depressions that trap rain water on the surface.

77

FYNBOS

THE SMALLEST KINGDOM

The mountains, valleys and coastal plains of the south-western Cape are the natural realm of the most varied assembly of plant species on earth – the Cape Floral Kingdom, smallest of the world's six floral kingdoms, but its richest.

Covering barely 18 000 square kilometres in a narrow belt of territory running parallel to the coast from the Olifants River, near Vanrhynsdorp, to the eastern Cape, it contains some 8 500 different species of flowering plants and ferns. Table Mountain alone, with 1 400 species, has almost as many as the whole of the British Isles. A century ago the area covered by the Cape Floral Kingdom was estimated to be three times the size to which human enterprise has now reduced it. On that area it was reckoned to have 1 300 species to 10 000 square kilometres, compared to a mere 420 for its nearest rival, the Neotropical Kingdom of Central America, which is 360 times its size.

Known also as the fynbos, or macchia, biome, the Cape Kingdom is typified by hard, stiff-leaved bush; heaths, or ericas, of which it has 600 species, against four for the whole of Europe; spiky sedges, called restios; and some 350 species of the protea family. The large number of endemic plant families is a source of particular interest to botanists, for whole families, such as the Bruniaceae, Penaeaceae and Grubbiaceae, evolved only here.

Small residual communities of Cape plants that survive in isolation on high mountains far to the north suggest that the smallest kingdom was actually once a larger floral region in Africa, entirely covering land now occupied by savanna and tropical grassland northward to Ethiopia. Gradually the fynbos retreated until at last it made a stand on home ground, among the mountains in the winter-rainfall area of the western Cape. Here it continued to flourish on the soils formed from the Cape Granite that builds Paarl Rock and the headlands at Langebaan Lagoon, but above all on soils from the sandstones and quartzites of Table Mountain, the Cedarberg and the great folded ranges overlooking the Little Karoo and Outeniqualand.

Today, the greatest variety of fynbos species is in the Caledon district. To the north and to the east the number of species decreases steadily, forming various combinations in different localities.

The evergreen shrubs of the fynbos have hard leaves with either leathery or hairy surfaces to protect them in summer. They go through a vegetative cycle in winter, when temperatures are low and the soil is wet. The smaller plants forming the ground cover have bulbs or tubers for storing water underground, or as annuals grow afresh each year, completing the entire cycle from germination to seeding within the first few weeks of spring, while the soil is still moist from winter rains. Thus August and September are the months for wild flowers, when countless 'daisies' weave a many-coloured tapestry wherever land has not been cleared and put to the plough.

The fynbos is generally thickest where the annual rainfall is between 500 and 800 millimetres. The tallest shrubs, mostly members of the protea family, grow to a little over two metres. Between and beneath them are densely packed smaller shrubs, such as ericas, perennial bush 'daisies' and brown-plumed clumps of reedy green Restionaceae, the so-called 'Cape grasses', or restios, that have been extensively used for thatching and making hardy brooms.

Cape vegetation is usually taller on mountain slopes than in valleys, because there it receives more rain and additional moisture from low clouds. It reaches its prime midway up the slopes facing the cloud-forming south-easterly wind in summer. Above 900 metres, however, larger bushes are confined to sheltered hollows, while the exposed areas are dominated by small heaths and 'Cape grasses', of which there are many varieties.

These 'Cape grasses' are also abundant on the seasonally waterlogged flats. They combine with palmiet to choke the channels of slow-flowing streams, imparting a brown colour to the water, while fluitjiesriet (*Phragmites*) and paapkuil (*Typha*) stand in shallow vleis.

In the drier parts of the Kingdom the vegetation is thinner and annuals more prolific. Small bushes with hard, flat leaves are dominant. There are fewer plants with erica-type leaves, more fleshy-leaved succulents and mesembryanthemum shrubs, of which crawling, large-leaved species, known as 'sour figs', often mat coastal sand dunes.

Fynbos species have long been part of the herbal lore of indigenous peoples. Used by Bushman and Khoikhoi as medicine and perfume, *Agathosma* species, popularly called 'buchu', are now cultivated for the recognized pharmaceutical properties of their pungent, oily leaves. The rooibos tea shrub, *Aspalathus linearis*, a legume with small yellow pea flowers that grows in the Cedarberg, has been domesticated for half a century and is widely used as a stimulant-free substitute for tea.

It took hundreds of thousands of years for rival floras to divest the Cape Kingdom of its vast African colonies and confine it to its original domain. It has taken man less than a century to reduce what remained by two-thirds. And it is not only its territory that man has appropriated for

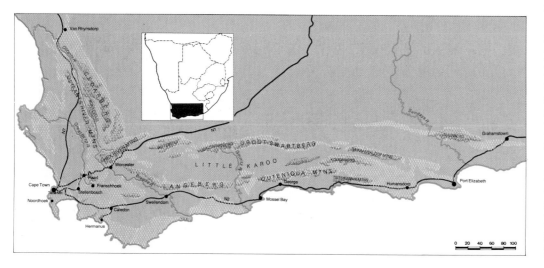

other purposes, but entire species that he has wiped out. With so many species in the realm, and a great number of them endemic to very small areas – perhaps only a single mountain-top, hillside or marsh – a species can easily be made extinct by a new road or a piece of land cleared for agricultural or urban development.

Some 1 500 recorded species are already listed as extinct, endangered or rare. One species of erica is found only on a single peak overlooking the Noordhoek valley, in the Cape Peninsula. In the late 1970s the last wild colony of golden gladiolus numbered only 23 plants. Until the Kenilworth Racecourse, in Cape Town, was rerouted a few years ago, the last known specimens of a water-living sorrel with delicate floating leaves grew in a pond near the track, and a few years earlier the last specimens of a rose-red

erica were seen nearby. The marsh rose, probably the most beautiful of all the proteas, has twice been pronounced extinct, and then rediscovered years later. There were only 300 known specimens of this plant left in 1960, and by 1968 the number had shrunk to 90. The marsh rose was only saved from imminent extinction when Forestry Department botanists undertook a special study of its life cycle and were rewarded recently with the successful regeneration of a number of populations amounting to several thousand individuals. The surviving population of another species, *Protea mucronifolia*, escaped obliteration in a wheatfield only because the farm boundary fortuitously turned back the plough less than 100 metres from it. A large green orchid, *Satyrium foliosum*, grows on two cliff faces, and is found nowhere else.

79. *Broad-leaved yellow leucadendrons, minute-leaved pink erica, and the brown-tufted 'Cape grasses', or restios, represent the three major elements of fynbos and are often seen together on south-western Cape mountains. Some 8 500 species make the Cape Floral Kingdom the richest for its size in the world.*

Veld fires have a curiously ambivalent role in the Cape Kingdom. Occasional fires in the natural course of events actually play a positive part in clearing the tangle of old vegetation for new growth. They also stimulate the growth of numerous species of bulbous and cormous plants, such as the familiar suurkanol, *Watsonia pyramidata*, which colours mountainsides with its vivid pink flowers after fires. Normally only five per cent of these plants flower each year, but an autumn fire, followed by good winter rains, will bring ten times as many to flower in spring, and an equivalent increase in the seed that germinates the next winter. There are also many small orchids that wait unseen underground for years at a stretch, before a fire creates the right conditions for them to surface again. On the other hand, the more frequent fires that are caused by man sap the vitality of the fynbos, and at the same time potentiate the seeds of noxious aliens, providing the exotics with a foothold from which to overrun large areas.

In their native habitats the spread of these exotics is checked by the natural balance they have struck with other plants over a long period. Freed from these natural restraints on their expansion, the exotics are in a strong position to usurp territory from the fynbos by upsetting the delicate natural balance of indigenous plants with their environment. The most menacing of these aliens are various species of Australian hakea, acacia, albizia, myrtle and eucalyptus, as well as cluster and other pines from the northern hemisphere. So far at least 24 per cent of the Cape Kingdom has been infiltrated, and to varying degrees overwhelmed, by these aliens.

Man's aggressive entry into the realm of the Cape Kingdom has also had the opposite effect of causing fynbos to spread into areas formerly inhabited by other types of vegetation, particularly into parts of the southern Cape and areas on Table Mountain where indigenous forests were felled for timber.

Conservationists are concerned not only for the future of the fynbos, but also for the insects, birds and other animals that depend on it for food and shelter. It is estimated that for every plant that dies, between ten and 30 other organisms also perish. At the same time, the plants rely upon the other organisms in a variety of ways. This interdependence is succinctly illustrated by sugarbirds in the Hottentots Holland Mountains that feed on high-altitude proteas in summer, and nest and breed at lower altitudes when another protea species flowers there in autumn and winter. To survive there, the sugarbirds require both species of protea, which in turn need the sugarbirds to pollinate them and distribute their seeds. If either plant falls below the birds' requirements, the birds will disappear from the area, to the ultimate detriment of both protea species, with a chain reaction of mortality among other organisms that depend directly or indirectly on them.

While there is much understandable gloom about the future of the Cape Floral Kingdom, enormous effort is being expended by individuals and institutions to save it from extinction. There are still

many areas of pristine fynbos among the mountains, and to a more rapidly diminishing extent on the coastal lowlands of the south-western and southern Cape. But their successes are temporary. They can win little more than limited respite for habitats from the mounting pressures of human population growth, economic expansion and strategic requirement. At best, they can only defer the Cape Kingdom's demise until a new ice-age changes the face of the earth more drastically than could man in his wildest fears.

80. One of the few proteas which does not occur in the south-western Cape, the broad-leaved protea prefers the mountains of the southern Cape and Little Karoo.   **81.** Named for the plume-like bristles of its flowers, the featherhead shrub grows a little over a metre tall.   **82.** Popularly known as the everlasting, or sewejaartjie, because its papery flowers maintain their appearance for several years indoors, this woolly shrub was formerly used to stuff mattresses.   **83.** One of some 600 species in the most numerous genus of the Cape Floral Kingdom, Erica abietina is endemic to the Cape Peninsula.   **84.** Growing up to two metres high, the blombos is a common shrub on the Cape mountains, flowering from April to September.   **85.** The lavender petals of Roella triflora are frequently seen on Cape mountains between December and March.   **86.** With massed styles bristling like pins, the plants of the Leucospermum genus are well named 'pincushions'. Although they are widespread, the greatest concentration of these plants occurs along the Bredasdorp coast.

87. *Kolkol is one of the more widespread members of Bruniaceae, a family which grows only on Table Mountain Sandstone formations of the western, south-western and southern Cape. This species' presence along watercourses or in seepage areas is a sure indication of perennial water. A large scarab beetle, one of the plant's pollinators, is at work.* **88.** *Wild watsonias demonstrate their ability to flower after a veld fire.* **89.** *Sissies, a member of the Penaeaceae family endemic to*

93

the south-western Cape, has an even more restricted distribution range as it occurs only in the Cape Peninsula. **90.** High on a mountainside overlooking the Cape coast, a large Felicia bush is dressed in its spring coat of pink. **91.** Its diaphanous brown plumes brilliantly backlit, Hypodiscus argenteus, one of 320 species of 'Cape grass', nods in the breeze. **92.** The only Mimetes species to be

found throughout the fynbos region of the south-western and southern Cape, the rooistompie thrives on well-drained acid soils derived from Table Mountain Sandstone. **93.** The natural habitat of the silver tree is in soil derived from Cape Granite on the eastern slopes of Devil's Peak and Table Mountain. A member of the Leucadendron genus, its leaves glitter brightly in summer, but lose their sheen in winter.

TABLE MOUNTAIN
BASTION OF THE FAIREST CAPE

For five centuries the mariner's western approach to the Cape of Good Hope has been signposted by the great block of Table Mountain, rising more than a thousand metres out of the sea, a flat-topped island on the seafarer's horizon. But often ships approach the Cape when a 'black Southeaster' has thrown a thick 'tablecloth' of dark cloud over the crags and buttresses. At such times, when according to early Dutch settlers the legendary tobacco addict, Van Hunks, is engaged in a smoking duel with the Devil, only the lower slopes are visible.

So it must have been when the early Portuguese poet, Luis Vaz de Camões, sailed in Cape waters a century before the Dutch settled. In the magnificent epic he wove around the voyage of Vasco da Gama, *The Lusiads*, he tells of an ominous cloud, 'something more than a storm', blacking out the sky. In the cloud, large as the Colossus of Rhodes, looms the towering figure of Adamastor, a giant son of Earth. Defeated by the gods,

disappointed in love, his flesh turned to soil, his bones to crags, he has been banished and transformed into 'that mighty hidden cape you Portuguese call the Cape of Storms'. There he guards the southern seas, vengefully menacing intruders with 'catastrophe of every sort, until death shall seem the lesser evil'.

But the gloomy seafarers' Cape of Storms became the Cape of Good Hope to optimistic merchant-adventurers, the 'Fairest Cape' to Sir Francis Drake. Ships putting into Table Bay for water, fresh meat and shelter from the south-easterly gales had a view of the mountain much as it appears from the bay today, but for the city and port of Cape Town at its foot and the exotic vegetation that has since infested its slopes. On either side are steep sandstone peaks, connected to the main body of the mountain by narrow, eroded 'neks'; Devil's Peak on the viewer's left, and on the right, Lion's Head, with the gently curved outline of Signal Hill running out towards the bay.

In the centre are the broad sandstone ramparts of Table Mountain itself, 1 082 metres high at Maclear's Beacon.

The face of Table Mountain looking down on the city is really the leading edge of the remnants of a sandstone island plateau forming the rocky backbone of the Cape Peninsula for 53 kilometres, from Mouille Point to Cape Point. The sense of being on an island is strongest at Maclear's Beacon, on the Upper Table. From here the lower Back Table declines towards Constantia Nek and Hout Bay; and beyond Vlakkenberg and Constantiaberg the mountains of the southern Peninsula are washed by the ocean on either side. To the west lies the wide Atlantic, curling round Cape Point into False Bay at one end, and round Mouille Point into Table Bay at the other. To the east, between the two bays, there is only the low driftsand causeway of the wind-swept Cape Flats linking the Peninsula to the distant blue ridges of the Groot Drakenstein, Stellenbosch,

Helderberg and Hottentots Holland mountains on the 'mainland'

Little imagination is needed now to visualize the Cape Flats submerged by a wide ocean channel, as they were in comparatively recent times, when the Cape Peninsula was indeed an island. It takes considerably more to envisage the entire space between the Peninsula and the distant mountains as a solid mass of rock which nature had to excavate to create the channel. Further back in time, our vantage point at Maclear's Beacon was buried under 500 metres of sandstone, and before that it was on a land surface planed and gouged by a vast ice-sheet. Still earlier it was a point suspended in the ocean, and in the beginning a mathematically determined point in space above an ancient shale and granite plain, where the geological history of Table Mountain has its genesis.

Some 700 million years ago, a vast quantity of fine-grained shale was deposited in a seabed depression extending over the south-western and part

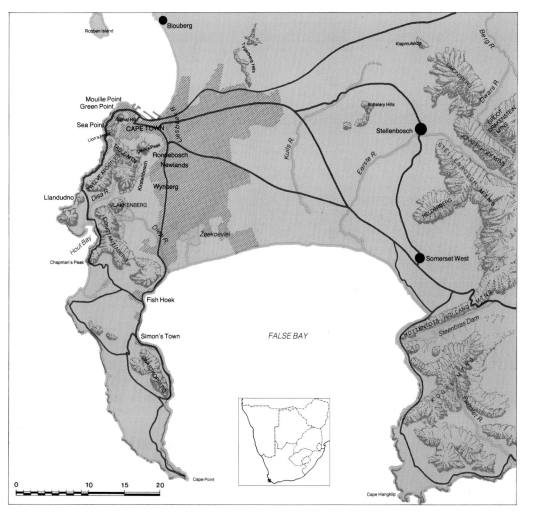

94. *The broad sandstone scarp of Table Mountain looms above the waves, its severe lines accentuated by cloud. Flanked by Devil's Peak on the left and Lion's Head on the right, it was a welcome sight to early seafarers after a long and dangerous voyage.*

95

of the southern Cape. About 100 million years later, molten rock from deep in the earth mushroomed beneath the shale and crystallized into granite plutons as it cooled. Probably before the granite hardened, the whole area was folded. Subsequent erosion reduced the folded eminences to a smooth plain, with surface areas of both shale and granite.

A granite pluton, similar to those of Saldanha Bay and Paarl Mountain, is the foundation on which Lion's Head and most of Table Mountain and the Peninsula range stand. Where the lower slopes are shaped in granite at Kloof Nek and below the sandstone heads of the Twelve Apostles, between Sea Point and Llandudno, it has weathered to soft, crumbly, cream-coloured stone. Concave slopes sweep down to a typically granite shoreline of small coves and rounded headlands, with lines of similarly rounded boulders forming points that run out from the land. Domes of granite break the surface on the lower slopes of Lion's Head above Sea Point. To the south, below Chapman's Peak, the Atlantic pounds fallen granite debris at the foot of precipitous granite cliffs.

Devil's Peak and the eastern face of Table Mountain, however, rise on shale foundations. Here the ancient Malmesbury shale provides the lower slopes and continues beneath the city, becoming prominent again on the other side as Signal Hill. On the seaward flank the hill slope levels out under Green Point and Sea Point, ending in wave-cut platforms, with long arms of dark shale reaching out into the ocean.

On the slopes of Devil's Peak and Signal Hill, shale close to the slowly cooling

granite was baked into hard slate. The contact between the two rocks is most dramatic at Sea Point, where the distinct shale and granite shorelines meet. Here, at a spot visited and recorded a century and a half ago by the eminent naturalist, Charles Darwin, the once-molten granite veined and mingled with, softened and recrystallized the shale, creating a spectacular occurrence of mixed rock, called migmatite, in which large white feldspar crystals have grown in a matrix of dark Malmesbury rock.

About 500 million years ago, the sediments that built the ramparts of Table Mountain and all the other major mountain ranges between the Great Karoo and the southern and south-western Cape coast first started accumulating on submerged portions of the ancient shale and granite plain.

At that time the landmass continued westwards for a considerable distance into what is now the Atlantic Ocean, and a great river flowed out of the north-west, bringing sediments from these highlands and depositing them in a flooded depression open to the sea in the south-east. Its northern shore, between Calvinia and Bitterfontein, and its western shore, running southward to about 150 kilometres west of Cape Town, embraced a large bay, which gradually broadened and developed into a tidal flat. Over this the ebb and flow washed purple clay and fine sand.

By then the Atlantic highlands had been eroded away, and the original river no longer flowed. Eventually, the ocean broke through at the north-western end, and the bay became a sea passage, swept by powerful bottom currents and

pummelled by heavy surf. For the next 50 million or so years the area of present-day Bushmanland was denuded of its mountains. Rivers carried the sand and pebbles away to the shore of the passage, where they were dragged out by the surf, and deep currents spread them over the bottom, layer upon layer, at a rate of about one metre of sediment every 30 000 years. This amounted to over 40 000 cubic kilometres of quartz sand.

Within the relatively short span of the next million years this whole region was covered twice by an ice-sheet centred on the Bushmanland area. The sheet advanced well to the south of the present land surface, retreated as far as Klawer, and then returned. The first time, the ice bore heavily on the floor of the depression, cut deeply into the sediments beneath it, and filled the hollows with sandy glacial tillite as it retreated. When the ice returned, bringing with it a clayey rubble, it floated on the sea above the depression, depositing shale on the floor.

After the ice melted, the depression again became a sea passage, and for the next 30 million years, quartz sand was agitated by the surf as before and distributed over the seabed by currents. Then disturbances in the earth's crust plunged the floor of the channel into deeper water, and black mud accumulated on the white sand of the seabed.

Not all these layers of sediment that built up over about 100 million years are visible on Table Mountain today. The

96

95. *Looking across the misty Cape Flats to the Hottentots Holland Mountains, it takes little imagination to envisage the sea covering the flat plain as it once did, making an island of Table Mountain and the Cape Peninsula.*
96. *Flowering from January to March, the red disa, pride of Table Mountain, is a ground orchid which grows in wet clefts in the rock and on the banks of mountain streams.*
97. *From Signal Hill the famous tablecloth, herald of the Southeaster, is seen billowing over Table Mountain.*

first deposits from the ancient Atlantic highlands were not distributed this widely. But the purple clay that once washed over the old tidal flat now forms a thin strip of shale between the older foundation rocks and the massive sandstone cliffs. On the Upper Table near Maclear's Beacon are traces of the tillite left by the first retreat of the ice-sheet. The great thicknesses of sandstone and shale, deposited after the ice floe finally receded, still form features in the other ranges of the western and southern Cape, such as the Cedarberg, Swartberg and Outeniqua. But in the Cape Peninsula they have been removed by erosion, and on Table Mountain no trace of them remains.

The story of how Table Mountain was shorn of several hundred metres of sandstone and shale and became isolated from the other ranges only really begins about 100 million years after the last of the sediments was deposited. At this time, the pressures that were producing the folded mountains of the southern Cape also caused a broad, arched ridge to develop from north to south in the surface of the south-western Cape. The mountains running northward from Cape Hangklip to the Cedarberg today are remnants of the base of the eastern side of the arched ridge, while the mountains of the Cape Peninsula are all that remains of the base on the western side.

Erosive forces were most effective on the curved top of the ridge. Once they broke through the upper sandstone crust they were able to excavate the softer, older rocks in the core far faster than they could reduce the hard sandstone sides. But as the arch had originally been tilted more towards the west, and the greater volume of drainage was concentrated on this side, less of the western flank has survived.

Later subsidence of the whole of this region let the sea into the broad lowland created by the erosion of the sandstone arch and the softer rock below. From the vantage point of the Upper Table, the eastern vista was then a wide ocean passage. The only land between Table Mountain and the distant blue krantzes was provided by the harder masses of granite and heat-tempered shale that, being more resistant than the softer shale around them, had remained as eminences in the broad lowland. The tops of the Tygerberg hills, Paarl Mountain, Perdeberg and Dassenberg were then islands in the passage that had also turned the Cape Peninsula itself into an island.

After a long time the sea-level began to drop, and most of the previously submerged area reappeared. But a narrow strait remained between Table Mountain and the 'mainland' until eventually the beach sands thrown up by waves closed it too, and sand from the beaches blew inland to build the low dunes of the Cape Flats.

Table Mountain owes its bold outline and massive features to the strong quartz cement that binds the sandstone particles together, making a hard quartzite highly resistant to weathering. But the stresses the quartzite was afterwards subjected to by earth movements produced a pattern of vertical and horizontal weaknesses in the rock. Percolating water widened the weaknesses into cracks, and gave erosion the foothold needed to split the rock into the familiar tabular shapes on Table Mountain today. The widely spaced horizontal bedding planes formed prominent ledges. Vertical weaknesses produced the sheer cliff faces and permitted the erosion of the gullies and gorges between the buttresses. Lichens clinging to the surface of the quartzite impart to it a dark shade of grey, while the freshly exposed rock is lighter grey, except where iron and manganese oxides have stained it brown or black and softened it at the surface.

From early Stone Age times, men recognized the pale grey quartzite as the hardest rock available in the area and fashioned it into primitive tools. These they left behind in many places on the lower slopes of the Peninsula mountains, and in caves overlooking beaches that are well above the reach of the sea today.

When the first Dutch settlers made their camp in 1652 beside the stream of fresh water flowing from Platteklip Gorge into Table Bay, there were still Bushmen living in the mountains. Cattle-herding Khoikhoi clans were gathered at Rondebosch and on Wynberg Hill. Small groups of people known to the settlers as Strandlopers, who included both Bushmen and Khoi, scraped their subsistence from the rocks between the

tides and made dams of tidal pools in which fish were trapped when the water ebbed.

If we compare Cape Town today with paintings of the way it was during the early years of settlement, the most striking contrast is in the vegetation. Then dense forests of ironwood, stinkwood, yellowwood, rooiels and other indigenous trees and undergrowth crowded the wetter slopes from Newlands almost to Constantia Nek. They filled the valley above Hout Bay and Orange Kloof, and climbed wherever possible up sheltered gorges on the drier western side. The lower slopes were spread thickly with fynbos, dominated by proteas and, in the heavy red soils formed on the old granite on the eastern side, by silver trees, which do not occur in nature anywhere else. Small fynbos shrubs clung to the cliffs, while the whole plateau was covered with proteas that flourished on the additional moisture wrung from the 'tablecloth'.

After severe clashes with the settlers, the earlier inhabitants either moved away, succumbed to alien diseases or submitted to cultural extinction, finding ways of gleaning their subsistence at the bottom of the new social order. Meanwhile, the newcomers quarried the old heat-hardened shales on Signal Hill and Robben Island for building stone, developed brickfields to exploit the rich red clay on the slopes of Devil's Peak, and cut down the indigenous hardwood forests above Wynberg and Hout Bay for timber and fuel.

Under pressure from the aggressive newcomers, the red hartebeest, zebra and eland that had browsed and grazed on the lower slopes began to disappear. So did the elephant, buffalo, rhino and hippo on the flats, leaving only the smaller solitary and secretive antelopes, such as the grysbok, crafty baboons and creatures that were small enough to escape notice. The last lion was shot after the British occupied the Cape in 1806; the last leopard followed 70 years later. Exotic forests were planted on the lower slopes and parts of the plateau, and rampant alien plants spread of their own accord, commandeering range from the fynbos, climbing on to krantzes and threatening the last refuges of indigenous forest in the kloofs.

A report published in 1976 by the Department of Botany at the University of Cape Town found that 25 per cent of the mountain was already covered by dense stands of introduced undesirables, and that much of the remaining natural area was in poor condition due to erosion and too-frequent burning. The forecast for 75 years hence was even more disturbing. Although there would still be vestiges of indigenous forest in ravines and gorges, the rest of the mountain would, without management, be completely overrun by cluster pine, hakea and other exotics. Widespread concern was translated into action by the authorities. A long-term programme to eradicate the aliens and foster the rejuvenation of fynbos and forest has begun to show visible results on

Devil's Peak, but ultimate success cannot be taken for granted, and the danger of re-infestation will never be removed.

When we look down over the Back Table from Maclear's Beacon today, we see the reservoirs that once supplied Cape Town among pine plantations in the broad valley of a mature river that flowed across the plateau 70 million years ago. Behind us rises the hum of a city of a million people. Far below, the stream of fresh water from Platteklip Gorge, at which mariners filled their water kegs centuries ago, now flows forgotten beneath the busy streets of central Cape Town.

Today, Table Mountain is linked to the rest of the continent by every modern means of communication. But there are misty mornings when low fog rolling in from the Atlantic piles up against the slopes and blankets bay, city and flats. Then, between Table Mountain and the distant blue krantzes, only the tops of Blouberg, Tygerberg, Perdeberg and Paarl Mountain show above the fog, as they showed above the sea long ago. And until the fog lifts, the illusion of still being on an island is almost complete.

98. *The sheer ramparts of Table Mountain form the leading edge of the remnants of a sandstone plateau stretching more than 50 kilometres southward to Cape Point.*
99. *From the sandstone buttresses of the Twelve Apostles above Camps Bay, concave granite slopes fall gradually to a shoreline cluttered with rounded granite boulders.*

99

100. *Below Chapman's Peak, Atlantic swells surge and break at the feet of granite cliffs daubed with sunset tints. Across Hout Bay the cone of Little Lion's Head dents the flushed western sky.* **101.** *Survivors despite the proximity of man, baboons are still frequently encountered on the mountains of the Cape Peninsula.* **102.** *The craggy sandstone cliffs below Cape Point bear the scars of being continually lashed on three sides by wind and wave.*

100

101

102

THE CEDARBERG
MOUNTAIN WILDERNESS

Etched into the sky east of the Olifants River, the rugged peaks and ridges of the Cedarberg range rise some 1 800 metres above the riverbed, running parallel to it from Citrusdal to Clanwilliam at a distance of a few kilometres. Here, within sight of the main road north to Namibia, a magnificent tract of wilderness encompasses 700 square kilometres of rocky mountainland, cleft by deep valleys with crystal pools and waterfalls, and gouged into fantastic shapes by wind and rain.

In a geological sense, it can be said that the Cedarberg range takes over from where Table Mountain leaves off. The quartz-sandstone that forms the massive upper cliffs of the Peninsula mountains also furnishes the greater mass of the Cedarberg. Here too it forms lofty peaks, such as 1 744-metre Krakadouw and 1 618-metre Middelberg, but in much of the range it is surmounted by later sedimentary formations already eroded away on Table Mountain.

Where the surface of the earlier sandstone is uncovered at the northern end of the Cedarberg, in Pakhuis Pass, it resembles a ploughed field because of the deep grooves scoured in it by the first of the two ice-sheets that once covered the whole region. Elsewhere, this surface lies directly beneath a thin layer of mudstone deposited by the second ice-sheet. But even there the imprint of the first sheet is visible in a number of places, where the sandstone immediately beneath the mudstone was pushed up into surface folds by the movement of the ice.

When the second ice-sheet retreated northward, it left a large accumulation of moraine material around its outer edge. For a time this sheltered the basin from vigorous surf action, allowing the silt washing out of the retreating ice to be deposited as shale and siltstone. The well-preserved fossils in them testify to the relatively tranquil marine origin of these shales, which form a conspicuous green band of grass-covered slope, known locally as Die Trap, 'the step'. This runs below Sneeuberg, all the way from

103. *The Stadsaal (town hall) Caves have been grotesquely carved by rain and running water in the sandstone of Truitjieskraalberg, at the south-eastern end of the Cedarberg range.*

Sanddrif in the south, past Tafelberg to beyond Sneeukop.

The bold cliffs below Die Trap are hewn from the pre-glacial sandstone, but the broken slopes above and the summits of peaks like Sneeuberg (2 026 metres) and Tafelberg (1 969 metres) are made of the redder, extensively jointed sandstone. This was deposited after erosion of the protective moraine barrier once more exposed the basin to the open sea, and the pounding of surf on the shoreline left nothing of the sediments but the particles of white quartz sand.

Weathering along the multiple weaknesses in the upper sandstone has in places left grotesquely carved pillars and upstanding rock masses, such as the grey sculptured columns of the Sneeuberg, the honeycombed orange rocks around Tafelberg, and the 10 metre-high natural sandstone arch crowning the Wolfberg at 1 608 metres. And on the same peak are the so-called Wolfberg 'Cracks', deep chasms cut through the sandstone, some too narrow to admit a man, and others so wide that they open into large caverns below, while their precipitous sides almost close overhead.

Winter rainfall, supplemented by occasional thunder showers in summer, yields annual totals ranging from 760 to 1 270 millimetres in different parts of the Cedarberg. The valley bottoms and lower-lying areas receive substantially less rain than the peaks and higher slopes, which are drained on the western side by tributaries of the Olifants River, and in the north-east by the Doring River system.

On the 'Cape grass' flats in the lower valleys, between 500 and 1 000 metres above sea-level, the drier conditions favour the prevalence of shrubs and bushes, such as the silky conebush and aromatic geelmargriet, generally less than three metres tall. The laurel protea may attain six metres and the sand olive five, as may the rockwood and mountain maytenus growing there on stony outcrops. On debris slopes at this altitude throughout the area the dominant plant is the unmistakable waboom, a species of protea that grows as a hardwood tree up to seven metres tall.

Higher up, the plants are generally shorter. 'Cape grasses' here are less than a metre tall on level sandy areas, while on stone kopjes and mountain slopes they mix with ericas and leucadendrons perhaps half a metre taller, and are also associated with the contorted Clanwilliam cedars that give the Cedarberg range its name.

Believed capable of living for 1 000 years, these unique so-called 'cedars'

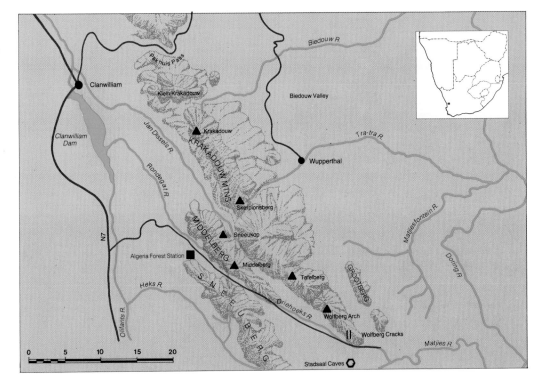

grow both singly and in scattered groups on rocky outcrops and mountain-tops below 1 400 metres. Although they may grow to 20 metres in protected positions, they are usually less than seven metres. The old trees expand sideways, and become spreading and gnarled, with heavy twisted limbs. Most of the older branches become dry and hard, and may die off, but the fresher tips continue sprouting new leaves. Sadly, few of these 'cedars' realize their full potential for longevity, and the dead trunks and branches of those destroyed by veld fires litter the mountains like driftwood.

Grass is tallest and most plentiful on the soil of the shale band between the sandstones. Here the most prevalent taller plants are the grey-green renosterbos and four species of protea, including the water white sugarbush.

Broad-leaved shrubs and small trees, such as lance-leaf waxberry, lance-leaf myrtle, kloof brachyleana and wild almond, crowd the lower-lying courses of perennial rivers. On west-facing boulder slopes, and around seasonal streams in narrow clefts and kloofs, where large boulders clutter streambeds, are dense stands of trees up to ten metres tall, including spoonwood, rockwood, silky bark, mountain maytenus, Breede River yellowwood and wild olive.

The tallest trees grow in the deep shade of well-watered kloofs, as at Helskloof and Duiwelgat, and in the higher courses of the Boskloof and Heks rivers, where 30-metre rooiels, witels and African holly rub shoulders with shorter Breede River yellowwood, hard pear and Cape beech.

Above the snow-line, their woolly white flowers growing directly out of the ground, are rare snow proteas, found here and nowhere else.

Crisply defined against the sky, Krakadouw Peak drops more than 1 200 metres on its north-eastern side to the broad Biedouw Valley. Here, on the southern fringes of Namaqualand, the springtime floral display rivals that of the Richtersveld, and the panorama of daisies includes the varieties known to the Khoikhoi as *bietou* (variously spelt), from which the valley gets its name. Further south, the eastern slopes of Skerpionsberg (1 617 metres), Sneeukop, Tafelberg and Wolfberg feed streams that join the Tra-tra River, which flows through the little mission village of Wupperthal.

Wearing the pigments and textures of spring, Wupperthal seems the nearest thing to an earthly paradise that the Rhenish missionaries Von Wurmb and Leipoldt could have created about themselves in this fertile valley in 1830. And for the 2 000 inhabitants living there today under the benign rule of the Moravians, who replaced the Rhenish missionaries, the hands of the clock appear to have barely moved in a century and a half. Above the streambed their terraced white cottages look out from under thatched eaves over front gardens freshened by vine and pomegranate, and an orchard of peach and pear blossom. Across the river, poplars, oaks, palms, beech and syringa trees shade the outspan and donkey paddock. The store, mission houses, church, post office and shoe factory enjoy views over the produce

104

104. *Caught by a shaft of sunlight, a cluster of leucadendron (conebush) adds a bright splash of colour to the drab shades of the Ganskloof valley above Algeria Forest Station.* **105.** *The sheer face and littered debris slope of the Sneeuberg exemplify the extensive jointing of the upper sandstone.* **106.** *Weathering of multiple weaknesses in the sandstone has produced many unusual rock formations, including several rugged stone arches, such as this one in the vicinity of the Stadsaal Caves.* **107.** *Gnarled, twisted and weather-whitened, the spreading older limbs of the Clanwilliam cedar give the impression that the tree is dead. Younger branches nevertheless continue drawing sustenance from the soil to sprout new leaves. With the potential to survive a thousand years, the trees' lives are generally foreshortened by veld fires.*

gardens dotted with trees in blossom and men in brightly coloured shirts cultivating with long hoes. Donkeys in pairs and teams trot ahead of carts and wagons through mountain byways.

Before European settlement at the Cape, the Cedarberg area was inhabited by Bushmen and, where there was grazing for the cattle and fat-tailed sheep, by Khoikhoi. On the walls of caves in the vicinity of Pakhuis Pass, Bushman artists chronicled the arrival of the white people in paintings of sailing ships, mounted men with guns, and women wearing long dresses and bonnets and riding in four-wheeled vehicles drawn by horses.

Farmers settled on the banks of the Olifants River early in the eighteenth century. By 1860 all the agricultural ground beside rivers and on open flats was taken. The State lands in the Cedarberg were given limited protection in 1876 by the appointment of a 'Forest Ranger' at Clanwilliam, and a few years later of a 'Superintendent of Woods and Forests', who lived in the mountains at the Algeria forest station. Almost a full century after the first appointment, the greater part of the Cedarberg was given

maximum official protection in 1973, when it was proclaimed a Wilderness Area, to be kept in its natural state, with all traces of civilization removed and access limited to small parties on foot.

Black eagles soar in the updrafts among the peaks, baboons roister in the wooded kloofs, and leopard and rooikat hunt klipspringer, grey rhebuck, red rock hare, and dassie.

The Cedarberg commands breathtaking views in all directions. To the south, other ranges complete the chain that runs finally through the Hottentots Holland to Cape Hangklip, forming the eastern base of the sedimentary arched ridge that once covered the south-western Cape. And far away to the south-west across the Swartland the great sandstone block of Piketberg rests on the horizon, a slab of that ancient arch protected by subsidence while the rest of the arch was eroded away, and which was then exposed when the softer shales around it were removed. To the west the thirsty Sandveld reaches to the sea, and to the east the dry plains of the Bokkeveld lead on to distant ranges that, in a geological sense, can be said to take over where the Cedarberg leaves off.

THE GARDEN ROUTE

LAND OF THE OUTENIQUA

The major Khoikhoi clan that once inhabited the luxuriant coastal belt from the southern Cape shoreline to the first range of folded mountains were known to other tribes as Outeniqua, 'people carrying bags'. They came to barter bearing skin bags of honey from the hives of wild bees that drew copious nectar from the flowers of forest and fynbos in their region. Although the Outeniqua disappeared as a clan more than a century ago, their name is perpetuated in the mountain range, while the coastal area straddling the Garden Route, from the mouth of the Great Brak River to the Storms River, is spoken of today as Outeniqualand.

A region of rocky, wave-cut headlands and tranquil lakes, yawning river gorges and quiet estuarine lagoons, it possesses one of the richest assortments of vegetation south of the Limpopo.

Although much of the original forest has fallen to the land developer's axe, some 65 000 hectares, interrupted by farmland and plantations of exotics, stretch 250 kilometres from Mossel Bay to Humansdorp, the largest natural forest complex in South Africa and most southerly outlier of the high mountain rain forests of East Africa.

Rising to 1 579 metres on Cradock Peak, north of George, the krantzes of the

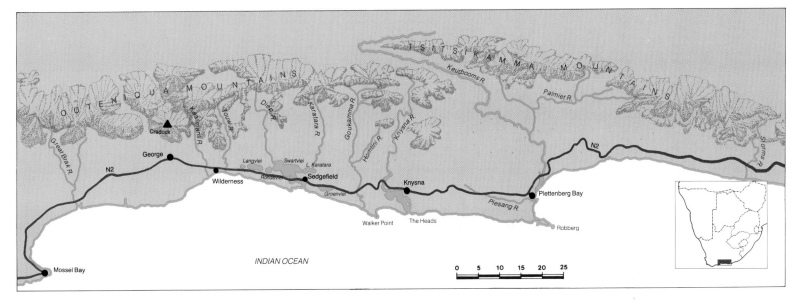

Outeniqua mountains have been chiselled from Table Mountain Sandstone of the Cape System, heavily contorted by the folding that gave rise to the range. At their foot a massive fault exposes a broad area of older pre-Cape rocks and Cape Granite.

The foothills were etched from a former plateau of sandstone and older rocks. The narrow ridges extending outward from the mountainside today are remnants of this upper plateau, now separated by the broad valleys of river catchments.

Between the foothills and the sea the older rocks underlie an erstwhile coastal platform. Levelled originally by sea action, this lower plateau now forms a wide plain, in which the Kaaimans, Touw, Homtini, Goukamma and Knysna rivers have incised deep gorges, and terminates in cliffs cut by waves along another former shoreline. The town of George lies on the broadest part of the plateau, which ends here in granite cliffs close to the present coast west of the Kaaimans River. East of the river mouth the line of old sea cliffs swings inland to ten kilometres from the sea, and then curves back towards the coast, forming the rocky margin of an old embayment. This one-time bay is now occupied by ridges of sandy limestone, marine terraces, loose surface sand and the lagoons and lakes of the Wilderness area.

All these features were produced by changes in sea-level. The lower plateau itself was cut by surf action more than five million years ago, when the sea was over 200 metres higher than now. When the sea dropped to about eight metres above its

108. *Sand dunes behind the long beach at Wilderness give a clue to the existence of the lakes behind. The sand bar at the river mouth sends fresh water flowing back into the Wilderness Lagoon.*

present level, the surf cut the cliffs and planed a broad beach, shelving gently into the sea. As the ocean withdrew further, lines of sand dunes began accumulating on the broad sandy shelf in the embayment, not only where they are visible today, but to 55 metres below present sea-level, then dry land. Local rivers, diverted into the valleys between the dune ridges, formed early lakes and alluvial flats, while the dune sands were cemented into the calcified 'dune rock' forming the limy-sandstone ridges today.

In the course of the last two million years, fluctuations of the polar ice-caps caused the sea to rise and fall several times. Where the sea's advance and retreat were arrested long enough, waves cut ledges in the steep seaward slopes of the 'dune rock' ridges and hollowed out caves in rocky headlands. Four tiers of former beaches were abandoned as the sea finally withdrew.

As the ocean drew back from its previous coastline 120 000 to 20 000 years ago, the rivers, cutting down towards a lower sea-level, broadened and deepened the valleys between the ridges. These low-lying parts were again flooded about 5 000 years ago, and remained inundated for another thousand years, before the sea eventually retreated to where it meets the land today. Drowned estuaries and depressions that continued to hold water were forerunners of the present lagoons and lakes of the Wilderness.

The white sands on the lake margins today were initially blown into the hollows from the dunes, before they were stabilized by vegetation. Later fine muds, exceptionally rich in decayed plant matter, accumulated in a 40 metre-thick layer on the lake bottoms. When the sea was still a few metres higher, so too were the levels of the lakes, which were

consequently larger. As the sea-level fell the lake levels also dropped, and previously continuous stretches of water shrank, breaking up into separate, smaller lakes linked by narrow channels, or were reduced by drainage to marshes and fens.

In the old embayment today, all but one of its six lakes owe their continued existence to being nearly at sea-level on a coast where the mouths of the rivers that ultimately connect them with the sea are often closed by sand bars. Fresh water rises behind the bars and ponds back into the lakes. When the river mouths are unbarred, however, the inland waters ebb and flow with ocean tides.

At the western end of the embayment, fresh water ponds back into the Wilderness Lagoon, behind the sand bar at the mouth of the Touw River, and begins flowing in reverse up the tortuous channel of the Serpentine, a former outlet of the Touw, now leading into Eilandsvlei. As Eilandsvlei rises, the fresh water floods further back through another channel into Langvlei, from where it occasionally finds its way up a narrow, reed-choked channel to Rondevlei. The salinity of these lakes depends on the extent to which they are refreshed by rivers. Rondevlei, although the most remote from the sea, is the most saline, benefitting least from the reverse flow of fresh water from the Touw River.

Lying further east, only Swartvlei, the biggest of the lakes, receives a plentiful supply of fresh water from perennial rivers. When the mouth of its estuary is closed by a sand bar, the rising waters of Swartvlei back up a wide channel into tiny Lake Karatara, which on rare occasions spills over into the freshwater fens of Ruigtevlei, once also a lake.

In contrast to the other lakes, Groenvlei is completely landlocked, its one-time link with Swartvlei smothered near Sedgefield by wind-blown sand some 3 000 years ago.

Cleft by the valley of the Goukamma River is a large outcrop of Table Mountain Sandstone, which surfaces again to form the cape at Walker Point and Knysna Heads. Beyond Knysna the granites and old pre-Cape rocks are not extensively exposed, and the coastline is cut in sandstone. Where rivers flow over resistant sandstone on this coast they cut deep, narrow gorges of the kind typified by the precipitous valley of the Storms River. In comparable fashion, the Knysna River incised only a narrow gap in the

109. *Year-round rainfall brought by onshore breezes contributes to the diversity and lushness of forest vegetation.*

110

sandstone for its spectacular outlet at the Heads. In the softer conglomerates deposited in a fault depression behind the Heads, however, it scooped out a broad valley, which was 'drowned' by subsequent fluctuations of the sea-level and became the remarkable stretch of water known as Knysna 'lagoon'.

At Plettenberg Bay, the Bietou and Piesang rivers also approach the coast in fault depressions similarly filled with conglomerates, and a conglomerate spit forms the prominent Robberg Peninsula. When the sea-level was lower and Plettenberg Bay dry land, the Keurbooms River flowed straight across the bay and cut the Robberg 'gap' in the peninsula.

Outeniqualand reaps the benefit of lying between the winter and summer rainfall areas. It is virtually without seasons, being favoured with mild temperatures and good rainfall throughout the year. The coastal mountains check the progress of onshore breezes, wringing from them their moisture. The amount of moisture increases as the breezes rise towards the mountains, and as a result, rainfalls of between 700 and 800 millimetres a year at the coast increase to 1 000 millimetres on the plateau, 1 300 millimetres on the mountain slopes, and as much as 2 500 millimetres on the peaks. This has a marked effect on the vegetation pattern at different altitudes.

The low-lying coastal strip, despite its lakes and waterways, is hot and dry. The vegetation fringing these waters varies with their salinity. Reeds and bulrushes crowd less saline shallows, but only salt-accustomed grasses prosper on saltier verges. The dunes, however, sustain a host of drought-resistant scrub species. Many would grow into small trees under more favourable conditions, but here they are stunted, gnarled and bushy. Spike-thorn, pincushion, bastard saffron, milkwood and many others form thickets of shrubs, with occasional dwarfed trees,

surrounded by herbaceous ground vegetation. But on windswept coastal cliffs, and where fire has reduced the dry scrub on the dunes, fynbos is gradually taking its place.

On the hot, dry, lowest levels of the lower plateau, scrub gives way to 'dry scrub forest', and Cape cherry and bastard saffron form a dense tangle with other small trees and tall shrubs. Ground vegetation here is sparse, as the canopy of intertwining branches excludes sunlight. Yet, where the low canopy is pierced by tall yellowwoods, ferns and small herbs spring up beneath in gaps in the foliage.

'Tall forest' growth thrives best where rainfall is neither too low nor too high, in a belt between the middle of the lower and the middle of the upper plateaux. Even within this belt rainfall differences produce a tiered succession of distinct types of 'tall forest'. A 'dry' form, at lower levels, gives way higher up to 'temperate', 'moist' and eventually 'wet' forms, each with a typical arboreal arrangement.

Along the lower fringe of the 'tall forest' belt, 'dry scrub forest' frays into 'dry tall forest', where small to medium-sized trees form a fairly dense canopy some ten to 18 metres high. Here the candlewood is the most common tree among many species, which include yellowwood and ironwood. Beneath the canopy is a lower storey, in which ironwood and kamassi prevail. Monkey ropes trail from their branches, and strangling twiner wraps around the trunks of young trees. Thorny shrubs form a scrub layer, while ferns, short grasses and herbs carpet the ground.

'Temperate tall forest', at a slightly higher altitude, sports a canopy 16 to 22 metres above the ground, composed chiefly of the same species as in the 'dry tall forest', but here ironwood and yellowwood dominate. A six- to eight-metre lower storey consists largely of younger trees of the same species waiting for space to reach maturity in the canopy, as well as several smaller species, kamassi being most prevalent. Beneath them, a dense underbush of witch-hazel stifles ground cover.

Higher up, where it is moister, the forest canopy has three storeys. In the upper are yellowwood, stinkwood, white elder, white pear and Cape beech, thrusting up to 30 metres, with great ironwoods breaking through, and towering yellowwoods reaching 50 metres. Quar, saffron, candlewood and witels make up an intermediate storey, mixed with immature trees of the upper canopy, and wild pomegranate, rock alder, forest monkey plum and kamassi comprise the lowest level. Thinner witch-hazel

underbush allows a rich, dense ground flora, while stunted tree ferns grow in wet depressions and beside small streams.

'Wet tall forest' occupies the rain-drenched higher parts of the upper plateau and foothills, raising a 20-metre canopy of mainly stinkwood, rooiels and yellowwood. Assegai, tree fuchsia and ironwood form a lower storey, over a dense jungle of tree ferns.

The still wetter, cold, lower mountain slopes are clothed in a 'wet scrub forest' which includes stunted rooiels, stinkwood and yellowwood, with tree fern and mountain saffron in the lower scrub layer, and a thick ground cover of ferns.

On the cold, misty, higher mountain slopes, the scrub is three to five metres high, consisting chiefly of scrubby mountain cypress, rooiels, keurboom and yellowbush. Between the scrub thickets are ferns and 'Cape grasses', with splashes of colour added by red-hot pokers and several watsonia species. The steep slopes above 480 metres are covered with fynbos.

In nature, the distinctions between these specific levels are often blurred, the orderly arrangement disrupted where the foothills and plateaux are dissected by broad and narrow valleys, ravines and gorges, with variously pitched slopes facing different ways, and varying degrees of exposure and protection. Thus a complex multiplicity of mini-climates allows different forest and scrub types to extend along valley slopes and bottoms to other levels, where particular situations suit them best.

This range of climates is largely responsible for the southern Cape being particularly well endowed with plant species, from both the Cape and Tropical kingdoms. Some 125 tree and major shrub species, introduced to Outeniqualand by the southward migration of tropical vegetation many thousands of years ago, later found that favourable conditions persisted here after the general northward retreat of tropical vegetation in response to widespread climatic fluctuations. These tropical species occur mostly in the 'dry scrub forest' and warmer localities of 'dry tall forest' nearer the coast, although some species – including white pear, saffron, forest monkey plum, wild peach, wild elder, Cape beech and Cape holly –

110. Found in indigenous forest and beside mountain streams, the Knysna lily is becoming rare. **111.** *The Knysna River could cut only a narrow, stormy channel through the sandstone to form the impressive Heads.* **112.** *Streaks of sunlight illuminate the tranquil waters of Swartvlei, largest of the Wilderness lakes.*

113. *A zone of weakness in the hard sandstone permitted the Storms River to cut the narrowest of channels to the sea. The steep, rugged cliffs of the gorge are softened by vegetation which clings tenaciously to the bare rock.*

realistically estimated to be between 600 and 800 years old, instead of the 1 000 to 2 000 years frequently claimed for them.

Although the potential of the Outeniqua forests as a source of much-needed timber was known to the Dutch settlers at the Cape by 1668, it could not be vigorously exploited for some time, as the many deep and precipitous river valleys running north to south between the mountains and the sea were too great a discouragement to west-east travel. Until the time the first village, George Town (for King George III), was laid out in 1811, the only settlers living in the area were a few impecunious farmers and woodcutters, who exported the produce of their labours through a special timber port at Plettenberg Bay.

George Rex, a man of obscure origins who was erroneously rumoured to be the natural son of George II, settled near Knysna 'lagoon' in 1809, and the small community that grew up around him became Knysna town. After the Royal Navy took charge of the forests in 1812, the exploitation of the timber to supply Simon's Town dockyard intensified to such an extent that the navy opened a second timber port at Knysna. As sailing ships on the coastal run were gradually replaced in the 1860s by steamboats, safer to handle in the treacherous waters at the entrance to the estuary, the importance of Knysna as a port increased.

Inexorably, the great forests were decimated, as was the wildlife of the region. Red hartebeest, bontebok, Cape buffalo and spotted hyena disappeared from the coastal plains, and the bluebuck and Cape lion became extinct. The hippo wallows no longer in the lakes and rivers. Of the former elephant herds, only a few individuals linger on in the forests north and east of Knysna, their gene pool already too depleted for their number ever again to increase. Only the smaller and more reclusive animals have been able to hold their own in the dwindling forests. Here genet and Cape wild cat, serval, caracal and leopard still prey on mice and shrews, dassies, vervet monkeys, baboons and small antelopes. Clawless otters fish in the streams and the honey badger still seeks out the hives of the wild bees whose honey was instrumental in giving Outeniqualand its name.

Fragmented by agriculture, reduced by industry and menaced by freeway development, the Knysna and Tsitsikamma forests retain their magic and majesty despite their depletion. Outeniqualand remains a place of beauty and wonderment, all that is left of a unique part of our natural legacy – to be squandered, or conserved for posterity.

are among the main trees in most Outeniqualand forest types.

More widely distributed are subtropical species, such as stinkwood, candlewood and ironwood. These evolved from tropical species, but are better suited to cool, moist conditions than their parent species. Most versatile of all, however, are the remnant species that were part of the ancient, distinctively Cape, forest vegetation that flourished in this area several million years ago. Such are the assegai and kamassi and the great yellowwoods. Dominating the forests, these yellowwoods grow taller and live longer than any other species, although the age of the giant specimens selected as 'big trees' to impress tourists are more

THE LITTLE KAROO
A FOLD IN THE MOUNTAINS

Between the mighty ranges of folded mountains that run west to east across the southern Cape lies the valley of the Little Karoo. 'Little' because it is small compared to the wide plains of the Great Karoo beyond the fringing northern range, and 'Karoo' because its surface is hard and dry, as the word in its original Khoikhoi form implies.

On the northern side of the valley, Anysberg, Klein Swartberg and the colossal Swartberg proper (2 325 metres) are links in a mountain chain that is continued further to the east by the Baviaanskloof and Winterhoek mountains all the way to Uitenhage. The southern side of the Little Karoo is bounded by the Langeberg chain, persisting eastwards in

the Outeniqua, Long Kloof, Tsitsikamma and Kareedouw mountains for some 480 kilometres to Humansdorp.

Both mountain chains are formed from huge folds in layers of the earth's crust, each made up of multiple lesser folds, tilted on the northern side, as if pushed over from the south. Between the major chains, rising from the valley floor, are

minor ranges, such as Touwsberg and Warmwaterberg, shaped from smaller folds.

At the western end of the valley, these intensely folded chains run into the more gently folded north-south trending ranges between the Cedarberg and Cape Hangklip. In the confused area of conflict between the two trends they create superb mountain scenery, at its most spectacular in the Hex River Mountains.

The crags of ranges cradling the Little Karoo are of the familiar resistant sandstone of the upper faces and rocky summits of Table Mountain and the Cedarberg. However, the Bokkeveld shales, deposited to a thickness of several

hundred metres on top of the sandstone, have also been preserved in the Little Karoo, not above the sandstone krantzes but at their feet, underlying the valley floor. On the Karoo side of the Swartberg chain, the shales also underlie a narrow valley separating the chain from the bare white quartzite ridges of the Witteberg, a smaller parallel range. The Witteberg gives its name to the quartzite, formerly deposited more extensively on top of the shale to complete the Cape System.

More than 250 million years ago, immense pressures exerted from the south by readjustments of the earth's crust caused widespread folding. The younger shales and quartzites then naturally formed the upper layers of the crests of the upfolds as well as the troughs of the downfolds, and therefore the bedrock of the valley floors. For the next 100 million years or so, erosion worked on the surfaces of both upfolded masses and hollows, deepening the valley of the Little Karoo and completely denuding the emerging folded mountains of their younger rock covering. And as the great sandstone ranges were revealed by weathering, the gravels, sands and muds into which the younger rocks decomposed were carried away by streams and rivers. The valley became choked with deposits of closely packed pebbles in a sandy matrix, cemented into reddish and lighter coloured conglomerates.

The Little Karoo is drained by tributaries of the Gouritz River. The major of these, originating in the Great Karoo north of the Swartberg range, have sliced narrow, sinuous, sheer-walled poorts

114. *In strong contrast to the pale grey sandstones of the folded ranges on either side, features on the valley floor are generally carved in reddish conglomerates. These coarse sediments derive from decomposed upper series of the Cape System that formerly capped the grey sandstones.*

through more than a thousand metres of hard sandstone, down almost to the level of the valley floor. Entering at the western end of the valley, the Touws River is joined by the Prins, which breaches Anysberg. It later links up with the Groot, which has forged a passage through Klein Swartberg. Seweweekspoort, incised by the Huis River, cuts Klein Swartberg off from Swartberg proper, which is cleft by the Gamka north of Calitzdorp. It is breached again by Meiringspoort at De Rust, and by the Olifants River at the eastern extremity of the range. Flowing from opposite ends of the valley, fed by many small tributaries on the way, the Groot and the Olifants rivers join with the Gamka south of Calitzdorp to form the Gouritz, which breaks through the Langeberg range north of Albertinia and flows into the sea between Stilbaai and Mossel Bay.

A landscape with essentially similar features to those of the present had evolved here by 100 million years ago. Renewed folding and huge faults along the southern flanks of the mountains caused a massive displacement of rock. In a number of localities this displacement exposed strips of older rock between the sandstone slopes and the fallen valley floor. The Cango fault, in the foothills of the Swartberg, is an extension of the great Worcester fault, which can be traced as far east as Uitenhage. Thirty kilometres north of Oudtshoorn the fault exposes a band of older, pre-Cape, dark grey crystalline limestone, 548 metres thick and some 24 kilometres long. Here the showpiece of the Little Karoo, the world-famous Cango Caves, has developed.

Created by the same process of carbonate solution in underground water that hollowed out the Sterkfontein and other cave systems in the dolomites of the Transvaal, and expanded in places by roof collapse, the Cango Caves present one of the world's most extensive and

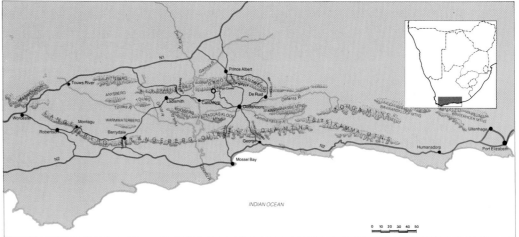

beautifully varied dripstone assemblages, in an amazing labyrinth of connected cavernous halls, smaller chambers, galleries, catacombs, passages and low crawlways.

Discovered in 1780 by a herdsman working for a farmer named Van Zyl, while either tracking a wounded antelope or searching for strayed stock, the Cango Caves today receive nearly 200 000 visitors every year.

Although these magnificent caves have been systematically explored over a long period, their full extent is still not certain. Until a little more than a decade ago the known caves penetrated 775 metres into the limestone hillside, but another 165 metres were added in 1972, when spelaeologists uncovered a small, rubble-hidden aperture opening into the so-called Wonder Caves, whose crystal splendours had never before been seen by human eyes.

Not even the justly celebrated beauty of the previously known caves can match the graces of the new halls and chambers. Warm air exhaled by millions of tourists over the years has dulled the radiance of the dripstone formations in the former, while the Wonder Caves, unviolated by man since the time they were formed, reflect a sparkling brilliance of crystalline reds and ambers, russets, creams, pinks

and purest white. Snowy gypsum flowers carpet the floor, calcite roses 'bloom' in shallow pools retained by rimstone, and flowstone 'waterfalls' tumble perpetually in arrested motion on to floors and ledges. Folded dripstone curtains hang like unfurled flags from the ceilings, amid miniature forests of intertwining straw stalactites and pale helictites in massed clusters. Stalactites and stalagmites, thick as tree trunks, unite in towering columns. Here no signs of life were found, save the bones of three genet cats and the skeletons of bats, embedded in the flowstone floor after they were trapped inside perhaps 50 000 years ago by an earthquake that sealed the exit with rubble. So that all this may be preserved for serious study, the Wonder Caves have not been opened to the public.

Water has played a part in forming not only the caves themselves and their adornments, but also their name. 'Cango' was adopted for the caves from the Khoikhoi name for their locality, and means 'water mountain'. Within a few days after rain, water falling here percolates down to fill the pools on the cave floor 182 metres below the surface. On the ceiling above, stalactites continue forming from minute carbonate residues left behind by drops of water when they fall into the pools.

The western part of the Little Karoo is an imbroglio of small brown stony hills, but towards the east, around Oudtshoorn, a series of valley-plain terraces slope gently down towards the centre on both sides of the valley, from the Swartberg and the Outeniqua. Both slopes then fall away more than 100 metres to the valley-plains of the Kammanassie and Olifants rivers, which flow westward on either side of the Kammanassie mountains towards their confluence in the Oudtshoorn basin, two kilometres south-east of the town.

With a thinly distributed perennial rainfall of 155 to 300 millimetres annually, Little Karoo vegetation is dominated by succulents, particularly a prolific assortment of bushy mesembryanthemum species. Grasses are correspondingly scarce, but dwarf trees and shrubs, like the ubiquitous guarri, are plentiful in the rocky parts, where the bare rock funnels rainwater run-off into pockets of soil, effectively increasing the rainfall they receive. Where conditions are propitious, thorn-tree thickets along river banks occasionally grow into forests of tall sweet thorn. The often troublesome renosterbos, whose leaves secrete a wax that makes them highly inflammable, is common on the highest hills and ridges

115

115. *Patterns in the rock on either side of the road illustrate the intense folding that created the southern Cape ranges. The Swartberg Pass opens an entrance to the Little Karoo from the north.* **116.** *Thorn-tree thickets disclose the path of a river in the broad, scantily vegetated expanse of the Little Karoo's valley floor.*

116

117. *Bounded by the Swartberg in the distance, this area of the Little Karoo forms part of the ostrich farmers' realm. It was they who introduced to the landscape the striking garingboom, the leaves of which could be used as fodder in times of drought.*

in the Little Karoo. Round its margins, renosterbos forms scrubland with several other species, including geelmelkbos, which grows in clumps and makes mounds of the wind-blown soil it traps in its dense growth at ground level. Non-succulent scrub associated with renosterbos is generally mixed with succulent scrub on the higher dry plains; but up the sides of the mountains moister conditions exclude the succulents. Mountain renosterveld includes trees such as the sweet thorn, sand olive and shiny-leaved rhus. This Karoo type of scrub finally gives way to fynbos on the upper slopes and summits.

Like most of the Cape Province, the Little Karoo was inhabited by Bushmen and Khoikhoi before white farmers began moving into the area. Small caves and rock shelters throughout the folded ranges preserve a rich tracery of Bushman art, most prevalent in the foothills of the Swartberg, between Meiringspoort and the foot of the Swartberg Pass, at Boesmanskloof, De Hoek and Skildergat.

Many of the place names here are either variants of the original Khoikhoi names, or translations. The *touw* of Touws River, for instance, was the Khoikhoi name for the bush *Salsola aphylla*, commonly called asbos, because its alkaline ash was used in making soap. Kammanassie means 'water for washing', Gamka is Khoikhoi for 'lion river' and the Gouritz

was named for the Gouriqua, a tribe which lived near its mouth.

The main road between Mossel Bay and Oudtshoorn today crosses the Langeberg range a few kilometres from Attaquas Kloof, where an old elephant track provided the first European explorers and frontiersmen with access to the Little Karoo. This route was pioneered in 1689 by Izak Schrijver, sent by Simon van der Stel to trade for livestock with the local Khoikhoi. Other routes were developed through Kogmans Kloof, near Montagu, and Tradouw Pass, near Barrydale, and by the 1730s a number of farmers were looking for suitable situations in the valleys between the folded ranges.

Those who settled in the Little Karoo lived in virtual isolation behind the forbidding mountains, and had to rely principally on Attaquas Kloof for communication with the world outside their valley. It was not until 1815 that a way across the Outeniqua between George and Oudtshoorn was opened by the hazardous Cradock Pass. In 1848 it was superceded by the Montagu Pass, which crosses the mountain 736 metres above sea-level. In 1869 the Attaquas Kloof route was diverted over Robinson Pass, 860 metres at its summit, and in the 1950s the Outeniqua Pass, which climbs a spectacular 799 metres, replaced Montagu Pass as the chief link between George and Oudtshoorn.

Early farmers found the indigenous vegetation unsuitable for grazing and turned to grain and fruit culture. Although their agricultural products gained a good reputation outside their enclosed area, the high mountains and poor means of communication remained a handicap to commerce. The change in the Little Karoo's fortunes was brought about by the domestication of the ostrich in the latter half of the last century and the international fashion craze for ostrich feathers that reached its zenith before World War I. Some 358 000 domesticated birds on farms in the area in 1904 had increased to 750 000 a decade later. Although the demand for feathers slumped, and there are only about 90 000 birds on 200 farms in the Little Karoo today, the wealth produced by ostrich feathers at the turn of the century laid the foundations for the whole of the diverse regional economy of the present day.

South of the Outeniquas lie the coastal lands of the southern Cape, leading on eastward through the Wilderness lake district, the Knysna 'lagoon' and the Tsitsikamma forests. On the northern side of the valley, Meiringspoort and Seweweekspoort allow passage through the Swartberg range, and from the 1 500-metre summit of the tortuous Swartberg Pass, built by convicts in the 1880s, there are glimpses beyond the Witteberg of the dry plains of the Great Karoo.

118

119

120

121

118. *Growing in a small pocket of earth among the rocks, succulent plakkies derive their name from the fact that the leaves of certain species were used as dressings for drawing wounds.* **119.** *The long, slender spines are the sharp armament of the sweet thorn, which forms tree thickets along the banks of Little Karoo rivers.* **120.** *A familiar sight in the Little Karoo, ostriches freely roamed the arid regions until the latter half of the last century, when they were domesticated to provide feathers for the fashion world.* **121.** *Moisture retained in the aloe's thick, fleshy leaves ensures the plant's survival in dry, rocky conditions.* **122.** *Still in regular use, one of the earliest routes into the Little Karoo was through Kogmans Kloof, near Montagu.*

122

123

123, 124, 125. *Hollowed out of crystalline limestone by carbonate solution in water, the Cango Caves are the showpiece of the Little Karoo. The first sequence of caves, known as Cango One and open to the public, penetrates some 775 metres into the hillside, and two more sequences extend even further. In Cango One alone, the array of dripstone formations is one of the most extensive and beautifully varied in the world.*

124

THE KAROO
A DESERT IN THE MAKING

Viewed from a car speeding over the dry flatlands of western-central South Africa, the Karoo is probably the average person's idea of a desert. Upon transients it leaves a composite impression of small, dusty towns, lonely railway sidings, gaunt windmills, and remote farmhouses in shading clusters of tall bluegums, roofs painted silver to shrug off the sun's heat. Dirt road turn-offs seem to lead nowhere across barren plains, broken along the skyline by isolated, flat-topped kopjes and table-lands. Everything about the Karoo – the land, the plants, the conditions of life – is hard and dry, as its name implies.

But it is not the same to all men. To the geologist, the Karoo is a system of rocks, to the botanist, a type of vegetation, both extending far beyond the geographical limits of the region. Familiar with the Karoo itself, geographer and inhabitant subdivide it into areas with names like Hantam Karoo, Tanqua Karoo, Roggeveld Karoo, Moordenaars Karoo and, of course, the Great Karoo.

The region known as the Great Karoo lies in the angle of the western and southern Cape Folded Mountains, its eastern limit defined by the valley of the Sundays River, flowing southward past Graaff-Reinet and Jansenville. Its northern boundary is the almost continuous wall of the Great Escarpment, formed by the Roggeveld, Komsberg, Nuweveld, Camdebo and Sneeuberg ranges.

Before the erosion of the Great Karoo to its present level, the plateau above the Escarpment extended uninterrupted to the Cape folded ranges. As rivers excavated the plateau surface, they formed the cliff-like edge of the Escarpment where thick sheets of dolerite, capping the softer sandstones and shales, resisted further headward erosion. The only major break in the abrupt scarp face is the 95-kilometre Biesiespoort gap between the Nuweveld and Camdebo ranges, at Beaufort West. Here the absence of a thick dolerite sheet enabled the Kariega and Salt rivers, headwaters of the Groot River, to cut wide valleys into the plateau.

The Klein Roggeveld range, projecting southward from the Komsberg, divides the Great Karoo in two. West of it, rivers drain north-west, passing from the Tanqua to the Doring and ultimately the Olifants River, which carries their combined waters to the Atlantic Ocean. East of the projection, rivers drain southward, slicing deep gorges through the folded ranges, to the Indian Ocean.

West of the Klein Roggeveld, the basin is known as the Tanqua Karoo (from *sanqua*, meaning 'Bushman') or Hantam Karoo, for the Hantam Mountains, near Calvinia, at the northern extremity. Cut off from rain by the enclosing mountains, the broad, flat valleys of the Tanqua and Doring rivers receive less than 150 millimetres of rain a year. Virtually the whole area between these rivers is a desert, eroded down to bare shale. Where there is topsoil, Bushman grass may spring up after rare good showers, but the scant perennial vegetation is dominated by succulents, chiefly stemless varieties of mesembryanthemum. Except where the dry courses of infrequent streams are picked out by twisted karee, sweet thorn and occasional wild tamarisk, tree and shrub growth is sparse.

The southern end of the Tanqua Karoo is called Ceres Karoo and Bokkeveld Karoo. Between the Tanqua and Doring rivers the plain is broken by the low Koedoesberg range, running north-west from the end of the Klein Roggeveld Mountains. Across this region lies the route to the interior taken by travellers two centuries ago. North-east of Ceres they entered the Bokkeveld Karoo through the Karoopoort gap in the Bonteberg and continued across the plain, passing beneath the aptly named Hangklip and through the Gousbloem (marigold) Kloof in the Koedoesberg. Finally they climbed to the Roggeveld Karoo above the Escarpment by way of Verlaten Kloof, followed today by the road to Sutherland.

East of the Klein Roggeveld range, the Great Karoo presents a bleak vista of undulating rocky ridges and rough stony plains, with large areas completely denuded of soil, except in valleys. Outcrops of bare rock are exposed

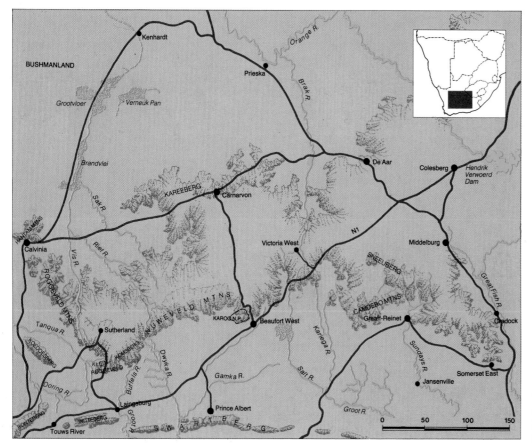

126. *Prickly pear and aloe overlook a portion of the Valley of Desolation. The turret-top of Spandaukop rises from the plains of Camdebo, and the Tandjiesberg almost fills the horizon.*

127

128

South of Matjiesfontein, the Witteberg range (127) is composed of the white quartzite and sandstone of the uppermost series of the Cape System, the Witteberg Series. To the north (128) eminences have the characteristic flat tops formed by dolerite sills that intruded Karoo sedimentary rocks.

between clumps of scrub. Westward, in the tract called Moordenaars Karoo between Laingsburg and the Komsberg escarpment, flat-topped hills, raised plateaux and rugged, angular buttes are prominent in debris-strewn plains. Between the Nuweveld escarpment and the Swartberg range is the central area, known as the Koup, a Khoikhoi word meaning 'flat land'. At the eastern end, near Graaff-Reinet, spectacular columns of weathered dolerite stand guard over the Valley of Desolation. In the extreme south testimony lingers of advance ripples pushed out into the Karoo rock by the thrust waves that folded the Cape mountains. Here parallel east-west ridges and shallow valleys formed in the thick glacial tillite deposits.

Between the Cape and Escarpment ranges, this entire region lies in the rain-shadow that separates the winter and summer rainfall areas. Annual precipitation, mainly in autumn, increases from 125 millimetres in the west to about 250 millimetres in the east. The vegetation is adapted to these semi-arid conditions and consists largely of drought-resistant scrub that can subsist in the thin, stony soil. Grasses may be widespread in wet years but succulents are rare, except along the northern foot of the Swartberg and the mountains ranging eastwards, where conditions are similar to those of the Tanqua Karoo.

Despite its sparseness, often limited to stunted shrubs in rocky crevices, Great Karoo vegetation is rich in variety. Over 40 Karoo bush species dot the plains and hillsides, and some 20 principal shrubs and trees are concentrated in the thornveld along watercourses. Though often difficult to find, there are more than 20 perennial grasses, which, together with a host of annual grasses and other ephemerals, sward tracts of wasteland after isolated showers. In the central area, the silty flats and broad floodplains around Beaufort West are fairly densely covered with low shrubs, such as doringkapok, blomkoolganna and ankerkaroo, whose branches curve over to anchor in the soil. Following the valleys of the Kariega and Salt rivers, this thicker cover extends northward through the gap in the Great Escarpment.

Upper Karoo is the name usually given to the huge plateau area behind the Escarpment, basined by streams and rivers that eventually feed the Orange River when they carry enough water. Bounded in the east and north-east by foothills of the Lesotho highlands and the Highveld, it grades down through ever-broader plains formed on Karoo shales and sandstones. Intrusion by dolerite raises dark ridges in the plains and the topmost palisades of turret- and table-topped kopjes. Towards the west the Upper Karoo shades into the great flatlands of Bushmanland, planed on older rock formations, dominated finally by the granite peaks of the Kamiesberg. Spilling from yet another great basin, the Kalahari Sandveld fringes the north.

Rainfall decreases westward across the Upper Karoo from 625 millimetres in the highland foothills, where mountain grassland gradually gives way to true Karoo scrub, down to 125 millimetres where the Karoo region borders on Bushmanland. In the eastern, central and other higher areas of the basin immediately behind the Great Escarpment in the south and south-west, a few mountains and many dolerite hills interrupt the terrain. Singly and in ranges, they pimple stony shale and sandstone plains, covered in places with thin deposits of red, sandy loam. A relatively dense and uniform growth of bush mantles the plains, while the slopes of hills and mountains are often better grassed with blousaadgras and steekgras.

To the north-west, the larger portion of the Upper Karoo receives less rain and is almost a desert, a flat country crossed by wide river tracts. Hills swell up chiefly in the south, along the northern foot of the Roggeveld range where it is cut by the Sak River and its many tributaries. After the autumn seasonal showers, stiff breezes send silver ripples among the silky plumes of white desert grasses on the plains. In the lower courses of the rivers, however, internal drainage has produced extensive brak, silt-spread *vloere*, or 'floors', such as Brandvlei, Grootvloer and Verneuk Pan, between Calvinia and Kenhardt. Some are partly covered with asbos ganna, but most remain bare. Internal drainage also speckles the plains with deposits of surface limestone, and calcrete pans proliferate westward into Bushmanland.

The name 'Karoo' is also applied to an immense, lava-capped geological system of sedimentary rocks deposited in a vast basin. Not only were all the present-day Karoo regions included in this basin, but it extended far beyond the contemporary coastline on to what are now other continents, overlapping Cape rocks in the south and east, older rocks in the north and west. The basin was centred on the Lesotho highlands, where today the full Karoo sequence of shales and sandstones, mudstones, dolerites and lavas is thickest and most complete. Around them the landscape is moulded in the older Karoo formations.

Some 620 000 square kilometres in South Africa are covered by Karoo rocks. Remnant outcrops are scattered in distant parts of the continent, but not all the layers in the full Karoo geological sequence are present today in the Karoo geographical region. The earliest sediments, Dwyka Tillites composed of coarse, angular fragments in a blue, silty matrix, deposited by ice-sheets some 270 million years ago, are most conspicuous in the extreme south of the Great Karoo, and are named for a minor river in that area. At Nooitgedacht, near Barkly West, the ancient lava floor over which the ice scraped is preserved in a 'glaciated pavement'. The lava has a smooth, polished surface, in which pebbles held by the moving ice gouged fine parallel striations, subsequently embellished with petroglyphs scratched in the rock by Bushman artists. But the uppermost series, the Cave Sandstone of Golden Gate and the basalts of the Drakensberg, have been removed from the Karoo by headward erosion of highland

129

129. *Succulent aloe and crassula species abound among the rocks at the foot of the Swartberg along the southern edge of the Great Karoo.* **130.** *Despite its sparseness, Great Karoo vegetation is rich in variety. More than 40 species of bush dot the plains in the central area.*

rivers, and its chief physical features are carved from the underlying Beaufort Series of brightly hued red, purple, blue and green shales and mudstones, interleaved with yellowish sandstones.

Ashimmer in summer noons, crisply detailed in the chill of icy winter dawns, the Karoo's empty arid plains awe with their sense of boundless space, timeless moments and wind-whispered silences. Shaven steadily deeper into their horizontal sedimentary beds, their standing features are isolated, cliffed table-lands, the fragments of former plateaux marooned hundreds of metres above the present plains, and smaller, often rounded, buttes. Weathering has reduced many of the great mesas to these characteristic flat-topped Karoo kopjes. Like the Escarpment itself between the Great and Upper Karoo, most receive their typical outlines from resistant dolerite intrusions, injected into the sediments as molten magma some 150 million years ago. Squeezed upward through vertical cracks and weaknesses in the sediments, the molten rock spread out horizontally between the easily parted layers of shale and sandstone. It cooled as tough dolerite sills, from less than a metre to 300 metres thick, covering up to 14 000 square kilometres. Where host-rock erosion has exposed dolerite hardened in vertical cracks, it strikes dark ridges across the plains. The steep cliffs topping the southern Escarpment, the raised table-lands and the kopjes are all weathered edges of dolerite sills.

The dolerite capping these eminences protects the underlying sediments from erosion. Weathering of the free faces above drops rock fragments on the slopes below, building up a protective layer on the bedrock and grading down in a concave sweep from large boulders near the top, to progressively finer material near the bottom. Uninhibited by vegetation, the rapid run-off produced by occasional violent storms results in sheetwash. This spreads debris over the broad, flat pediments, which dip barely perceptibly towards the centre of drainage in the plain. Other dolerite sills and hard sandstone layers below the capping may step the scarps. Kopjes of shale and sandstone layers that have lost their capping have a ragged conical shape, determined by the harder sandstone bands, while those consisting wholly of shale flatten into low mounds.

The period of more than 30 million years during which the Beaufort sediments were deposited coincided with the great Age of Reptiles, when these early forms of life developed and throve in the

swampy Karoo environment of the times. Since the pioneer road-builder Andrew Geddes Bain discovered the skull of a mammal-like reptile, known today as Therapsida, near Fort Beaufort in 1838, these sediments have yielded countless fossil remains. Denizens of the ancient Karoo included reptilian ancestors of yesterday's dinosaurs and today's lizards, snakes, crocodiles, birds and mammals.

The vast fertile plain of the Karoo in Beaufort times, with its great rivers and lakes in which freshwater sharks, coelacanths and lungfish flourished, vanished millions of years ago in the natural course of faunal succession and climatic changes. But even as recently as two centuries ago it was still a far more fertile region than it is now, although the climate has not changed significantly.

Few traces of topsoil are left in the Karoo, but the little remaining suggests that it was not always a stony wilderness. Extensive areas now taken over by Karoo bush and reduced to desert wasteland

130

were once great grasslands. Early travellers crossing these plains recorded immense herds of springbok, blesbok, mountain zebra and black wildebeest. These huge concentrations of game followed the rain, migrating over hundreds of kilometres from one temporarily lush area to another. After they left an area denuded of grazing, the veld had sufficient time to recover before they visited there again. During the dry winter months the plains were rested, as the herds moved into the mountains where the vegetation was greened by melting snows.

As sheep farmers replaced Bushman, lion and cheetah as dominant predators in the Karoo, they shot out the game, fenced the land and restocked it with sedentary domestic flocks. Lacking knowledge of vegetation, they subjected the veld to continuous over-grazing, frequently burning the grass in spring and autumn to stimulate nutritious fresh growth. But the tender, new green shoots were gained at

the expense of the root systems binding the soil. Run-off increased and less water was retained by the soil, as it evaporated faster from bare surfaces. Unable to survive, the grasses were replaced by drought-resistant bush whose roots are ineffectual in checking the removal of topsoil by erosion. Thus scrub takes over from grassland, and desert takes over from scrub, in a continuing process which, if unchecked, will convert half the surface of South Africa into desert and scrubland by the middle of the next century.

When this ominous warning was sounded in the 1950s there was hope that the process could be halted. For the areas already depleted of topsoil there could be no redemption – here the grasslands had gone for all time – but perhaps the remainder could still be prevented from going the same way. Tremendous effort was poured into educating farmers in responsible veld management, checking harmful selective grazing and other destructive practices. Some 30 years later,

with little evidence of success, the view has gained ground that the sheep is an antagonistic ecological factor, and that there is no prospect of conserving the Karoo while it is used for sheep farming. Banning sheep from the Karoo might save it in the long run, but to do so would be a short-term political risk no government could afford to take.

Although no workable solution to the larger problem has been found, steps have been taken at least to preserve and restore representative portions of the Karoo. The Karoo National Park, near Beaufort West, was proclaimed in 1979, and a nature reserve incorporating the Valley of Desolation, at Graaff-Reinet, has been created under the auspices of the Cape Department of Nature Conservation.

Elsewhere, the Karoo remains a place of serene, barren beauty; of stony plains detailed with dwarf shrubs, occasional herds of sheep and solitary, creaking windmills, turreted kopjes and table-land fortresses – a desert in the making.

GOLDEN GATE

CROWN OF THE 'CONQUERED TERRITORY'

Majestic above the bubbling perennial headwaters of the Little Caledon River, the scalloped sandstone cliffs of Golden Gate crown the edge of the broad interior plateau in the north-eastern Orange Free State. Here, between parallel ridges of the Rooiberg range, streams have cut rolling valleys, their steep south-facing sides weathered by frost and snow. Above hazy half-lit dales, sunlight slants red and gold on the flanks of mushroomed eminences. To the south-east, the mighty Maluti Mountains build the roof of southern Africa over the heartland of Lesotho.

Running westward from its source for 11 kilometres, the Little Caledon curves southward for the remaining 46 kilometres to its confluence with the Caledon River at the Lesotho border, near Butha Buthe. From source to confluence it descends through the full layered sequence of Stormberg Series rocks topping the Karoo System.

In the upper catchment, Stormberg-capping basalt forms the highest peaks of the Rooiberg. Ribbokkop (2 840 metres) and the slightly smaller Generaalskop tower some 1 200 metres over the lower reaches of the river. Its channel near the confluence is in shales and sandstones of the underlying Beaufort Series, which shoulder Karoo kopjes and table-land further west.

Upstream, riverbed and banks are cut in the brilliant Red Beds. These fine, purple and red sediments, deposited more than 180 million years ago in shallow water covering inland alluvial flats, dried and hardened into thick mudstone bodies. When arid interludes suspended the accumulation of mud, wind-blown sand provided material for thin sandstone layers in the mudstone. Being more resistant to erosion, these sandstones are conspicuous as the ledges of low waterfalls in the river and tributary streams.

At the time the Red Beds were deposited, dinosaurs roamed the land. Five-toed footprints of the mighty *Massospondylus* are preserved in one of the sandstone layers, and incomplete fossil skeletons of three of these dinosaurs have been found in the area.

The Age of Dinosaurs culminated in a period of extreme aridity, when desert winds massed huge sand dunes on the eastern side of the Karoo Basin. Here they were compacted into massive Cave Sandstone, up to 245 metres thick, between the earlier Red Beds and the immense basalt capping produced by subsequent lava flows. Golden Gate's

most striking and characteristic features, its creamy-coloured scarps, bluffs and buttresses, have been shaped from these petrified dunes. Protruding dolerite sills, domed with slope debris, lip the pale yellow sandstone cliffs, giving them their mushroom-like appearance. These bold features mark the steeper, south-facing slopes of the valley, which rise almost directly out of the river, and have been weathered by frost in the teeth of snow-bearing winds. On the southern side, broad alluvial terraces separate the river from the gentler north-facing slopes.

Summer thunderstorms shed 700 to 850 millimetres of rain yearly in the valley, but frost and snow from May through August impose a cold, dormant period. Although the easily eroded, powdery red soil from mudstone and the shallow sandy sediment from Cave Sandstone have low fertility, rich basalt soils grass hills and valleys in the upper catchment with a dense growth that checks erosion of the steep slopes. Here the vegetation comprises over 50 grass species, chiefly ones common to high mountains, but including tolerant temperate and tropical species, reminders that the Golden Gate highlands lie on the old floral migration route. Abundant wild clover on upper slopes associates with fynbos and temperate herbs, ferns and grasses, members of genera more at home in the western Cape. In season, the grasslands are tinted by the flowers of bulbous annuals, gladioli, berg lily, red-hot poker and watsonia. The violet heads of agapanthus dot rocky positions and arum lilies, bulrushes and 'Cape grasses' line streams.

The abundance of bulbous plants indicates that over a very long time periodic grassfires have swept these slopes. Trees and shrubs grow where boulders shelter them from the blaze. Pockets of forest survive in deep valleys and protected gorges incised in the Cave Sandstone. Here ouhout, kershout and sagewood dominate mixed communities of katbos and taaibos, lightning bush, cabbage tree, Cape myrtle, protea, tree fuchsia, bramble and aromatic wilde-als.

A century and a half ago, these high grasslands attracted vast numbers of game and attendant predators. Lion, leopard, hyena and wild dog hunted eland, hartebeest, blesbok, springbok, reedbuck, wildebeest, klipspringer, oribi and zebra. At the beginning of summer, great herds of migratory species moved away to the

131. *The south-facing red and cream portal of Golden Gate has been shaped from the ancient sand dunes by icy winds.*

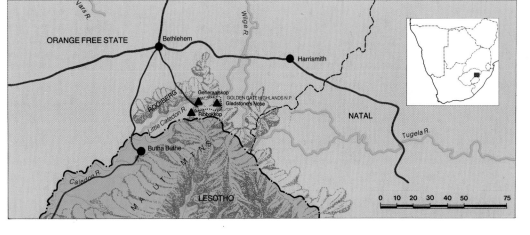

western Free State for sweet early grasses, returning to the eastern highlands in autumn, when the mountain grasses were most palatable. In winter some went down the mountains to warmer pastures in Natal.

Early Voortrekker communities establishing themselves in the north-eastern Free State made their living from hunting and trading hides. To them these grasslands, densely populated with game, were the Riemland, because hides of the many antelope shot here were cut up for multi-purpose rawhide thongs, called *rieme.*

The Cave Sandstone, named for the characteristic caves and rock recesses weathered at the base of cliffs, has from prehistoric times given shelter and refuge to man at Golden Gate. Here two centuries ago, Bushmen were still painting eland on rock-shelter walls.

When the rise of the Zulu kingdom under Shaka sent waves of violence and destruction through the land early last century, the Taung, led by Makwana, found sanctuary in these caves for a while. Later menaced by followers of Lesoeana, whom privation had driven to cannibalism, they eventually came under the Tlokwa chief, Sekonyela, who expelled Lesoeana and ruled the highlands in the 1830s.

In exchange for some cattle, Makwana ceded his interest in the district to the trekker leader, A.H. Potgieter. Sekonyela, though deemed a vassal by the Boer trekkers, continued exercising his authority. After the Orange River Sovereignty was proclaimed in 1848, however, the British treated him as an independent ruler, carefully defining his territory, including Golden Gate. But five years later he was vanquished by Moshweshwe, whose Basotho took possession of Sekonyela's land. After constant friction with the Boer Republic that came into being the following year, the Basotho were finally driven out in

1865 by Free State commandos. Four years later the Second Aliwal North Convention proclaimed this 'conquered territory' an integral part of the Orange Free State.

Shots echoed again from the krantzes of Golden Gate during the Anglo-Boer War at the turn of the century, and once more the sandstone caves provided sanctuary for fugitives. This time it was Boer families hiding to avoid being sent to British concentration camps.

Sixty years after peace was restored, farms allocated in the upper catchment of the Little Caledon River were repurchased by the South African government, and some 43 square kilometres were proclaimed the Golden Gate Highlands National Park. Many animals that had disappeared from the area were re-introduced, but the big predators were not among them. Nor could springbok and blesbok return in their former numbers, for agricultural subdivision of the interior plains had closed the old routes of annual migration between the highlands and the western Free State.

While human sovereignty over the highlands has shifted through the years from one tribe or nation to another, Golden Gate has remained the territory of one lammergeyer (bearded vulture) pair. Powerful birds, with beaks of eagles, flat claws of vultures and wings spanning up to three metres, they tolerate no encroachment on their domain by others of their kind. When one dies, the other seeks a new mate to share nesting sites in shallow caves high on the sandstone cliffs. Magnificent in flight, they glide at great speed along ridges, searching for carrion and unwary small mammals. Their whistle calls ring out over rest camps, tarred access roads and caravan parks today, as they did long ages before Makwana, Sekonyela or the Parks Board came to this highland valley of red and yellow stone, and grassland gold with ripening seed.

NATAL DRAKENSBERG & LESOTHO HIGHLANDS

ROOF OF THE SUBCONTINENT

Quathlamba, meaning 'massed assegais', was the name Zulus gave the soaring basalt peaks, buttresses, rock walls and pinnacles of the mighty escarpment bearing the Lesotho plateau high above the coastal lands and foothills of Natal. To the Voortrekkers, this rugged lava barrier, towering over 3 000 metres for more than 200 kilometres, resembled rather the profile of a dragon's back, for which they named it the Drakensberg.

Even its moods seem draconic. Three, four times a day in summer, thunder may roar among the lofty peaks as violent electrical storms assail these heights, spitting fire at crags, whitening hollows with hailstones, making runnels brim. From May through August, continual heavy snowfalls blanket summit landscapes, and frosts attack the south-facing cliff-sides of deep gullies untouched by winter sun.

Today, the name applies to almost 1 000 kilometres of the Great Escarpment, from near the Limpopo in the northern Transvaal to the Stormberg in the eastern Cape. The northern part, exemplified at Blyde River, is made of Transvaal System quartzites and underlying Basement granite. Where the range enters northern Natal at Laing's Nek, however, Ecca shales of the Karoo System compose the scarp face. Further south these are topped by progressively younger Karoo formations. Beaufort shales and sandstones are succeeded by isolated residual uplands capped with Cave Sandstone or basalt, becoming larger and more numerous in the approaches to the Maluti Mountains and High Drakensberg through Rydal Mount, Witzieshoek and Golden Gate. This is still the Low Drakensberg; the scarp itself is little more than 300 metres high and the range seldom rises above 1 550 metres, from Laing's Nek to Gudu Pass, where the High Drakensberg, the true 'Berg' begins.

The massive wall of the 'Berg rises abruptly from less than 1 500 metres among the Natal foothills to between 3 000 and 3 480 metres at the summit on the Lesotho plateau. The scowling black cliffs are the edge of a 1 400 metre-thick remnant of volcanic basalt that began forming some 150 million years ago. Immense volumes of fluid lava, welling from long cracks in the earth's surface, spread outward, burying the Karoo sediments, filling valleys and submerging ridges beneath lava plains, over a vast area of old Gondwanaland.

Horizontal lines marking the cliff faces reveal that the Drakensberg basalt was built up by successive flows, from about a metre to 50 metres thick, pouring out upon one another so quickly that a flow surface hardly had time to weather before it was covered by the next. Rising higher than the scarp itself, the uppermost peaks of the Lesotho plateau are crowned with flows between 90 and 180 metres thick. Since the last flow cooled and hardened, the basalt mass has always been the roof of southern Africa. No younger geological formation has ever been laid upon it.

By the time the ancient continent of Gondwanaland began splitting up some 135 million years ago, denudation had levelled the surface of the lava plain, removing perhaps another 10 000 metres of basalt. Thereafter, the plain was lowered scarcely at all by 'down-weathering' of the basalt, denudation being principally by headward erosion of rivers and streams cutting down to the new coastline after the continents parted. On the highlands today, relics of that ancient Gondwana plain form the upper skyline along the watershed and the crests of basalt-capped ridges, breaking away in perpendicular cliffs, between river valleys. The rolling plateau landscape between the upper skyline and the lip of the Escarpment was produced by river erosion in early post-Gondwana times.

But the major features of the Drakensberg and Lesotho highlands, including the Escarpment itself, were sculpted in the basalt very much later. They are the result of four major uplifts over the past 65 million years. These raised the plateau 2 760 metres to its present height, greatly intensifying the erosive power of rivers and streams cutting down to a lower sea-level.

Draining westward, the headwater streams of the Orange River incised profound valleys in the highland plateau, cutting it up into narrow interfluves and isolating the Maluti Mountains as a separate range from the Motai Plateau. Where they have removed the basalt completely, they now flow through broad valleys in the underlying yellow Cave Sandstone, as at Golden Gate.

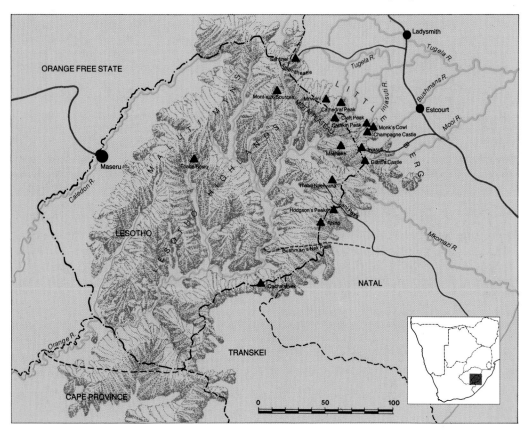

On the eastern side, the former extent of the high Lesotho plateau was reduced to the full width of Natal. The Escarpment was cut back 150 kilometres from the coast to its present position by the heads of countless rivulets eroding the face of the easily weathered basalt. Beneath the dark krantzes of the 'Berg, Cave Sandstone forms the broad ledge of the Little 'Berg, which is deeply dissected into great rambling spurs reaching out towards the coast between the wild gorges of major rivers. Close to the 'Berg the spurs may be topped with basalt or Cave Sandstone. Further out, the lower crest-lines are determined by older Beaufort sandstones. Up the river valleys, the basin plains of the Natal midlands invade the mountain foreland, narrowing the Little 'Berg, and adding the thickness of the Cave Sandstone to the majestic upward sweep of the Escarpment.

From end to end the face of the 'Berg is a continuous, repetitive sequence of rock walls, buttresses, peaks, gullies, pinnacles and towers. Even the Little 'Berg and spurs extending beyond it change only in detail, not character. In the high, thin air on the summit plateau, rigorous conditions restrict vegetation to scattered clumps of erica, heath and hardy grass. Beneath the basalt cliffs, the emerald grassland clothing talus slope, Little 'Berg and spur is sprinkled with highveld protea and silver protea in drier localities, berg cycad, mountain cypress, assegai and fynbos in protected valleys. In river gorges below 1 200 metres, yellowwoods dominate the forests of white stinkwood, African holly, Cape chestnut and Cape beech which swarm up the cooler, south-facing slopes under the Cave Sandstone.

From its commencement above the Royal Natal National Park, the 'Berg escarpment trends generally towards the south-east. Posted in the north-west by the mighty Beacon Buttress and the outlying Sentinel peak, in the south-east by the free-standing Eastern Buttress, Devil's Tooth and Inner Tower, the crescent-shaped basalt wall of the Amphitheatre rears 500 metres above the Little 'Berg, almost 3 000 metres above sea-level. On the flat summit land behind the Escarpment, known to Zulus as emPhofeni, 'place of the eland', are several hills, the highest of which is Mont-aux-Sources, 250 metres above the surrounding plain, 3 282 metres above sea-level. Aptly named in 1836 by the

French missionaries, T. Arbousset and F. Daumas, it is the source of the Western Khubede headstream of the Orange River, the Eland, which descends north into the Orange Free State, and the Tugela and its tributary the Eastern Khubede, which tumble over the edge of the Amphitheatre into Natal. Here, in the five spectacular leaps of the Tugela Falls, the river plunges 850 metres down to the deep gorge it has incised in the Little 'Berg.

As the range continues from Eastern Buttress there are several prominent peaks and buttresses on the edge of the Escarpment, among them Mount Amery, Ifidi Buttress, Mbundini and

132. *Across the Amphitheatre from Sentinel, Eastern Buttress (left), Devil's Tooth and Inner Tower serrate the basalt skyline.*

Ncedamabutho. Where the Mnweni River and its tributaries have cut back deep into the mountains a number of detached peaks – the Ifidi Pinnacles, Mnweni Pinnacles, Mnweni Needles, Mponjwana, Rockeries and North-west Peak of the Saddle – stand out.

Beyond the Saddle, the 3 004-metre spire of Cathedral Peak dominates a long line of free-standing peaks which juts out four kilometres at right-angles to the Escarpment, along the watershed between tributaries of the Mnweni and Mlambonja rivers. Further south are Mount Helga, Pyramid, Column and Camel. Next to

3 281-metre Cleft Peak the many thin columns of Organ Pipes extend in a row from Castle Buttress, at the head of the Thuthumi River. The foot pass to the summit was used in the days of Shaka for parleys between Basotho and Zulu, as they could call to each other from a safe distance, their voices amplified by echoes. Far below, the Thuthumi flows into the great gorge cut in the Little 'Berg by the Ndedema River, sheltering the largest natural forest in the Drakensberg and reckoned to be the richest rock art area in the world.

Below Vultures' Retreat another file of

134
135

133. *Backed by the great rock wall of the Amphitheatre, the Tugela River winds among the grass-covered slopes of the Little 'Berg.* **134.** *A bright red spearhead on a hairy shaft before it opens, this species of Haemanthus is found in forested river gorges of the Drakensberg.* **135.** *Sometimes called geeltulp, or yellow tulip, this species of Moraea favours damp places.*

136. *In the highlands of Lesotho the flat top of Thaba Bosiu, 'mountain of night', is surrounded by precipices, making it a natural stronghold. In troubled times Moshweshwe and his Basotho people withdrew to the summit and from there were easily able to repulse invaders at the head of the only pass.* **137.** *The Icidi valley ascends between the emerald slopes of the Little 'Berg to the cleft of Icidi Pass, flanked on the right by Ifidi Buttress.* **138.** *Against a misty background, the column of Umkulunkulu overlooks the Mbundini River as it plunges into a forested gorge en route to join the Mnweni.* **139.** *Early snowfalls dust the summit and ledges above Organ Pipes Pass.*

free-standing peaks forms Dragon's Back, reaching out to Intunja, a mountain with a hole the size of a double-storey building through it. Separated from Dragon's Back by Grey's Pass, a similar range projecting from 3 377-metre Champagne Castle includes the descriptively named Monk's Cowl, the great square block of Cathkin Peak, Sterkhorn and two very much smaller points, Tower and Amphlett.

South of Champagne Castle the array of buttresses and peaks on the Escarpment includes the highest point in South Africa. From 3 409 metres Injasuti (the full dog) Dome looks down over the crest of Red Wall into the wildest part of the Drakensberg, where the Little 'Berg is webbed by tributaries of the Injasuti River. Detached from the Escarpment, the Injasuti Triplets, all higher than 3 150 metres, rise between Red Wall and 3 353-metre Trojan Wall. On the Lesotho plateau, standing back 12 kilometres from the Trojan Wall scarp, the second highest peak in southern Africa, Makheke, reaches 3 461 metres.

Many foot passes crossing the Great Escarpment in this area were blasted by settlers in the last century to make them impassable to highland Bushmen rustling Natal cattle. At the head of the Bushmans River is the pass through which Langalibalele and his followers fled the British in 1873, beating off their pursuers in a sharp engagement at the summit.

Also topping 3 300 metres, massive Giant's Castle juts out three kilometres

from the main Escarpment. Here the bearing of the 'Berg swings sharply from south-east to south-west. There are no free-standing peaks from here to Sani Pass, but the summit area is more broken and changes in the relief are greater. In Lesotho, five kilometres from the main Escarpment, rises Thaba Ntlenyana, 'beautiful little mountain', the highest peak south of Kilimanjaro. On a clear day, with half of Natal laid out in panorama below, its 3 482-metre summit commands views northward as far as Mont-aux-Sources, and to Qacha's Nek in the south.

In a narrow valley at the head of the Mkhomazana River, flanked by Phinong and Sakeng buttresses, Sani Pass is the only road which enters Lesotho from the east, crossing the Escarpment at 2 843 metres. A little beyond Sakeng are Hodgson's Peaks, last repose of Thomas Hodgson who was accidentally shot by a companion while making a reprisal raid on the Bushmen over a century ago. Rhino is the last of the better-known peaks. Thereafter the escarpment wall, topped by less familiar eminences, continues to Qacha's Nek, where a detached segment of the 'Berg forms an isolated basalt range east of the Tsedike Valley, in Lesotho.

Inaccessibility and a harsh climate have spared the 'Berg much human depredation. The remote summit area is a silent world. Occasional mountain reedbuck and grey rhebuck nibble temperate grasses and browse in the fynbos, while furtive jackal stalk hare,

rodent and bird. Here the brightest colours are glimpses of malachite sunbirds, the deepest shadows beneath the spread wings of black eagles and lammergeyers swooping on prey, and man is a rare, blanketed herdsman or a mountaineer. The sheer escarpment face is forbidding to most mammals other than baboon, klipspringer and dassie, but eland, red hartebeest and blesbok mount the slopes to its foot. The rooigras slopes of the Little 'Berg offer more plentiful grazing for black wildebeest, southern reedbuck find cover in the reeds and tall grass beside streambeds, and bushbuck and grey duiker favour forested gorge and riverine scrub.

Bushmen lived here for thousands of years before being driven over the 'Berg to cultural extinction by black and white pastoralists in the last century, leaving their finest artworks behind them on the walls of their former Cave Sandstone shelters in the Little 'Berg. For centuries black herdsmen have brought their cattle to graze these rooigras slopes in summer, and in some areas tribesmen and commercial farmers still cultivate valleys. But today some 2 000 square kilometres (74 per cent) of 'Berg slope and Little 'Berg are protected as wilderness areas, game parks and nature reserves, and more land is earmarked for inclusion. Crowning the subcontinent, the Drakensberg, most majestic of southern Africa's natural wonders, is receiving the attention it commands.

137

138

140

141

142   143

140. *Mists trail through the valleys between the spurs of the Little 'Berg below flat-topped Greater Injasuti Buttress and pointed Scaly Peak.*
141. *The Bushmans River flows from the pass between Long Wall (right) and Giant's Castle, one of the most prominent features of the Drakensberg.*   **142.** *Mitre and Chessmen, part of a row of free-standing peaks above Mlambonja Pass.*   **143.** *Umkulunkulu, in the foreground, is small compared to the two Mnweni Pinnacles. The broader Outer Pinnacle offers mountaineers one of the most challenging climbs in the Drakensberg.*

145

144

144. Like many other members of the Amaryllidaceae family, these cormous plants with grass-like leaves and six-petalled pink flowers are known as sterretjies, 'little stars'.   **145.** Beyond the ragged brown ridge of the Dragon's Back rises the table-top of Cathkin Peak, flanked on the left by Mount Memory.

THE VALLEY OF A THOUSAND HILLS

MAZE OF THE MGENI

Lying north of the main Pietermaritzburg-Durban highway, the Valley of a Thousand Hills is one of southern Africa's most accessible natural wonders. The flat land dips downward only 12 kilometres from Pietermaritzburg, and open fields give way to rolling hills and green valleys. Here the Msunduzi and Mgeni rivers, their beds incised far below the level of the pre-existing plain, combine at the beginning of the great valley itself. The countless hills, and the deep, narrow valleys between them, are individually only subsidiary features in the chaotic landscape. Together, the confused mass of interfluves, some rising 600 metres above the riverbed, present a rugged panorama of breathtaking beauty on a magnificent scale, entirely the work of erosion by the Mgeni and its innumerable tributaries.

The Mgeni's meandering course was established at a time when it wound over a fairly flat sandstone plateau. The extensive incision that has since taken place in the valley is due to the river now cutting down vertically into the granite core of a gigantic fold over 30 kilometres wide and flanked by sandstone remnants of the former plateau. Isolated protective sandstone cappings to the granite preserve the wild ruggedness of the scenery.

Because of its great resistance to erosion, the sandstone has had a profound influence on the topography, usually standing out boldly above the lesser hills carved in the granite. It forms imposing plateaux with ragged outlines, bounded by pink, purple, red and brown krantzes 150 metres high. Overlooking valleys and plains, the plateaux rise above the complex river system that has cut down deep into the Basement granite.

This rock, comparable in age and kind to the old, early Precambrian granite of the Transvaal, is the foundation of the whole district. It embodies many scattered patches of schist and quartzite of even greater age, relics of very ancient mountain ranges, engulfed by the magma before it hardened into solid granite.

Nothing survives in the geological record of this area to indicate whether other rock systems were deposited here during the 2 000 million years that followed. The whole area was planed by erosion to a fairly even granite surface that finally was submerged in a shallow sea some 500 million years ago.

On this smoothed granite surface, in a

huge trough extending at least as far south as Port St Johns on the Pondoland coast, rivers from the north and north-east then deposited sediments. These built up into a massive thickness of sandstone, at the same time that the sandstones of the Cape System were laid down in the southern and western Cape. During the same period, muddy accumulations on the tidal flats of a great river delta left layers of maroon-coloured shale in the sandstone.

Over 300 million years ago, uplift raised the sandstone above sea-level, and erosion began cutting down the deposit. It was finally reduced to a level, ice-scoured surface, upon which Karoo sediments, the first being Dwyka Tillite, were deposited.

Towards the end of the period in which the Cape ranges were folded in the south and south-west, some 200 million years ago, there was also a folding movement here. It resulted in the formation of an immense monocline fold, curving down towards the coast in the eastern part of Natal. Its axis, or hinge, lay close to a line from Nkandla, north of the Tugela, to the mouth of the Mtamvuna River at Port Edward.

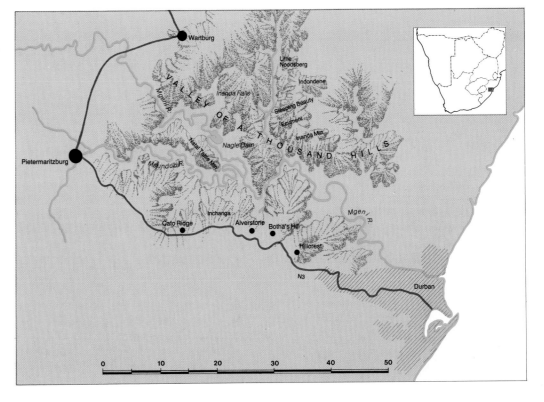

During the folding and in the period that followed, numerous faults, causing vertical displacements in the rock of 100 metres and more, dislocated the area on either side of the axis. The country was broken up into blocks, creating weaknesses where erosion could break it up further. Although Karoo rocks still cover the sandstone in neighbouring areas, here they were completely removed. Little by little most of the valley lost its sandstone cover, enabling rivers and streams to go to work vigorously on the softer granite underneath.

The surfaces of the plateaux on the surviving blocks are fragments of the original continuous plateau on which the now-absent Karoo sediments were deposited, although they stand at different heights today as a result of the faulting.

The bounding scarps of these residual plateau fragments correspond fairly closely to those originally produced by the faults. Weathering has cut them back very little in the time it has taken the Mgeni's tributary streams to carve the unprotected granite into a maze of valleys confined between steep slopes. The deep, narrow valley of the Mgeni itself indicates that the incision of the granite has been very rapid.

Hillcrest village is built on top of one of

146. Flat-topped sandstone mountains provide a sense of order above the confusion of watercourses and interfluves carved in the Basement granite of the Valley of a Thousand Hills by countless small tributaries of the Mgeni River.

the largest of the plateau remnants. The north-facing escarpment of reddish sandstone, 150 metres high and broken only by the Mgeni gorge, runs north-east for over 20 kilometres. Extending from Tyeloti, the 850-metre mass above Alverstone, to beyond Botha's Hill, it finally declines slowly to the Mzinyati Falls. West and north-west of Tyeloti, faulted masses continue inland, including Inchanga, the Dardanelles and Natal's Table Mountain, which is preserved by its sandstone capping on the axis of the monocline. To the north, the granite terrain is dissected by small valleys to a depth of more than 460 metres.

Across the Mgeni valley, plateau remnants build Inanda Mountain. From the river, steep granite slopes rise higher than 360 metres and are surmounted by superb krantzes of red sandstone, forming walls and columns that raise the plateau over 500 metres above the riverbed. To the east, it is separated from the Groenberg mass by the Mzinyati valley. Increasing northward from 850 to 915 metres, Ecumeni, Sleeping Beauty, Sangwana, Indondene and Shiaze Mountain stand out above the granite, with 1 045-metre Little Noodsberg at the northern end of the chain.

There appears to be no record of who first called this the Valley of a Thousand Hills, but the name must have received general acceptance very quickly. As one looks out over the infinitely broken scene from a vantage point on one of the plateaux, it seems the valley must have named itself.

THE WILD COAST

SHORES OF PARADISE

Although improved roads have made parts of the Wild Coast more accessible, long stretches of the shore bordering the land of the Xhosa and Pondo remain an untamed, subtropical paradise. Washed by the warm waters of the Indian Ocean, remote, deserted beaches of soft, creamy sand are interrupted by rocky juts, rugged points, cliffs, capes and headlands. Broad

147. *The sandstone layers of Hole in the Wall defiantly resist attempts to weather them, although waves have found a weak spot at the base and bored a hole through which they explode at high tide.* **148.** *The spectacular Mfihlelo Falls plummet some 160 metres directly into the ocean.*

lagoon-like estuaries of innumerable rivers snake among grassed and forested hills, ponding back behind sand bars that close the rivers' exits to the sea. Fringing the beaches, dune forests crowd almost to the high-water mark in tangles of red milkwood, Natal strelitzia, veld fig, white pear, wild silver oak and thorn pear.

Here it is nearly always warm, often hot and humid, with mean maximum and minimum temperatures of 24 and 15 degrees. But, while the air below is clear, moist sea breezes turn to mist around the hill summits, and rain falls on 90 days a year, precipitating a total of 900 to 1 200 millimetres annually, most of

it disgorged by summer's frequent, violent thunderstorms.

Mist and rain, brought by the south-east trade winds, water dense forests which lie up to 425 metres above sea-level, on ridge slopes facing the wind and the sides of valleys that open towards it. Smaller hills are crowned with yellowwood, red beech, white stinkwood and hosts of other trees, shrubs, herbs and climbers. At higher altitudes, on north-facing slopes and in valleys opening away from the wind, the vegetation is chiefly tall grassland dotted with proteas, aloes and scattered patches of forest. Found nowhere else in the world, Pondo coconut palms, also known

as Mkambati palms, line the northern banks of the Mtentu and Msikaba rivers, and bear miniature fruits which are similar in structure, smell and taste to true coconuts, but only two centimetres in diameter. On intertidal flats in some estuaries open to the sea, mangroves, normally confined to tropical parts, survive this far south under the warming influence of the Mozambique Current.

Described broadly, the Wild Coast is the whole of the 250-kilometre Transkei coastline, from the Great Kei River to the mouth of the Mtamvuna, extending almost to East London in the south-west, and a little way up the Natal coast in the north-east. But some regard Port St Johns, at the mouth of the Mzimvubu, as the north-eastern limit, for here the character of the coastal belt changes, although it loses nothing of its wildness.

To the south-west, the landscape along the coast is fashioned entirely from Karoo System rocks, while at Port St Johns

and further to the north-east the most prominent features are of tough, resistant sandstone, deposited at the same time as the sandstone of Table Mountain in the south-western Cape, and very like it in composition.

This sandstone is identical to that forming the major features in the Valley of a Thousand Hills, and, like it, rests on the crest of an enormous fold which runs from the Lebombo Mountains, through Zululand and Natal, to beyond Port St Johns. Trending south-south-west through Natal, the fold would cut the coastline in northern Pondoland and continue out to sea, but at the Mbotyi River a massive transverse fracture, the Egosa Fault, has shifted the crest several kilometres to the west. So south of the fault it continues inland, running parallel to the coast, to south of Port St Johns. There a second great fracture, the Umgazana Fault, has shifted the crest again, this time eastward into the sea, at the mouth of the Mgazana River.

North of the Egosa Fault, the flat-lying sandstone, formerly buried beneath Karoo rocks, now forms the whole of the coastal belt, ten to 16 kilometres wide. The fault-scarp is its southern edge, rising above the down-faulted Karoo and dolerite surface to the south of the fracture. Inland, the great Egosa Forest smothers the scarp, spreading out below and swamping over it on to the plateau near Lusikisiki, and reaching up narrow ravines cut back into the sandstone block. From where it meets the sea, the scarp boldly defines the coastline for some 13 kilometres to the north-east with a continuous zigzag of

148

precipitous cliffs. The first of these is the well-known Waterfall Bluff whose lip shelves dizzily over the turbulent shoreline and sends the Mkozi River crashing to the white water below.

Rivers such as the Ngogwana and Magwa, which drain the sandstone area north of the fault, trench through it in narrow, steep-sided gashes; the Magwa stream cascades down the vertical wall of the chasm to the incised riverbed 146 metres below. But south of the fault, rivers have eroded the softer Karoo formations differently, and the Mzintlava, Mntafufu and Mzimvubu have carved

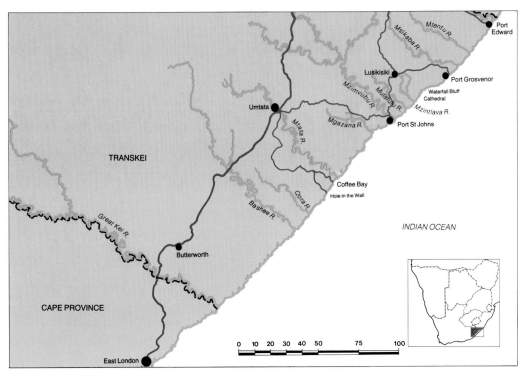

the former plateau into a maze of hills and sinuous valleys, with the summits of ridges towering 300 metres above sea-level.

In the midst of this intensely broken country, the table-top mass of St Johns Mountain is an isolated southern extension of the sandstone plateau. Rising almost 370 metres above the riverbed, this huge block of sandstone was left standing between two parallel fractures when the land around it subsided. It is cleft by the three kilometre-long Mzimvubu gorge into Mount Thesiger and Mount Sullivan, also known as the 'Gates' of St John because from the sea they give the impression of opening and closing the gap between them.

As much features of the Wild Coast as sweeping beaches, turquoise ocean and peaceful estuarine lagoons are the great stone sculptures carved by wind and wave from the living rock of the sea cliffs. Hole in the Wall, an offshore hill pierced by a hole through which waves explode at high tide, is only a few kilometres from Coffee Bay. Near Waterfall Bluff, the huge spray-misted rock stack of The Cathedral, complete with salt-stung spires and wave-cut arch, rises amid boiling seas hurled back by the unyielding sandstone cliffs.

Since Portuguese mariners first pioneered the sea route to India, the Wild Coast has claimed countless ships, the lives of the men who sailed them, and the treasures of the East they were bearing to Europe in their holds. One night in 1552 the *São Joao* (St John) drove ashore on the rocks at the mouth of the Mzimvubu, leaving its name to the town that developed there centuries later. The *São Bento* was wrecked at the mouth of the Mtata River in 1554, and in 1593 the *Santo Alberto* ended on the rocks near Hole in the Wall. But of the long succession of ships that have foundered on the Wild Coast, the most celebrated is the *Grosvenor*, the treasure-laden British Indiaman that broke her back on the reefs of Lambasi Bay in 1782, reputedly with the fabulous missing peacock throne of Persia stowed with the loot below decks. Though this was never confirmed, the prospect of finding the lost throne and the fortune in gold and diamonds that went down with the ship has lured treasure hunters to the Wild Coast for two centuries.

Although coins, trinkets and fragments of crockery from sunken hulks are still occasionally washed up along the shore, it is the natural wonder of the Wild Coast that attracts the majority of visitors, for whom the chance of finding treasure is an exciting but remotely possible bonus.

149, 150. *Jagged rocks repulse the waves'
assault along the northern part of the
appropriately named Wild Coast. But in
places the erosive power of the sea has
exploited weaknesses in the tough sandstone,
sculpting the arch and spires of The Cathedral,
one of several such dramatic offshore
formations.*   **151.** *Gulls are among the many
seabirds which wander the Wild Coast.*
152. *The waters of the Mkozi River thread their
way through the countryside, having made
little impact on the resistant rock. The shallow
valley ends abruptly at Waterfall Bluff and the
river tumbles down the precipice to join the
roiling surf.*

155

156

153. *A sweep of white beach, as much a hallmark of the Wild Coast as rocky cliffs, bars a river's exit to the sea.* **154.** *Watered by mist and rain, dense forest clothes the slopes of Mount Thesiger and Mount Sullivan, the 'Gates' of St John, between which the Mzimvubu River has carved a passage to the Indian Ocean.* **155, 156.** *Crashing waves contrast sharply with the tranquil waters of the Mzimvubu River behind the sandstone 'Gates'.*

LAKES AND FLOODPLAINS OF ZULULAND

LAND OF THE THONGA

For over a century and a half, the men living on the coastal plain of northern Zululand, between the Lebombo Mountains and the Indian Ocean, have spoken among themselves a different language from their women. A legacy of their subjugation by Shaka's impis, Thonga men speak Zulu, the language of the conqueror, while the women continue to speak and preserve their traditional tongue.

Their land extends 250 kilometres southward from the Maputo River floodplain to Lake St Lucia. The flat, featureless, sandy plain that is Tongaland seldom rises more than 100 metres above sea-level. The sand, accumulated over the past five million years, blankets older marine sediments which were deposited when the whole coastal plain of Mozambique and Zululand lay beneath the Indian Ocean and waves beat against the slopes of the Lebombo range. In places, lines of dunes mark former shorelines, abandoned inland as the sea haltingly withdrew eastward.

From the west, four main rivers cut through the Lebombo Mountains to the plain. The Mkuze turns southward into the St Lucia lake system, while the Pongola winds northward on the western side of the plain. Combining with the Ingwavuma and Usutu, it becomes the Maputo River for the rest of its course to Delagoa Bay. In the east, large lakes and lagoons fill depressions in the sand near the coast, separated from the sea by high dunes.

The many vleis and marshes lining the floodplains of these rivers suggest that they now follow the beds of erstwhile lake chains and lagoon systems. These developed near former coastlines when the sea-level was higher than today, and were similar at the time to those bordering the present coast.

On the Pongola drainage system south of the Mozambique border, some 11 000 hectares of floodplain, lake and river have protection as the Ndumu Game Reserve. Spared competition with tribesmen, crocodile and hippo thrive here, and small herds of rare nyala antelope browse in dense tropical bush at the water's edge.

In the rainy season, from October to March, rivers and countless smaller streams pour into swamps and pans, creating wide, shallow, ephemeral lakes. Along its course, brown floodwaters of the the Pongola spill into Tete, Sivunguvungu, Namanini and about 40 other pans. The wide, sandy flats, covered mostly with thorn scrub, are generally infertile, but spreading sycamore figs, meshed in riverine thickets, shade clear streams and brood over dark swamp waters. Tall fever trees fringe floodplain vleis. At the coast, tidal lagoons are edged with mangroves, reedbeds and salt marshes.

The fluctuations of these waters regulate the lives of the Thonga. During the dry season they cultivate strips of fertile soil beside the rivers and graze their cattle on the sweet floodplain grassland. When the rains come, they gather water-lily bulbs and water-chestnuts for food. In autumn, as the floodwaters subside, they set fish traps and organize communal fish drives, in which long lines of wading tribesmen use baskets to harvest the shallow pools.

Like the Thonga on the river floodplains, those living at the coast are fishermen. But while the former's fishing is a seasonal activity, the tides are harvested all year round by those fishing the estuaries, lagoons and lakes connected to the sea. In the Kosi lake system, open to the sea at the Mozambique border, they paddle about on rafts made from the frond stalks of raffia palms, setting their nets and tending their basket fish traps in sheltered tidal waters. From bank and island, the fences of their 'fish kraals' loop out across the mudflats to filter the ebb tide in the shallow estuary, directing mullet and grunter, perch and yellowfin bream into the valved mouths of staked trap enclosures.

Comprising a shallow tidal basin and four lakes with channels connecting them to one another and the sea, the Kosi system parallels the coast for 12 kilometres. Behind the narrow outlet, the estuary broadens into the tidal basin. Close to the northern and western shores, the permanent channel is two to three metres deep. On the eastern and southern sides, however, low tides expose extensive sandbanks. Here, too, are

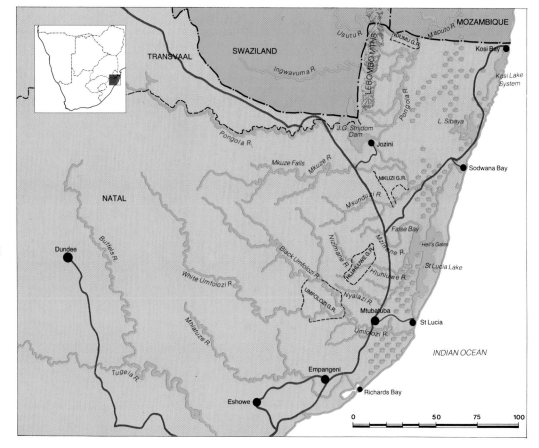

several small, mangrove-covered islands, most of them submerged at high tide.

Steeply banked near the mouth by the coastal dune wall, the eastern shore flattens as it curves round south of the tidal basin. At levels reached only by some spring high tides, the flats are rush-dominated salt marsh, separated from bare mudflat and open water by mangroves. Reedbeds and rushes on swampy ground line the northern shore, which, sloping more steeply into deeper water, does not have an intertidal strip suitable for mangroves.

Although mangroves grow in estuaries on the eastern seaboard as far south as the Wild Coast, only at Kosi estuary and further north do they form thick woodland over large areas and include all the mangrove species of southern Africa. These trees and shrubs are unrelated, but independently they have evolved common characteristics. All can cope with high salinity, grow exclusively in the muddy zone between mean sea-level and the high-water mark of spring tides, and have distinctive root systems adapted to these conditions. Instead of deep tap roots, they have 'cable' roots spreading horizontally under the mud, reinforced above ground by 'prop' roots, 'knee' roots, 'buttress' roots, 'pencil' roots or 'stilt' roots.

Probably the oddest inhabitant of the 'tidal forest' in the Kosi estuary is the tiny mudskipper. An amphibious fish, generally seen out of water on the roots and low branches of mangrove trees, it has raised, bulbous eyes on top of its head, behind which its brown, fleshy body tapers to the tip of its tail. Reminiscent of a large tadpole in an advanced stage of metamorphosis, it has fins shaped like forelegs on either side behind the head. On the underside, fan-like fins can be spread like wings, enabling it to skip over the surface of the water in rapid alternation of swimming and flight. Fiddler crabs, asymmetrically deformed by one greatly enlarged nipper, swarm yellow, red, pink and blue on the mud at low water, retreating into deep burrows for safety when the advancing tide brings marine predators. Whelks, with their elongated spiral cone shells, and periwinkles climb the trunks of mangrove trees, which have oysters and barnacles clinging to their roots. In the shaded, shallow waters, pistol shrimps loudly snap their claws, producing sharp cracking sounds that stun the minute aquatic organisms on which they feed. Upper branches are similarly busy. To pied, mangrove and malachite kingfishers they offer convenient lookout posts, and serve as casual perches, roosts, and in some cases nesting places, for herons, egrets, flycatchers, purplebanded sunbirds, golden weavers, fish eagles and many other species.

Mangroves continue up the Kosi estuary. Thinning out southward along both banks, they crowd islands in the broad Kongozu channel, that connects the tidal basin to Mpungwini, smallest of the four lakes. On its western side the bank is steeper, the channel deeper, and the influence of less saline water permits inclusion among the true mangroves of the so-called 'freshwater mangrove'. Well named the powder-puff tree, it trails pendulous sprays, over half a metre long, of pale pink flowers. Further south, the lakes themselves are fringed with rushes, reeds, grasses and occasional palms. Mangroves still occur here and there in small clumps or as scattered individual trees, but are concentrated only beside the channels linking the lakes.

Not quite a kilometre in diameter, Mpungwini lake is linked by two short channels to Sifungwe, four times as large. At its south-western end, a narrow, winding channel joins Sifungwe to the largest of the lakes, Nhlange, seven kilometres long, five and a half wide. It is fed by the Nkanini stream in the west and

157. *Its placid surface broken by the curving lines of Thonga fish kraals, the Kosi estuary provides a shallow sandy channel well suited to the use of palisade fish traps. Linked by guide fences to form a kraal, the traps capture fish returning to the ocean from upstream, and supply the local people with a major source of food.*

158

159

the Malangeni in the south, from both of
which underwater valleys continue across
the bottom to the deep north-eastern
corner. On the south-eastern side, a low
sand bar, only a few hundred metres
wide, seals a former exit to the sea. The
fourth, and southernmost, lake of the
series, Amanzimnyama, lies 16 kilometres
from the estuary and contains fresh water.

While the surfaces of the saline Kosi
lakes are near sea-level, further south the
landlocked waters of Lake Sibaya rise
21 metres higher. South Africa's largest
freshwater lake, Sibaya covers an area of
more than 65 square kilometres. Its main
basin, eight by six kilometres, reaches
long arms northward and westward,
filling deep valleys which continue
underwater to enter a trough, 25 metres
deep, running north-east to south-west
across the basin floor. At the southern end
is a smaller basin, its connection with the
main one reduced by a sandspit to a
narrow channel. This is kept open by the
movement of surface water, shifted from
one end of the lake to the other by
alternating northerly and southerly
winds.

Until the early 1950s, Lake Sibaya's
fever-ridden shores were inhabited
exclusively by Thonga fishermen. They
spread their nets in the shallows, set traps
at the mouths of creeks and inlets, and
speared barbel on marginal, sedge-
covered terraces inundated by heavy
summer rains. The late advent of less
conservative peoples has left much of
Sibaya's natural wonder relatively
unchanged. Although cut off from the sea
some 5 000 years ago, several marine and
estuarine fishes and crustacea left behind
have adapted to the lake's fresh waters.
Crocodile and hippo remain plentiful in
the wilder northern and western parts of
the lake, and over 200 bird species, 40 of
them permanent residents, have been
recorded on the shore. Snakes glide
silently over the surfaces of pools in the
bordering marshes. In the neighbouring
dune forest, gaboon vipers lie unseen

158. *Overhung by weaver nests, the muddy
Pongola winds its way sluggishly through
riverine forest on its northward journey to
Mozambique.* **159.** *The alluvial soils of its
floodplain nourish a mosaic of vegetation
types which in turn support a great variety of
animal life. Grazers feed on the nutritious
grasses, and the reeds provide a nesting
habitat for many birds, among them the
ubiquitous weaver and the openbilled
stork.* **160.** *Home to a cluster of whelks, the
mangrove trunk is supported by buttress roots
which anchor it firmly in the unstable
mudflats. Seedlings in the mud develop
quickly from seeds which germinated while
still on the tree.*

160

among the fallen leaves, where duiker, bushbuck and bushpig forage, and genet, polecat and jackal hunt. Pythons coil among the branches, while vervet and samango monkeys romp in an arboreal canopy enlivened by the calls and colours of purplecrested loeries, trumpeter and crowned hornbills, rollers and flocks of smaller woodland birds.

Pointers to the origin of Tongaland's coastal lakes and estuaries are the valleys running across the floors of Sibaya and Nhlange. That their bottoms are well below present sea-level indicates that the lakes lie in valleys cut by rivers when the sea-level was more than 30 metres lower. 'Drowned' when subsequently the sea rose again, the valleys were gradually silted up by the movement of sand along

161

the coast and soil brought down by rivers. The original deep watercourse of the Kosi estuary was reduced to a series of lakes, which became progressively shallower towards the mouth. The channels connecting the lakes were kept open by the inflow of fresh water into Nhlange, at the head of the system. At Lake Sibaya, however, the inflow was too weak to keep the outlet open, and sand dunes formed across the former exit, sealing it off permanently from the sea.

South of Lake Sibaya, similar processes formed the better-known St Lucia system. Comprising three highly saline lakes, it spreads over some 415 square kilometres and is about a metre deep, connected to the sea by a long, winding channel. In the upper part of the system, elongated False Bay opens through Hell's Gate, a broad breach in its eastern shoreline, into North Lake St Lucia, which is linked by a narrow channel at its southern extremity to South Lake St Lucia. The Mzinene, Hluhluwe and Nyalazi rivers flow into False Bay, while the Mkuze enters at the northern tip of North Lake through a marshy, crocodile-haunted delta.

Below the narrow exit from South Lake, the main channel, about 100 metres wide and up to two and a half metres deep, snakes southward for nearly 20 kilometres to the sea. Its muddy banks bordered with reeds and occasional small patches of mangroves, the channel broadens and becomes very shallow and muddy near St Lucia village, before swinging eastward about two kilometres from the estuary. Steep and wooded at first, the northern bank flattens into a large reedbed. On the southern side, tangled mangrove swamps throng the bank to the edge of the mudflats.

Today the estuary is about 50 metres

wide and less than two metres deep, but a hundred years ago the area was a large lagoon, which shipwrecked Portuguese sailors named St Lucia Bay in 1554. When *HMS Goshawk* sailed into the bay 330 years later to claim Zululand for Britain, ocean swells still surged through the entrance and broke on the shore where mangroves now flourish.

Soft sediments introduced by the Umfolozi River accumulated in the estuary for thousands of years, causing severe siltation. Rising tides temporarily checked the outflow, and muddy Umfolozi water trapped inside was pushed back several kilometres up the St Lucia channel by incoming sea water. At slack water, when the tide began to turn, the silt was deposited as sticky mud on the channel floor. To begin with, the amount of silt deposited was small, as the Umfolozi waters were filtered by papyrus swamps before reaching the estuary, but poor farming methods practised in the river's catchment caused extensive soil erosion and an enormous increase in the burden of silt carried to the coast. The condition was aggravated by sugar farmers, who in 1913 reclaimed the papyrus swamp for sugar-cane and dredged a direct channel for the river. Consequently it poured mud into the estuary at a high speed, converting the deep, clear waters of the bay into mudflats and mangrove swamps. The growing mud banks restricted the tidal flow that kept the estuary open and smothered aquatic vegetation and bottom fauna that were vital links in the food chain. Drastic steps had to be taken to rectify the situation, and in 1952 the course of the Umfolozi River was changed to flow directly into the Indian Ocean.

162

Water salinity also affects the density of life in the lakes. Though tidal fluctuation is measurable in the channel, the lakes themselves are not tidal. In the dry season, when the loss by evaporation exceeds gains from rains and rivers, the levels fall and water from the sea moves up into the lakes, increasing their salinity. In times of severe drought the lakes are not seasonally refreshed by rivers and the concentration of salt in them becomes greater than in the sea. Normally, when the drought breaks, the lakes are flushed by fresh water and a salinity level acceptable to aquatic life is restored. The damming of the rivers in the west for agriculture, however, has drastically reduced the flow of fresh water to the lakes, inhibiting revival after dry spells and regularizing salinity levels that are too high to maintain aquatic life.

Although man greatly accelerated the salination and silting of the St Lucia system, it is probable that these would eventually have been accomplished by nature. Unaided by man, natural events changed Sibaya from an open estuary, like Kosi Bay, to a landlocked lake that no one would want to restore to its former state. Before humans appeared on the scene, chains of estuarine lagoons and lakes were converted into river floodplains far from the sea. In the blink of an eye, compared to the aeons in which the face of the subcontinent has been transformed countless times, the coastal wonderland became a wonderland of seasonal waters. Though worthy and desirable, concern for conserving St Lucia is, like the Thonga women's preservation of their language, a longing for the immediate past, a wish to prolong another moment in eternity.

163

161. *The tiny mudskipper fish, an inhabitant of the mangrove swamps, lives almost entirely out of water and may provide a clue to the way aquatic creatures have adapted to life on land.*
162. *A great white egret stands solitary at the edge of a reedbed at St Lucia, which also provides a rich fishing ground for white pelicans (**164**).* **163.** *A white rhino stands guard over his lush territory of nutritious red grass. In the background the Black Umfolozi River is one of the few reliable water sources for animals in the dry season.*

164

165. *Like many of the Zululand rivers, the broad Usutu is gradually being affected by siltation. Once it flowed smoothly to its confluence with the Pongola River and thence to Delagoa Bay, but now the stream is impeded by silt deposits in the dry season.*

165

166. *Fever trees, such as these on the banks of the Nhlonhlela Pan in the Mkuzi Game Reserve, were long thought to cause malaria, the bane of Zululand. However, the association stems from the fact that the trees grow well in swampy areas, the ideal breeding ground for the malarial mosquito.* **167.** *Cattle egrets pluck parasites from the backs of hippo which spend most of the day submerged. Their movement in the water keeps channels open and free of vegetation.* **168.** *A black mass of aerial roots is one means of survival used by mangroves in the waterlogged, saline environment of an estuary.*

166

167

168

VICTORIA FALLS

SMOKE THAT THUNDERS

'Scenes so lovely must have been gazed upon by angels in their flight.' So waxed the Scots missionary-explorer, David Livingstone, pressed by his publisher some years afterwards to embellish his recollection of that moment when, on November 16, 1855, he first glimpsed the greatest curtain of falling water in the world and named it the Victoria Falls for his queen.

Doubtless Livingstone's angels had been first to gaze upon many things more and less lovely, but he is generally regarded as the first mortal European to see the entire width of the Zambezi River tumbling over the lip of the basalt precipice 1 700 metres from bank to bank and to hear it roaring through the narrow chasm 100 metres below and, in places, only 60 metres wide.

By that time other mortals had been gazing upon the wonders of the mightiest of waterfalls for perhaps 500 000 years, but we have no idea by what names they knew it. At one time Shongwe, meaning 'seething cauldron', appears to have been used by some. The Kololo tribesmen, who had invaded the area from the south less than 20 years earlier, told Livingstone that in their language, which was foreign to those parts, the Falls were called Mosi oa

Tunya, meaning 'the smoke that throbs'. Although the Kololo were overthrown by the Lozi not long afterwards and disappeared from the area, the name they gave to the Falls has been preserved as a more evocative unofficial alternative – since then more freely translated as 'the smoke that thunders'.

Great clouds of spray, carried aloft by the updraft of air displaced in the chasm by the descending torrent, rise more than 300 metres above the Falls. Like five columns of pure white smoke, they are visible 50 kilometres away when the Zambezi is in flood. At half the distance, on a still night, the thunder of the floodwaters in the chasm is like the throb of a far-off diesel engine.

When the floodwaters of the Zambezi's distant headstreams reach the Falls in March or April, at the end of the rainy season, flows of more than 700 000 cubic metres a minute have been recorded. Even at peak times in average years, some 550 000 cubic metres of water, stained yellow and red-brown by sediments, plunge into the chasm every minute, completely hiding the Falls in a dense fog of spray. The flow slackens steadily through the dry season until, by the time the new rains start in November, it has

shrunk to a mere 20 000 cubic metres a minute. No longer burdened with sediments, the water is sparkling, transparent and white, and the full spread of the Falls is revealed.

At these times scarcely any water at all flows over the lip of the 304 metre-wide Eastern Cataract, on the Zambian side of the river. There is also little water to obscure the cliff-face beneath the ridge of the Rainbow Falls, which extends for 350 metres to the west of it. Still further west, beyond the interruption of Livingstone Island, the flow is stronger over the 830-metre front of the Main Falls. Then, between Cataract Island and the Zimbabwean bank, a weakness in the rock concentrates the surging waters in a gap only 27 metres wide, which has been cut down to ten metres below the level of the other sections of the Falls. Despite its size, this ever-turbulent cutting, given the name Devil's Cataract, is a key to the history of the Falls and a projection of what will become of them. How the Falls came into existence and came to be where they now are is a chapter in the long story of the Zambezi River itself.

The Zambezi, carrying more water than any other river in southern Africa, flows some 2 700 kilometres to the Indian

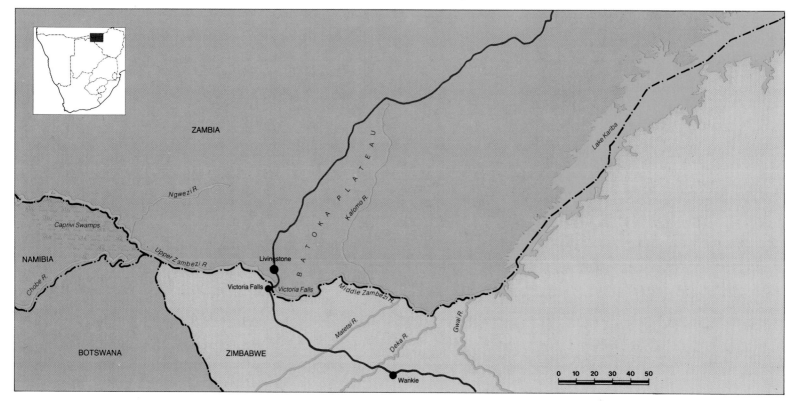

Ocean from its source as a small stream near where the present borders of Zambia, Angola and Zaire meet. Almost half of this distance has been covered, and the Upper Zambezi has grown to a river nearly two kilometres wide before it plunges over the Falls and races through the zigzags of the narrow Batoka Gorge into the Gwembe trough of the Middle Zambezi, now flooded at its eastern end by man-made Lake Kariba.

But the Zambezi we know today was not always a single, continuous river. The Upper and Middle courses were in fact once parts of completely separate river systems. The joining of the two, and the nature of the rock beneath the connecting channel, are responsible for creating the Falls.

Swollen by the contributions of many tributaries, the headstream of the Upper Zambezi flows first west and then generally southward, passing through the sandy flats of the Barotse Plain, seasonally covered with shallow water. From there the river runs through several rapids in rocky country and enters the Caprivi Swamps at Katima Mulilo, in which its waters are joined by those of the Machili, Ngwezi and Chobe rivers.

Two million years ago the Upper Zambezi continued flowing southward from there, crossing Botswana and linking up with the Limpopo, and possibly at one stage the Orange River, so reaching the sea. Movements in the earth's crust in central Botswana subsequently severed the connection with the southern river systems, however, raising a barrier behind which the dammed waters of the Upper Zambezi and other rivers created a huge lake. The outlet of this enormous lake was at its north-eastern corner. Here the overflow spilt into a shallow trough, which conducted it eastwards across the Batoka Plateau. When later the climate became more arid, the lake started to shrink and withdrew from the outlet. The Upper Zambezi nevertheless continued to escape from the Chobe Swamps through the channel, flowing in a broad stream, as it still does above the Falls today. Finally it hurled its full width over the edge of the

plateau, dropping 250 metres into the valley of the Matetsi River, until then the chief source of the Middle Zambezi.

It was here, at the edge of the Batoka Plateau, more than 100 kilometres downstream from where they are now, that the Victoria Falls began. The curtain of water that cascaded down the left flank of the Matetsi Valley was the first in the succession of mighty waterfalls that slowly cut a deep zigzag gorge back through the plateau to where the Falls are presently situated. The course they took was determined by the structure of the plateau rock.

The thick, red sand covering of the Batoka Plateau, and the thin layers of sandstone and chalcedony that underlie

169. *Split by rocky projections, the Main Falls plunge into the turbulence of the gorge below. Devil's Cataract, at the bottom of the picture, cuts a narrow separate channel between Cataract Island and the Zimbabwean bank to the head of the gorge. Incised more deeply than the other falls, Devil's Cataract, though only 27 metres wide, draws off proportionally more of the Zambezi's flow. This is the beginning of a new gorge that will be excavated upstream of the present Falls millennia from now.*

it, rest on a massive basalt shield, spread more than 300 metres thick over the land during a prolonged period of almost perpetual volcanic activity. At the same time similar lava flows were hardening into the upper basalts of the Drakensberg, some 150 million years ago. As the Batoka basalt cooled and solidified, shrinkage produced intersecting systems of deep vertical cracks in the rock. The dominant cracks, running roughly west to east, were afterwards widened into fissures by

earth movements and filled with soft sediments. The lesser cracks cut across them at right angles.

Very much later, after the flow of the Upper Zambezi was redirected across the plateau, it began cutting back from the edge of the basalt shield. The curtain of water falling into the Matetsi Valley started to concentrate more and more at a weakness where one of the lesser cracks allowed faster erosion of the lip, much as is happening in the Devil's Cataract today.

The growing flow at this point opened up the weakness until eventually it sliced through upstream into one of the sediment-filled fissures. Once the flow had been captured by the fissure running across the riverbed, the soft sediments were scooped out and carried off by the torrent, leaving a deep, narrow gorge between sheer-sided basalt cliffs. The gorge cut off the supply of water to the original falls, and the edge of the cliff on the upstream side of the gorge became the

170

lip of a new curtain of falling water that now thundered into the freshly excavated chasm below. This occurred many times as the Falls retreated to their present position. Each time the water cut back into another sediment-filled fissure further upstream, the old fall was abandoned and a new stretch of gorge was added.

Below the Falls today, the Zambezi follows a tight zigzag course for about eight kilometres, in which seven broad

waterfalls, each equal to the present Falls, have been successively formed and abandoned. Further downstream the gorge becomes progessively deeper, until eventually its bottom is 250 metres lower than the chasm beneath the Falls, and 350 metres below the level of the plateau in which it has been incised. But the sides are no longer vertical, as they still are further upstream, because here they were cut much earlier, and in the intervening time they have been weathered to steep slopes.

On the surface of the plateau above, remnants of the old bed in which the broad Zambezi once flowed are still visible in the upper sandstone and chalcedony. Early Stone Age implements found along the former banks show that primitive men lived beside these waters anything from a quarter to half a million years ago. Middle Stone Age implements further upstream suggest that in the past 35 000 years the Falls have occupied eight different positions across the Zambezi and that the gorge has been cut back 18 kilometres in that time.

Eventually the water passing through Devil's Cataract will slice back into the next sediment-filled fissure upstream. Then the ridge of the present Falls will become another dry precipice rising vertically from the gorge, and the broad curtain of the new Falls will thunder into another chasm.

As the Falls worked their way upstream their drop has become progressively shorter. A point will finally be reached when the Falls will disappear altogether, and the Zambezi will flow over a series of rapids through the extended system of zigzag gorges to the Gwembe trough.

But for the next few thousand years the great clouds of spray will continue to rise from the gorge below the present Victoria Falls, and the water they deposit as heavy 'rain' will still maintain over 400 species of trees, shrubs, grasses, sedges, ferns and climbers, many of which have not been recorded elsewhere, in a narrow belt of 'rain forest' along the bank. Here vervet monkeys chatter among the vines trailing from tall African ebony, muchiningi, wild fig and sausage trees, beneath whose sun-pierced canopy delicate ferns, flame lilies, black arums and white ground orchids are reflected in shallow pools.

Beyond the fringing wild date palms, the chasm is spanned by great double rainbows by day and, at full moon, by night, creating a sense of primeval permanence in a scene that is continually changing, but so slowly that the changes accomplished in a human lifespan are imperceptible.

171

172

Even after the Zambezi floodwaters have subsided, spray rising on air displaced by falling water obscures the gorge at the foot of the Main Falls (170). But in the dry season, Rainbow Falls (171) may dwindle to a series of trickles and Eastern Cataract (172) cease altogether. Save for a chain of pools, the floor of the chasm becomes dry, although white water still foams through the gorge at the other end, turning abruptly into the whirlpool of the 'boiling pot' at the start of the next gorge downstream.

OKAVANGO DELTA & MAKGADIKGADI PANS

A VANISHING GREAT LAKE

Like the Kunene and Zambezi, the two rivers that combine to make the Okavango have their sources in the highlands of Angola. But while the Kunene empties into the Atlantic and the Zambezi crosses the subcontinent to the Indian Ocean, the Okavango never reaches the sea. The 8 000 million cubic metres of water brought yearly into northern Botswana by the second largest river in southern Africa all end in the sands of the Kalahari.

But it is a grand finale, for here in the heart of the thirstland, floodwaters of distant origin have created a verdant wonderland of waterways, islands, marshes and shallow 'lagoons', abounding with terrestrial, bird and aquatic life. Here tribal fishermen still silently pole their dugout *mekoro* over unruffled reaches and set their reed fish traps among the culms of papyrus that grow three metres tall at the water's edge.

Although difficult to visualize, this whole region, in the centre of the largest unbroken sand plain on earth, was once a vast lake, the size of Lake Victoria, extending from the Zambezi to the most southerly edge of the Makgadikgadi Pans.

Long ago the Okavango River flowed unhindered to the sea, linking with the Limpopo which then flowed westward, joining the Molopo and eventually discharging into the Atlantic by way of the Hygap channel and Orange River. For then the Limpopo was a truly great river, and its headstreams included also the Upper Zambezi, Chobe and Okwa, now a broad, dry, fossil river valley cut across the Kalahari from Namibia. But the link with the Limpopo broke about two million years ago, when earth upheavals in north-central Botswana barred the channel and diverted the Okavango and other headstreams into the Makgadikgadi basin, an enormous depression created by the earth movements.

Today several huge salt pans and countless smaller ones occupy the deepest parts of this depression. But when the climate of surrounding highlands was very much wetter, this was a 60 000-

square kilometre lake, covering not only the Makgadikgadi basin, but most of the Okavango Delta too. At its highest, the lake flooded northwards, uniting the Upper and Middle Zambezi rivers and initiating the Victoria Falls between them.

Subsequently, further doming of the earth's crust 25 000 years ago caused faulting in the underlying rock along a line between Lake Ngami and the Mababe Depression, which divided the ancient lake in two.

The upper part continued receiving Okavango and Chobe waters, but the Chobe was eventually captured by the united Zambezi. During a drier period the upper lake began filling up with silt and wind-blown sand, developing into the inland delta we know today. In the deeper hollows of Ngami and Mababe, smaller lakes lingered and slowly shrank, all but disappearing in recent times.

Meanwhile, the lower portion formed a separate lake covering nearly 34 000 square kilometres, 45 metres deep,

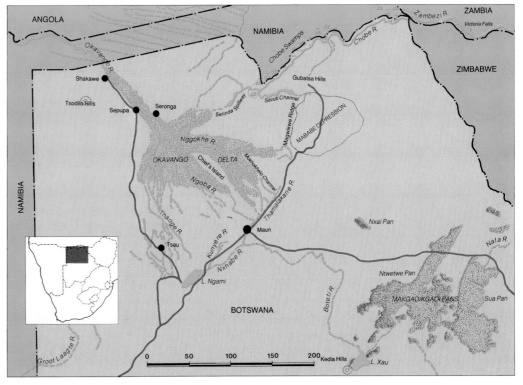

requiring more than six times the present annual flow of the Okavango River to maintain it. But in those days the Makgadikgadi basin was still fed from the highlands of present-day Namibia by powerful rivers like the Okwa, which have left deep gashes across the plains of the western and central Kalahari. As a more arid climate began to prevail, however, these ancient rivers ceased to flow, the lower lake also shrank and broke up into a series of smaller lakes. Eventually they too dried out and became the Makgadikgadi Pans.

Grasses able to survive the high concentrations of salt sporadically carpet these relics of the former great lake, but most are bare white expanses of alkaline mud. Only Lake Xau, on the south-western margin of the depression, has occasionally filled with water in historical times, while parts of the two largest pans, Sua and Ntwetwe, as well as many of the smaller ones, may be covered after heavy rains by very thin sheets of blue water. While they last these attract flocks of pink flamingoes and other wetland birds, but quickly dry up after the storm clouds depart. Salt bubbles and encrustations form, and the hot desert sun bakes the white mud hard, patterning the broad, flat surfaces with an intricate network of cracks.

173. *A verdant wonderland of waterways, marshes and islands is dotted with occasional fan palm groves. Trails left by fishermen's mekoro thread through the aquatic plantlife that spreads over still backwaters.*

Strange, crescent-shaped islands of sand ranging from 5 000 square metres to about eight square kilometres are found, particularly in the western part of Ntwetwe Pan. Rising five metres above the pan floor, they are usually grassed, and stand in sharp contrast to the lighter pan surface.

The margins of the ancient lake are still visible in places along the remnants of its former shoreline. As a wide arc northward across the sandy Kalahari plain for over 250 kilometres, it sweeps from Lake Xau and the Kedia Hills in the south to the Thamalakane River, at the foot of the delta. Climbing gradually to about 30 metres above the plain, this gently curved, two to three kilometre-broad band comprises sand finer and more uniform than that of the surrounding terrain. Lower down, the slope is marked by a layer of fine-grained rock, compounded from the minute silica cases of microscopic, plankton-like plants.

The Thamalakane River flows in the north-east to south-west trending fault that divided the original lake in two. Here a 200-metre displacement in the rock along the fault raised the eastern side as a barrier to the flow of water from the north. In a parallel fault 25 kilometres to the west the displacement was 500 metres, and again the higher eastern side became the bank against which the silt and sand forming the delta built up.

Okavango water that manages to cross the Thamalakane fault flows into the Boteti River system and may still reach the Makgadikgadi Pans, as in the past.

From where the Boteti leaves the Thamalakane at the rock bar near the town of Maun, it flows east-south-east some 250 kilometres to the pans, carrying water first to Lake Xau, and in high flood years continuing from there to Ntwetwe and Nata pans.

When the Thamalakane is in high flood, water flows past the Boteti feed-off and on through the Nxhabe River towards Lake Ngami, at the south-western extremity of the delta. Once three drainage lines – the Groot Laagte from the south-west, the Thaoge from the north, and the Kunyere from the north-east – converged here. Of the three, only the Kunyere still brings water to Lake Ngami. Now largely reliant on local rainfall, it is today a mere shadow of its former self. Old strand lines nine metres above the present level indicate that it must once have spread over some 520 square kilometres; a sand ridge further west suggests that even earlier it was twice that. But since the Thaoge stopped flowing into the lake in 1884, after a chief dammed the river to deprive his downstream foes of water, not more than a third of Lake Ngami's floor has ever been covered.

The Mababe Depression, also a remnant of the ancient lake, on the north-eastern side of the delta, is an oval hollow 80 kilometres long and half as wide, its floor 30 metres below the present level of the plain to the east. The western rim is a gently curved sand ridge – Magwikwe ridge – which is attached to the Gubatsa hills and continues north-west of the Savuti Channel. This conspicuous ridge appears to be a sandspit formed by the old lake, while the Savuti Channel may once have brought the Chobe into the depression, before the Zambezi captured it. Today the Mokhokhelo Channel leads water escaping from the Chobe swamps into the depression. Higher up the delta, in exceptional years, the floodwaters of the Ngoba overflow below Seronga into the Selinda (Makwegana) and Haignoma spillways and sometimes reach the Chobe swamps.

Of the 8 000 million cubic metres of water introduced to the delta yearly by the Okavango River, and an equivalent amount contributed by rain in the delta area, less than two per cent eventually reaches the Thamalakane and passes on to the Boteti and Nxhabe. The rest is lost along the way through the delta, by evaporation from inlets and 'lagoons' and transpiration by the lush plantlife it supports.

From Mohembo, where the Okavango River enters Botswana as a stream some 560 metres wide and almost four metres deep, until 100 kilometres south of Shakawe, it follows a single channel. In a 16 kilometre-broad riverine belt, it cuts across an ancient dune field, still bounded at a distance by fossil dunes that are now fixed by vegetation. South of Sepupa, the Okavango branches into the Thaoge to the west, and the Nggokhe to the east. They, in turn, flow into the permanent swamps, where they become

infinitely divided, fanning out over a 18 000-square kilometre delta comparable in size to the Nile Delta. About 10 per cent of this area is permanently inundated. Although the spread of water increases five-fold following the annual rainy season in Angola, abnormal flooding can result in as much as 14 000 square kilometres being under water.

When the floodwaters from Angola reach the permanent swamp in March and early April, dense aquatic vegetation impedes the flow, and the waters back up and spread out, forming a reservoir that later supplies the rest of the delta. The flow divides around Chief's Island, a ridge on a calcrete base at the centre of the delta. Two-thirds of the flow moves eastwards into the Moremi 'lagoon' areas, while the remainder continues south across the Xo flats and through the Thaoge, Kunyere and Boro outlets to the Thamalakane.

Moving slowly south and east, the floodwaters pass over white, sandy bottoms, through open channels 15 to 150 metres wide and five to seven metres deep, then spill over into the lesser channels of the perennial swamps and filter through thick beds of papyrus and reeds into the madiba. Wrongly called 'lagoons', these are actually oxbow lakes which developed in former river channels and now remain free of vegetation.

The sheet of water moving down the delta slope soaks into the dry sand ahead, rises again slowly as the sand becomes saturated, and continues its unhurried way. The slope being only between 20 and 40 centimetres a kilometre, the flow is easily interrupted by minor obstructions and takes four or five months to reach the Thamalakane.

Delta drainage patterns are continually changing. Once the water leaves the major channels it does not necessarily follow the same courses year after year. Lesser channels now flowing one way, may flow the other next year, or become so choked with vegetation that they cease to flow at all. Large masses of papyrus, torn living from the banks by the river upstream to ride like floating islands on the rising waters, can lodge in the shallows and take root when the flood subsides. Debris piling up behind the new growth may subsequently divert the flow, and the former channel will remain closed until cleared eventually by one of the fires that seem always to be sweeping through the papyrus somewhere in the delta.

These swamps offer a habitat for prolific plant and animal life. Blue water-lilies dance on crystal clear waterways which are edged with snake root, water

174. *The circular leaves of water-lilies form a sun-silvered pathway between the reeded banks of an inlet.* 175. *An air of tranquility settles over the unruffled waters of the madiba as the lowering sun illuminates a transient stormcloud.* 176. *The tranquility is momentarily broken as, with talons outstretched, an ever-vigilant fish eagle swoops on a fish that chose the wrong moment to break the surface.* 177. *As the sun sets behind the silhouette of fringing forest, a returning fisherman silently poles his mekoro across a channel of liquid gold.*

grass, reed and papyrus. Inhabiting these waters are an estimated 35 million fish of almost 80 species. The most abundant, three species of bream, are preserved from excessive predation by crocodiles feeding on the tiger fish that would prey on the bream.

Hippo flatten paths through the papyrus on their nocturnal forays to graze on the rooigras plains within the swamps. The shaggy, solitary sitatunga, long hooves developed to cope with soft marshy soil, snorts an alarm call among the reeds. Another wetland antelope, the gregarious red lechwe, raises ringed, lyre-shaped horns and whistles before taking refuge in the water. Small herds of waterbuck plunge through the shallows. Family groups of tsessebe roam grassland and floodplain. Fan palms cluster on islands, where heron, stork, ibis and cormorant form colonies in thickets of water fig.

Belts of forest fringe the swamps with tall trees. Dark, rounded crowns of ebony diospyros, yellow-barked sycamore fig, grey-green leadwood and russet bushwillow give shade to large herds of buffalo waiting to graze in the evening cool. Beyond the forest camel thorn,

mopane and leadwood form open savanna parkland, and these drier areas attract the greatest concentration of game and accompanying predators. Lion, leopard, cheetah, hyena and wild dog hunt where elephant and giraffe browse with antelope of almost every kind, from buffalo, wildebeest and kudu to sable, roan and impala.

Some 300 kilometres wide at its base, the green, brown and yellow world of the Okavango Delta is a huge oasis in the Kalahari, a maze of channels, 'lagoons' and backwaters, where the rhythm of life depends on the annual rise and fall of the floodwaters. But it is a changing world. The flow of the life-giving waters, so easily altered by minor obstacles, is also affected by the more deeply seated instability of the region. Beneath the swamps, huge cracks in the earth's crust may be an extension of the Great Rift Valley, and continual seismic activity – 30 earthquakes in 23 years – supports the theory that there is an active 'hot spot' under the delta. Already the eastern side of the swamps are becoming drier, and a time will probably come when the wonderland of the swamps has no more water than the Makgadikgadi Pans.

178

178. The stout web of a swampland orb-spinner set for larger prey. The webs of some species are strong enough to hold bats and small birds.   **179.** The pendulous grey fruit of the sausage tree may grow to a metre in length. It has numerous applications in traditional medicine and is frequently hung in huts to ward off whirlwinds.   **180.** Concentric circles of heaped sand mark the entrance to a termite nest. With over 2 000 termite species in Africa, the swamp islands have their quota.
181. A fresh water-lily, open to the sunlight, seems to be withered in its image mirrored by the clear blue water.

179

180   181

182. Due to the low gradient, channels that flow one way one year may flow the other way the next and easily become blocked, ceasing to flow at all for several years.   **183.** A pile of stranded driftwood provides convenient perches for a group of yellowbilled egrets to groom themselves and watch for their next meal.   **184.** A party of blacksmith plovers move about restlessly in the short grass, while nearby a solitary grey heron waits patiently for the tell-tale movement of fish, frog, insect or mouse.   **185.** Taking stock of the situation, two sentinel male impala consider alerting the grazing herd.

182

183

184

185

187

188

186. *Drawn up along the bank at the day's end are the mekoro of Mbukushu tribesmen. Painstakingly shaped with adzes from the straight trunks of hardwood trees, these dugout craft are the universal form of transport used by the Okavango swamp-dwellers. Essential in the principal occupation of fishing, they also provide local taxi services.*   **187, 188.** *Now bare, white expanses of alkaline mud, baked and blistered by the desert sun, the Mkgadikgadi Pans were once the floor of an ancient great lake that was deprived of its chief sources of water by climatic changes. In some areas vegetated accumulations of sand form dark 'islands' on the salty flats. Thin sheets of blue water, briefly covering parts of the surface after rain, attract migrant herds of wildebeest and other antelope.*

THE KALAHARI
LAST RANGE
OF THE BUSHMEN

Typical Kalahari landscapes have little in common with the conventional idea of a desert, although usually so described. Gently undulating sandy plains, surprisingly thickly vegetated, seem to extend to infinity in all directions. A flowering wilderness in spring, the Kalahari seems a pastoral paradise of tall green grass and leafy trees and bushes after midsummer rains. Even through the long dry months, in the subdued buffs and greys of withered foliage, the dried culms and fallen leaves bear testimony to cycles of life in greater abundance than is generally associated with deserts. Rainfall, though scanty, irregular, unevenly distributed and limited to a brief season, is higher than in truly arid regions.

More accurately described as 'thirstland', the Kalahari is covered everywhere with vegetation adapted to its seasonal austerities. Ranging from forest and swamp grassland on its north-eastern fringes, it varies through combinations of tree and bush savanna to mopaneveld and bushveld in the south-east, thornveld and arid shrub savanna in the south-west. Here the great herds of game that have disappeared elsewhere in southern Africa still range over the plains according to the seasons; animals hunt and are hunted,

much as they preyed and were preyed upon before men entered their world.

Kalahari sand, its characteristic red colour given by the thin film of iron oxide coating the grains, furnishes what is probably the largest continuous sand surface in the world. Covering almost a third of the African subcontinent, it is spread to a thickness of anything from three to more than 100 metres over an area of some 2,5 million square kilometres. From south of the Orange River it stretches to the Zaire watershed, and westward from the Wankie area in Zimbabwe to Etosha Pan in northern Namibia. More specifically, the Kalahari is the vast sandveld region of central and western Botswana, extending into eastern Namibia and the northern Cape.

The sands of the Kalahari have accumulated in a huge depression, the result of continental uplift more than 60 million years ago. This central area remained at its previous level, while the surrounding highlands grew in stature. In an ensuing prolonged period of extreme aridity, daily temperature fluctuations gradually broke down a good deal of the pre-existing sedimentary rock in the basin, reducing it to sand, which then collected in valleys and hollows in the bedrock. When climatic changes initiated

a wet period lasting many millions of years, the highlands were eroded by rivers and streams pouring into the basin from all sides, covering low-lying areas with river gravels, marls and clays. In a following period of aridity, the evaporation of standing water left a thick crust of surface limestone, called calcrete, and protruding sedimentary rocks were ground down to form a layer of sand over the calcrete.

The only eminences in the Kalahari today are relics of these rocks. Along the limestone Ghanzi Ridge, the sandstone Mabeleapodi, Khwebe, Makabana and Haina hills protrude between Gobabis and Lake Ngami. In and north of the Mababe Depression are the Gubatsa and Goha hills, with the sandstone Tsodilo and the dolomite Aha hills in the north-west.

Most of the southern Kalahari appears to be underlain by sheets of calcrete and calcareous sandstone. Borehole drillings have revealed that the calcareous layer is over 100 metres thick in places, and exposures of up to 30 metres are commonly seen in the banks of the now dry, but once powerful, 'fossil' rivers that cut their channels in it. In eastern Namibia, from Tsumis to Aroab, the western boundary of the Kalahari is marked for almost 300 kilometres by the

189

calcareous table-land and low escarpment of the Urinanib (white ridge) Plateau. Near Asab, an outlier undercut by weathering forms the amazing Mukorob, or 'Finger of God', an enormous block of rock precariously balanced, like a top, on an incredibly fine point.

Since sand first spread over the floor of the basin it has been redistributed many times. When the climate was wetter than now, rivers flowed swiftly throughout the year, and the sand was covered with vegetation. Then, in even drier periods than at present, the rivers dried up, vegetation disappeared and strong winds again blew the loose sand about the depression, here piling up high ridges, there reducing it to a level plain. Humid and arid periods, each lasting many millennia, have alternated several times over the past million years, and only in the last 20 000 years have the dunes assumed their present positions and been fixed by the vegetation that still binds their surfaces today.

A broad, flat-topped swelling, the Bakalahari Schwelle runs south-east from near Gobabis to Kanye. Here rainfall, instead of being borne away by streams, collects briefly during the short rainy season in pans which cluster in a wide belt from the Namibian border to Sekoma. These small ephemeral lakes and vleis vary from a few hundred square metres to about 16 square kilometres. Their clay floors, bare or partially vegetated, are generally from five to 20 metres below the level of the surrounding sandveld. Originally, seasonal water accumulated in the pans and, by inhibiting perennial

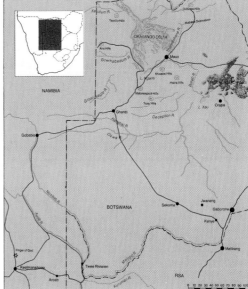

190

plant growth, enabled the wind gradually to remove dry surface sand in other seasons and heap it up as crescent-shaped dunes on their southern margins. Usually pans of this kind have two dunes. A large outer dune is composed of the reddish-brown quartz sand that the wind removed in hollowing out the original depression. A smaller inner dune of grey-brown sand, containing high proportions of calcium carbonate and fine clay particles, is made up of material later blown from the surface of the pan itself.

North of the Schwelle the drainage, in theory, is into the ancient 'fossil' watercourses of the Okwa, Hanahai, Deception and their former tributaries. At one time these were mighty rivers from the highlands of Namibia, filling the great

lakes that then occupied the area of the Makgadikgadi Pans. Deeply incised then into the calcrete and underlying rock, today they carry no water, their lower courses buried beneath the gentle, almost imperceptible undulations of the wide, sandy plains they traverse in the central part of the Kalahari. Further north, beyond Ghanzi Ridge, the Groot Laagte once flowed into Lake Ngami, and the Gcwihabadum, Xaudum and Ncamasere ran into the Okavango Delta region.

There are few well-defined dunes in the central Kalahari, apart from isolated crescents associated with pans, and low, rolling dunes along what were once western shorelines of the Makgadikgadi depression. In the north, however, an area of about 16 000 square kilometres, extending from western Zimbabwe to Etosha Pan, is marked by the remnants of former great dune ridges, 90 metres high, similar to those in the Namib 'dune sea'. Today, these ridges are best developed west of the Okavango River and its delta. They still form broad parallel ridges of brown sand up to 25 metres high, two kilometres apart and running roughly east to west, uninterrupted in some cases for 200 kilometres. Reckoned to be the oldest dunes in the Kalahari, they were bare, like

189. *Normally fairly well covered with vegetation, red sand dunes are dotted with camel thorn and grey camel thorn trees. The dry watercourse, now used as a road, is covered with sand which varies from pale brown and grey to white, partly because it has been introduced from other areas by floodwaters, and partly a result of the admixture of material weathered from the calcrete cliffs that bank much of the lower Auob's course.* **190.** *The stately gemsbok is well adapted to survive the dry conditions of the Kalahari.*

191. *Well-worn game paths indicate that this Kalahari pan is visited regularly by antelope for the salts deficient in their diet. In temporary occupation are a few zebra and a herd of wildebeest.*

the Namib dune ridges, at the time of their greatness. Their subsequent decline was arrested by vegetation, and today they support open savanna woodland, dominated by red syringa and kiaat trees on the ridges, with grass and scrub in the wide valleys between them.

South of the Bakalahari Schwelle, a basin-shaped depression filled with red sand extends some 125 000 square kilometres. In the northern and eastern parts of the depression the sand has a fairly flat surface, sparsely vegetated with grass and scrub. In the west and south-west, however, long parallel dune ridges rise to between five and 20 metres high, with 100 to 500 metres between crests. Although in places the ridges merge and diverge, complicating the pattern, their general alignment is north-west to south-east.

Four powerful rivers once converged on the centre of the depression. They carved channels up to a kilometre wide and more than 30 metres deep through not only the thick calcrete layer, but also, in several places, banded ironstones, schists and hard quartzites. All four originate outside the Kalahari. The Auob and Nossob, which enter the depression from the north-west, rise in the mountains around Windhoek. The longest, the Molopo, has its source far away to the east, issuing from a limestone 'eye' in the Transvaal dolomites, near Lichtenburg. The Kuruman rises from a similar 'eye' at the northern Cape town of the same name. The Auob meets the Nossob at Twee Rivieren, and some 90 kilometres south of their confluence the Nossob links up with the Molopo, which is joined by the Kuruman some 15 kilometres further on.

Long ago, their combined waters then flowed on through the Hygap channel to the Orange River. But in historical times the rivers have rarely run in their lower courses, and then only after exceptionally heavy rains in their upper catchment areas. The seasonal floodwaters of the Molopo seldom even reach the Kalahari nowadays, and not within human memory have they come as far as the confluence with the Nossob. On the few occasions that the Nossob and Kuruman have flooded all the way, they have been diverted by a large sand dune that has blocked the entrance to the Hygap for at least a thousand years. Redirected, they empty into Abiekwaputs, a large pan at the lowest point in the Kalahari, 853 metres above sea-level.

Its rainfall so low that it is nearly a desert by definition, this is the most arid part of the Kalahari; the struggle for survival is keenest, the adaptability of all living things most critically poised against death and extinction. Yet even here, except where over-grazing has caused blowouts, the dunes are well covered with grass, shrubs and occasional witgat, camel thorn and grey camel thorn trees. Life is most concentrated in the dry riverbeds, plants and animals being more plentiful in number and numerous in kind than in the surrounding sandveld. The sands of the old watercourses, far from uniform in texture and composition, furnish varied conditions favouring many plants unable to grow among the dunes and therefore providing food for animals that cannot subsist on dune vegetation alone. Springbok, gemsbok, red hartebeest, blue wildebeest and eland spend at least part of each year in the

riverbeds, and many are permanent residents. The channel floors are thus favourite haunts of lion, hyena, leopard and cheetah, as well as a host of smaller predators and scavengers who live by their wits on the fringes of larger animals' kills.

The diversity of thirstland life is the true wonder of the Kalahari, for the one thing it does have in common with deserts is the complete absence of any surface water for all but a month or two each year. The plants that grow here are those able to survive through not only the long dry season every year, but a succession of drought years.

In times of drought, most annuals do not appear at all. They preserve their life potential as seeds in protective shells, proof against summer's withering heat, when maximum daily temperatures average 30 degrees and sand temperatures push the mercury to twice that. Perennials rely on other means. Either, like the camel thorn, their roots are so deep that they remain in touch with moisture far below the surface, or they have large moisture storage organs and special root adaptations insulating them from the hot sand near the surface. The roots of the perennial grasses are covered with fine hairs, on which a protective sheath forms around the upper root. Bulbous plants have particularly succulent roots, storing enough water to keep them alive for three or four years. Some have roots that become shorter, instead of thinner, as they dry out, pulling the bulb deeper into the sand when they contract. Many slender-rooted plants expand their roots to develop extra storage tissue in times of need, while the roots of others are preserved by becoming thin, tough and wiry. Yet others develop different root structures for different seasons. When dry, they have only a few major roots, well protected against the heat and moisture loss by thick cork skins. But within hours of rain, a large number of fibrous roots, with no cork covering, grow from the major roots and suck up moisture from the sand. When the sand dries out, the fibrous roots die off, leaving the moisture stored inside the cork skins of the main roots.

Moisture retained by plants – particularly tsama melon, gemsbok cucumber and wild cucumber – is the key to animal survival in the thirstland. Antelope and other herbivores extract the moisture they need from fresh grass, browse, melons, bulbs and tubers. Meat- and insect-eaters also get some moisture from melons, but their principal source is the blood and body fluids of their prey.

Special adaptations enabling animals to

acquire and conserve moisture are products of physical and behavioural evolution. Natural selection has endowed some with bodies that make maximum use of moisture in their diet. Some can alter the temperature of their bodies, others limit sweat loss by having fewer sweat glands, or decrease evaporation from their lungs by cooling the air as it passes out through their noses. Others conserve moisture by producing more concentrated urine, or are equipped to reabsorb more from waste material in their colons.

Most adaptations, however, are in the habitual behaviour of the animals, such as the lion's characteristic laziness, and the way in which animals seek shade in the heat of the day. Many small creatures regulate their climate by withdrawing into underground burrows and tunnels, where temperature and humidity are constantly moderate. In summer herbivores generally feed in the evening, night or early morning, when sweat loss is least and they can chew the hygroscopic plants that absorb moisture readily from the slightly damper air at those times of day.

Northward and eastward moisture conditions improve, the vegetation is enriched by a greater variety of plants, migratory herds increase in number, swell in size, and animals not seen in the driest areas – kudu, zebra, giraffe, elephant – become part of the Kalahari landscape.

Man, too, has been a very small figure in this vast landscape for many thousands of years. Believing there was a time when all animals were 'people', Bushmen have lived in the Kalahari since Late Stone Age times. In harmony with the animal world, as hunters (predators), collectors (scavengers) and gatherers (browsers), they have occupied an ecological niche within the balance of nature, relying on tsama melons, bulbs and tubers for water.

Like the tsetse-fly belt, the Kalahari was a major obstacle to southward migration by black pastoralists from Central Africa.

Their migration routes skirted the thirstland to east and west. Sotho-speaking tribes reaching the Transvaal found further expansion limited by Zulu and other Nguni tribes in the east, the Korana and later Griqua and white frontiersmen in the south and south-west. Eventually population growth compelled them to spread west and north-west into dry areas bordering the Kalahari. The first of them, called Kgalagadi because they settled near the great salt pans, were later

192. *Sociable weavers build their large communal nests in the sturdy branches of camel thorn trees. These nests eventually grow so big that they fill entire trees, and it is quite common for branches to shear off under the weight.* 193. *A hyena prospects the remains of a gemsbok carcass.*
194 (Overleaf) *An outlier of the Urinanib Plateau, undercut by weathering, forms the amazing Mukorob, or 'Finger of God', an enormous block of rock precariously balanced, like a top, on an incredibly fine point.*

dislodged by other Sotho tribes, known collectively as Tswana, who drove them into the depths of the thirstland, reducing them to hunting and gathering for their livelihood in the arid region that assumed their name.

Ironically, the absence of surface water has been one of the Kalahari's greatest assets, discouraging permanent settlement, protecting the sensitive ecosystem from over-grazing by domestic stock, preserving the Bushmen and their way of life long after they were forced from all the better-watered parts of the subcontinent. But while it delayed settlement, it did not prevent it, and as the methods of tapping underground water improved, pastoralists were able to penetrate deeper into the thirstland.

Fences erected to check the spread of stock diseases have in places barred the migration routes of the great herds, causing thousands of animals to die cut off from water. The number of Bushmen still living in the old way dwindles rapidly as they are lured by the crumbs of relative affluence to seek menial jobs at cattle-posts, ranches and settlements. Diamond-rich kimberlite pipes at Orapa and Jwaneng have brought large-scale mining to the Kalahari, while politicians and technological visionaries talk of spanning the sands with railway lines and modern highways, and of draining the Okavango swamps to irrigate the thirstland.

Yet little change is visible in the absorbent immensity of the landscape. Flying over the thirstland, for hours on end one sees no sign of civilization, the scars left by man. All around, the rolling plains reach clear to the flat skyline, slight undulations banded from rise to hollow by subtle variation in the vegetation. Straggling game paths radiate from pans where antelope gather for salt-lick, as they did in 'old Africa', before the first herdsmen grazed their cattle on the desert grasses of the Kalahari.

GLOSSARY

Banded ironstone – rocks rich in iron minerals deposited as thin bands in layers of varying colour and texture.

Basalt – an igneous rock produced by lava flow, the fine-grained equivalent of gabbro.

Basement Complex – consists of deposits of mainly metamorphic and igneous rocks underlying sedimentary layers. Basement formations date back to the beginnings of geological time.

Batholith – a large mass of igneous rock, usually granite, the result of an intrusion of magma solidifying at great depth. Associated with mountain belts, batholiths are often exposed when less resistant overlying rocks have been eroded.

Bedrock – the lowest layer of solid, unweathered rock that underlies superficial formations.

Biome – a major ecological region, usually characterized by a dominant type of vegetation.

Breccia – a rock similar to conglomerate except that the large fragments in the matrix are angular rather than rounded. It may be sedimentary, or the result of crushing along faults.

Butte – a small, flat-topped hill with steep sides, formed when resistant material caps a softer rock.

Calcrete and **Calc-tufa** – essentially similar phenomena, these are deposits of soil or rock fragments which have been cemented by calcium carbonate transported by water from underground.

Chalcedony – a quartz mineral which forms chert and agates.

Chert – a variety of quartz composed predominantly of chalcedony.

Conglomerate – a coarse-grained sedimentary rock composed of relatively large, rounded fragments embedded in a fine matrix.

Craton – an area of the earth's crust that has been relatively stable during the last 1 000 million years.

Dolerite – a medium-grained igneous rock formed from basalt magma which has solidified near the earth's surface. Dolerites usually occur as dykes or sills.

Dolomite – a rock of chemical origin that is similar to the mineral dolomite (calcium magnesium carbonate) in composition.

Dripstone – a general term used to describe deposits of calcium carbonate precipitated by dripping water in underground caverns. Thus it refers to stalactites, stalagmites, flowstone and similar formations.

Dyke – a vertical body of igneous rock, usually dolerite, intruded into cracks in existing sedimentary rocks.

Fault – a fracture in the earth's crust resulting in the displacement of the rocks on one side relative to those of the other side.

    Fault-scarp – a steep, cliff-like slope above the surrounding land, the result of faulting.

    Thrust fault – a fault where a body of rock has been displaced over another, pushed upward over the lower block by horizontal stress.

Feldspar – a common mineral constituent of igneous and metamorphic rocks.

Flowstone – a feature of underground caverns, formed where water has moved slowly over large areas of rock and left a sheet-like deposit of calcium carbonate.

Gabbro – a dark igneous rock, the coarse-grained equivalent of basalt and dolerite.

Gneiss – a coarse-grained metamorphic rock composed predominantly of quartz and feldspar, with some mica.

Granite – a coarse-grained, and therefore plutonic, igneous rock, usually light in colour. It is composed chiefly of quartz and feldspar, with mica and several other minerals.

Helictite – a very delicate deposit of calcium carbonate in underground caverns, which looks like a miniature stalactite twisted in all directions.

Hygroscopic – refers to plants, or minerals, which can absorb moisture from the atmosphere.

Igneous rocks – are formed from molten magma pushed up from inside the earth. When the magma cools and solidifies very slowly beneath thousands of metres of older rock, it crystallizes out as coarse-grained, or plutonic, rocks such as granite and gabbro. When the magma reaches the earth's surface and cools rapidly, it forms fine-grained volcanic lava such as basalt. Magma which solidifies near the surface forms medium-grained rocks such as dolerite.

Inselberg – a large, dome-like hill of resistant rock rising abruptly from the surrounding plain.

Interfluve – the high ground between two rivers in the same drainage system.

Intrusion – a body of igneous rock which has intruded into older rock but does not reach the surface.

Khoikhoi – the name given to an indigenous people of southern Africa, also known as Hottentots. They were primarily nomadic pastoralists.

Kimberlite pipe – a cylindrical mass of rock formed when magma drilled from the interior of the earth to the surface by gas explosions cooled together with rock fragments plucked from the formations through which it passed. It is often a source of diamonds.

Kloof – a steep-sided valley, similar to a ravine.

Kopje – a small but prominent isolated hill, usually flat-topped.

Krantz – a rock precipice.

Lava – molten or partially molten magma disgorged by volcanoes, and the fine-grained igneous rock formed when it cools.

Leaching – the draining away of substances through soil by percolating water.

Limestone – a sedimentary rock which consists mainly of calcium carbonate. It can be formed from eroded rock particles, from the calcareous skeletons of organisms or from a chemical precipitate.

Magma – molten material beneath the earth's surface which consists chiefly of silicates. It crystallizes and solidifies to form igneous rocks.

Marble – a hard crystalline rock resulting from the metamorphism of limestone or dolomite.

Marl – a fine-grained sedimentary rock containing a high proportion of calcareous material.

Matrix – the fine-grained material of a rock in which the coarser components are embedded. In sedimentary rocks it is usually the cementing material which binds together the larger grains or pebbles.

Mesa – an isolated hill with a flat top resulting from a cap of hard rock. It often consists of alternate layers of resistant and less resistant rock which give a step effect when eroded.

Metamorphic rocks – have been transformed from their original structure and composition by the action of extreme heat and pressure below the earth's surface.

Monocline – a folding of the strata of sedimentary rock in such a way that two areas of horizontal strata lie at different elevations, connected by a steeply inclined series of the same strata.

Moraine – material deposited by ice-sheets and glaciers.

Mudstone – a fine-grained sedimentary rock similar to shale but less inclined to split along bedding planes.

Nek – a narrow pass.

Outlier – an outcrop of exposed younger sediments entirely surrounded by older rocks.

Oxbow lake – a crescent-shaped lake in a river floodplain. The remnant of a meander, it is formed when the river erodes the outsides of the meander bends and eventually cuts across the neck of the meander, leaving the oxbow lake to silt up.

Plutonic rock – the coarse-grained result of magma cooling slowly and crystallizing deep below the earth's surface. A **pluton** is an intrusive body of such rock.

Poort – a narrow pass through mountains, usually following a stream.

Porphyry – an igneous rock containing large crystals set in a fine-grained matrix.

Precambrian – the earliest division of time in the earth's geological history.

Quartz – a very common mineral, also known as silica or silicon dioxide. It is both an essential constituent of silica-rich igneous rock, such as granite, and the predominant component of sandstone, to which it lends its very resistant properties.

Quartzite – a very hard rock, produced by the metamorphism of pure sandstone.

Rimstone – a feature of underground caverns, formed where calcium carbonate has been deposited at the edge of a shallow pool.

Sandstone – a common sedimentary rock which, owing to the presence of quartz, is resistant to weathering and thus forms some of the most outstanding features of the landscape. It is composed of sand grains welded together by pressure or bound by a cement such as calcite.

Schist – a foliated metamorphic rock in which equally thin layers of micaceous minerals and quartz/feldspar alternate.

    Green schist – igneous rock metamorphosed at a low temperature and low pressure, which derives its colour from the presence of green minerals such as chlorite, hornblende and epidote.

Sedimentary rocks – are formed by the accumulation and lithification of organic and mineral sediments deposited by water, ice, wind or chemical precipitation. Sediments consisting of varying sizes of rock fragments which have been eroded, transported and deposited elsewhere are consolidated into strata, forming rocks such as mudstone, shale, sandstone and conglomerate.

Series – the body of rock laid down during the corresponding geological epoch. Several series are combined to form a system; thus the Ecca Series is a part of the Karoo System.

Shale – a dark, laminated sedimentary rock composed of very fine-grained particles such as clay.

Sill – a flat, usually horizontal body of medium-grained igneous rock, caused by the intrusion of magma between layers of sedimentary rock.

System – the body of rock laid down within the corresponding geological period. A system consists of a number of series.

Talus – the accumulation of weathered rock debris at the foot of a slope resulting from the erosion of the rock face above.

Tillite – a sedimentary rock composed of unsorted fragmental material deposited by ice-sheets and glaciers.

Vlei – an area of low, marshy ground.

Weathering – the process of breaking down or altering rock by weather conditions, usually wind, precipitation, extreme heat or extreme cold.

BIBLIOGRAPHY

Abercrombie, M., Hickman, C.J. and Johnson, M.L., 1973. *A Dictionary of Biology*. Penguin Books, London.
Acocks, J.P.H., 1975. *Veld Types of South Africa*. Botanical Research Institute, Dept. of Agricultural Technical Services.
Acocks, J.P.H. 'Karoo Vegetation in Relation to the Development of Deserts.' *Ecological Studies in Southern Africa*.
Andrag, R.H., 1977. *Studies in die Sederberge*. MSc thesis, University of Stellenbosch.
Berjak, P., Campbell, G.K., Huckett, B.I. and Pammenter, N.W., 1977. *In the Mangroves of Southern Africa*. Wildlife Society of Southern Africa.
Biggs, R. 'An Ecological Survey of Chief's Island and the Adjoining Floodplain.' *Botswana Notes and Records*, 1975.
Birch, G.F. and Du Plessis, A., 1977. *Offshore and Onland Geological and Geophysical Investigations in the Wilderness Lakes Region*. Geological Survey, University of Cape Town.
Bornman, C.H., 1978. *Welwitschia, Paradox of a Parched Land*. C. Struik, Cape Town.
Breen, C.M. and Hill, B.J. 'A Mass Mortality of Mangroves in the Kosi Estuary.' *Trans. Royal Society of SA*, 1969.
Brink, A.B.A. and Partridge, T.C. 'Transvaal Karst: some considerations of development and morphology, with special reference to sinkholes and subsidences on the Far West Rand.' *SA Geographical Journal*, 1965.
Broekhuysen, G.J. and Taylor, H. 'The Ecology of Kosi Bay Estuary System.' *Annals of the SA Museum*, 1959.
Buckle, C., 1978. *Landforms in Africa*. Longmans, London.
Callan, E. McC. 'Ecology of Sand Dunes, with Special Reference to the Insect Communities.' *Ecological Studies in Southern Africa*.
Campbell, A. and Child, G. 'The Impact of Man on the Environment of Botswana.' *Botswana Notes and Records*, 1971.
Clark, J. Desmond (Ed.), 1957. *Third Pan-African Congress on Prehistory – Livingstone, 1955*. Chatto and Windus, London.
Coates Palgrave, K., 1977. *Trees of Southern Africa*. C. Struik, Cape Town.
Cooke, H.J. 'The Origin of the Makgadikgadi Pans.' *Botswana Notes and Records*, 1979.
Cooks, J. 'Stadia van die Geomorfiese Siklus in die Wes-Transvaalse Dolomietgordel.' *SA Geographer*, 1968.
Davies, W.N.G. 'Southern Rhodesia.' *SA Geographical Journal*, 1933.
Day, J.H., Millard, N.A.H. and Broekhuysen, G.J. 'The Ecology of the St Lucia System.' *Trans. Royal Society SA*, 1954.
Day, J.H. 'The Biology of Langebaan Lagoon: a study of the effect of shelter from wave action.' *Trans. Royal Society SA*, 1959.
De La Cruz, A., 1977. *The Bedrock Basement of Saldanha Bay*. Geological Survey, University of Cape Town.
De Villiers, J. and Sohnge, P., 1959. *The Geology of the Richtersveld*. Geological Survey, Dept. of Mines.
Dorst, J. and Dandelot, P., 1972. *A Field Guide to the Larger Mammals of Africa*. Collins, London.
Du Plessis, E.J., 1973. *'n Ondersoek na die oorsprong en betekenis van Suid-Afrikaanse berg- en riviername*. Tafelberg, Cape Town.
Du Toit, A.L. 'The Evolution of the South African Coastline.' *SA Geographical Journal*, 1922.
Du Toit, A.L. 'The Mier Country'. *SA Geographical Journal*, 1926.
Du Toit, A.L., 1954. *The Geology of South Africa*. Oliver and Boyd, Edinburgh.
Du Toit, A.L. *The Geology of Pondoland*. Geological Survey, Explanation of Cape Sheet No. 28.
Fair, T.J.D. 'Hill-slopes and Pediments of the Semi-arid Karroo.' *SA Geographical Journal*, 1948.
Flemming, B.W., 1977. *Depositional Processes in Saldanha Bay and Langebaan Lagoon*. Geological Survey, University of Cape Town.
Flemming, B.W. 'Distribution of Recent Sediments in Saldanha Bay and Langebaan Lagoon.' *Trans. Royal Society SA*, 1977.
Frandsen, R. 'Project for the Conservation of the Flora of the Western Cape.' *The Conservationist*, 1979.
Fuggle, R.F. 'Review of a Symposium on Research in the Natural Sciences at Saldanha Bay and Langebaan Lagoon.' *Trans. Royal Society SA*, 1977.
Gebhardt, L. 'Sandwich Harbour, a Sanctuary in the Dunes.' *SWA Annual*, 1973.
Gevers, T.W. 'The Morphology of Western Damaraland and the Adjoining Namib Desert of South West Africa.' *SA Geographical Journal*, 1936.
Giddy, C., 1974. *Cycads of South Africa*. Purnell and Sons, Cape Town.
Goudie, A. 'Notes on Some Major Dune Types in Southern Africa.' *SA Geographical Journal*, 1970.
Grove, A.T. 'Landforms and Climate Change in the Kalahari and Ngamiland.' *SA Geographical Journal*, 1959.
Hall, A.L. 'The Transvaal Drakensberg.' *SA Geographical Journal*, 1925.
Harger, H. 'The Underground Erosion of the SW Transvaal Dolomite.' *SA Geographical Journal*, 1922.
Haughton, S.H. 'Geological History of South Africa.' *Geological Society SA*, 1969.
Henderson, M. and Anderson, J.G., 1966. *Common Weeds in South Africa*. Botanical Survey, Dept. of Agricultural Technical Services.
Hendey, Q.B. 'Fossil Occurrences at Langebaanweg.' *Nature*, 1973.
Hendey, Q.B. and Deacon, H.J. 'Studies in Palaeontology and Archaeology in the Saldanha Region.' *Trans. Royal Society SA*, 1977.
Hill, B.J. 'The Bathymetry and Possible Origin of Lakes Sibaya, Nhlange and Sifungwe in Zululand.' *Trans. Royal Society SA*, 1969.
Hill, B.J. 'The Origin of Southern African Coastal Lakes.' *Trans. Royal Society SA*, 1975.
Hyde, L.W. 'Ground-water Supplies in the Kalahari Area, Botswana.' *Botswana Notes and Records*, Special Edition, 1971.
Inskeep, R.R., 1978. *The Peopling of Southern Africa*. David Philip, Cape Town.
Irwin, P., Ackhurst, J. and Irwin, D., 1980. *A Field Guide to the Natal Drakensberg*. Wildlife Society of Southern Africa.
Jones, C.R. 'The Geology of the Kalahari.' *Botswana Notes and Records*, 1980.
Kerfoot, O. 'The Okavango Controversy: A Real Cause for Alarm.' *SA Journal of Science*, March 1975.
Kerfoot, O. 'The Okavango Delta Controversy – a follow-up.' *SA Journal of Science*, July 1975.
King, L.C. 'Notes on the Valley of a Thousand Hills.' *Annals of the Natal Museum*, 1942.
King, L.C., 1951. *South African Scenery: A Textbook of Geomorphology*. Oliver and Boyd, Edinburgh.
King, L.C. 'The Natal Monocline: Explaining the Origin and Scenery of Natal.' *SA Geographical Journal*, 1974.
King, L.C. 'Aspects of the High Drakensberg.' *SA Geographical Journal*, 1974.
King, L.C. 'The Geology of the Makapan and Other Caves.' *Trans. Royal Society SA*, Vol. 33, No. 1.
Kock, Dr. C. 'Living Sands.' *SWA Annual*, 1970.
Lancaster, I.N. 'Pans of the Southern Kalahari.' *Botswana Notes and Records*, 1974.
Lancaster, I.N. *Quaternary Environments in the Arid Zone of Southern Africa*. Environmental Studies Occasional Paper No. 22, University of the Witwatersrand.
Leistner, O.A. 'The Plant Ecology of the Southern Kalahari.' *Botanical Survey Memoir* No. 38, 1967.
Le Roux, J.S. 'Enkele Aspekte van die Serie Stormberg in die Clocolan-Gebied, OVS.' *SA Geographer*, 1969.
Lewis, A.D. 'Sand Dunes of the Kalahari within the Borders of the Union.' *SA Geographical Journal*, 1936.
Liebenberg, L.C.C. 'Die Grotere Soogdiere wat Vroeër Dae Voorgekom het in die Omgewing van die Golden Gate Hooglandpark.' *Koedoe*, 1964.
Logan, Dr. R.F. 'The Strangest Climate.' *SWA Annual*, 1970.
Lombard, G.I. 'Blyderivierspoort.' *Fauna and Flora*, 1972.
Mabbutt, J.A., 1952. *The Cape Peninsula*. Maskew Miller, Cape Town.
Macfarlane, D.R. 'On the Causes of Submergence and Re-emergence at Plettenberg Bay.' *SA Journal of Science*, 1958.
Marker, M.E. and Moon, B.P. 'Cave Levels and Erosion Surfaces in the Transvaal.' *SA Geographical Journal*, 1969.
Marker, M.E. and Brook, G.A. *Echo Cave: a tentative quaternary chronology for the Eastern Transvaal*. Environmental Studies Occasional Paper No. 3, University of the Witwatersrand, 1970.
Marker, M.E. 'Karst Landform Analysis as Evidence for Climatic Change in the Transvaal.' *SA Geographical Journal*, 1972.
Marker, M.E. 'Aspects of Desert Geomorphology.' *SA Geographer*, 1978.
Marker, M.E. 'A Systems Model for Karst Development with Relevance for Southern Africa.' *SA Geographical Journal*, 1980.
Martin, A.R.H. 'Evidence Relating to the Quaternary History of the Wilderness Lakes.' *Trans. Geological Society SA*, 1962.
Maufe, H.B. 'Some Factors in the Geographical Evolution of Southern Rhodesia and Neighbouring Countries.' *SA Geographical Journal*, 1935.
McLachlan, G.R. and Liversidge, R., 1978. *Roberts Birds of South Africa*. John Voelcker Bird Book Fund, Cape Town.
Moll, E.J. and Campbell, B.M., 1976. *The Ecological Status of Table Mountain*. University of Cape Town.
Moolman, J.H. 'The Orange River, South Africa.' *The Geographical Review*, 1946.
Moon, B.P., 'Factors Controlling the Development of Caves in the Sterkfontein Area.' *SA Geographical Journal*, 1972.
Mossop, Dr. E.E. *Old Cape Highways*. Maskew Miller, Cape Town.
Mountain, E.D., 1968. *Geology of Southern Africa*. Books of Africa, Cape Town.
Nicol, I.G. 'Land Forms in the Little Caledon Valley, OFS.' *SA Geographical Journal*, 1973.
Nienaber, P.J., 1971. *Suid-Afrikaanse Pleknaamwoordeboek*. Tafelberg, Cape Town.
Nienaber, G.S. and Raper, P.E., 1977. *Toponymica Hottentotica*. SA Naamkundesentrum, Raad vir Geestewetenskaplike Navorsing.
Pearse, R.O., 1973. *Barrier of Spears*. Howard Timmins, Cape Town.
Phillipson, D.W. (Ed), 1975. *Mosi-oa-Tunya*. Longman.
Pike, J.G. 'Rainfall over Botswana.' *Botswana Notes and Records*, Special Edition, 1971.
Raffle, J.A. (Chairman), 1981. *Report of the Place Names Commission*. Republic of Botswana.
Raper, P.E., 1972: *Streekname in Suid-Afrika en Suidwes*. Tafelberg, Cape Town.
Rautenbach, I.L. 'A Survey of the Mammals occurring in the Golden Gate Highlands National Park.' *Koedoe*, 1976.
Reavell, P. 'The Okavango Delta: Planning for the Future.' *SA Journal of Science*, 1978.
Roberts, B.R. 'The Vegetation of the Golden Gate Highlands National Park.' *Koedoe*, 1969.
Robertson, T.C. 'St Lucia need not die and other articles.' *The Caltex Circle*, Vol. 12, No. 2.
Rogers, A.W., Hall, A.L., Wagner, P.A. and Haughton, S.H., 1929. *The Geology of the Union of South Africa*. Heidelberg.
Rogers, J., 1977. *Sedimentation of the Continental Margin of the Orange River and the Namib Desert*. Joint Geological Survey/UCT Marine Geoscience Group, Bulletin No. 7.
Ross, Dr. E.S. 'Wonders of Africa's Namib Desert.' *SWA Annual*, 1974.
Russell, G.E. and Biegel, H.M. 'Report on Botanical Collecting Trips to Maun and the Northern Okavango Delta.' *Botswana Notes and Records*, 1973.
Russell, J.R. 'Some Characteristics of Free Faces in the Magaliesberg of the Southern Transvaal.' *SA Geographer*, 1976.
Rust, I. 'The Western Cape some 450 million years ago.' *SA Geographer*, 1969.
Scientific American, Special Issue on Evolution, September 1978.
Seely, Dr. M.K. 'Namib Research.' *SWA Annual*, 1972.
Seely, Dr. M.K. 'The Namib.' *SWA Annual*, 1975.
Seely, Dr. M.K. 'The Oldest Coastal Desert in the World?' *SWA Annual*, 1976.
Simpson, E.S.W. and Davies, D. 'Observations of the Fish River Canyon in South West Africa.' *Trans. Royal Society SA*, 1957.
Smith, C.A., 1966. *Common Names of South African Plants*. Botanical Research Institute, Dept. Agricultural Technical Services.
Sneesby, G.W. 'Eastern Pondoland: A Geographical Study.' *SA Geographical Journal*, 1933.
Sparrow, G.W.A. 'Observations on Slope Formation in the Drakensberg and Foothills of Natal and East Griqualand.' *Journal for Geography*, 1965.
Spies, J.J. 'Die geologiese en geomorfologiese geskiedenis van Golden Gate-Hoogland Nasionale Park.' *Koedoe*, 1969.
Spilhaus, M.W., 1950. *Indigenous Trees of the Cape Peninsula*. Juta, Cape Town.
Standish-White, D.W. 'Watch on the Okavango.' *Optima*, 1973.
Stiegeler, S.E. (Ed.), 1976. *A Dictionary of Earth Sciences*. Pan Books, London.
Swanevelder, C.J. 'Granietmorfologie: Enkele waarnemings op Paarlberg.' *SA Geographer*, 1968.
Sweeting, M.M. 'Karst Landforms and Limestones.' *SA Geographical Journal*, 1973.
Tinely, K.L. 'Fishing Methods of the Thonga Tribe in North-Eastern Zululand and Southern Moçambique.' *Lammergeyer*, 1964.
Tlou, T. 'The Taming of the Okavango Swamps – the Utilization of a Riverine Environment 1750 to 1800.' *Botswana Notes and Records*, 1972.
Tredgold, R. (Ed.), 1956. *The Matopos*. Fed. Dept. of Printing and Stationery, Salisbury.
Tromp, R.D. and Fuggle, R.F. 'Die Verwantskap tussen Struktuur en Topografie in die omgewing van Pretoria.' *SA Geographer*, 1969.
Truswell, J.F., 1970. *An Introduction to the Historical Geology of South Africa*. Purnell and Sons, Cape Town.
Twidale, C.R. and Van Zyl, J.A. 'Some Comments on the Poorts and Pediments of the Western Little Karoo.' *SA Geographer*, 1981.

Tyson, P.D. (Ed.). 'Outeniqualand: The George-Knysna Area.' *SA Geographical Society*, 1971.

Tyson, P.D. and Seely, M.K. 'Local Winds over the Central Namib.' *SA Geographical Journal*, 1980.

Van Rensburg, A.P.J., 1967. *Golden Gate: die geskiedenis van twee plase wat 'n Nasionale Park geword het.* National Parks Board, Pretoria.

Van Rooyen, T.H. and Burger, R. du T. 'Physiographic Features of the Central Orange River Basin, with a note on Pan Formation.' *SA Geographer*, 1973.

Van Rooyen, T.H. and Burger, R. du T. 'Plant-ecological Significance of the Soils of the Central Orange River Basin.' *SA Geographical Journal*, 1974.

Van Wyk, Dr. W. 'The Geological History of South West Africa.' *SWA Annual*, 1971.

Von Breitenbach, F., 1974. *Southern Cape Forests and Trees.* Government Printer, Pretoria.

Von Koenen, H. and E. 'Namib Desert Life.' *SWA Annual*, 1963.

Wayland, E.J. 'More about the Kalahari.' *SA Geographical Journal*, 1953.

Weare, P.R. and Yalala, A. 'Provisional Vegetation Map of Botswana.' *Botswana Notes and Records*, 1971.

Weare, P.R. 'Vegetation of the Kalahari in Botswana.' *Botswana Notes and Records*, Special Edition, 1971.

Wellington, J.H. 'The Topographic Features of the Witwatersrand with Special Reference to the Evolution of the Present Witwatersrand Surface.' *SA Geographical Journal*, 1924.

Wellington, J.H. 'The Physical and Economic Geography of the Central Magaliesberg Region of the Southern Transvaal.' *SA Geographical Journal*, 1926.

Wellington, J.H. 'The Vaal-Limpopo Watershed.' *SA Geographical Journal*, 1929.

Wellington, J.H. 'Notes on the Surface Features of Natal.' *SA Geographical Journal*, 1932.

Wellington, J.H. 'The Middle Course of the Orange River.' *SA Geographical Journal*, 1933.

Wellington, J.H. 'Zambezi-Okavango Development Projects.' *Geographical Review*, 1949.

Wellington, J.H., 1955. *Southern Africa: A Geographical Study.* Cambridge University Press.

Wellington, J.H. 'The Evolution of the Orange River Basin: Some Outstanding Problems.' *SA Geographical Journal*, 1958.

Werger, M.J. and Coetzee, B. 'A Phytosociological and Phytogeographical Study of the Augrabies Falls National Park.' *Koedoe*, 1977.

Whitten, D.G.A. with Brooks, J.R.V., 1972. *A Dictionary of Geology.* Penguin Books, London.

Wilson, B.H. 'Some Natural and Man-made Changes in the Channels of the Okavango Delta.' *Botswana Notes and Records*, 1973.

Zaloumis, Dr. E.A. and Cross, Robert, 1974. *A Field Guide to the Antelope of Southern Africa.* Wildlife Society of Southern Africa.

INDEX